GODREJ: A HUNDRED YEARS

Also by B.K. Karanjia:

RUSTOM MASANI: PORTRAIT OF A CITIZEN

A MANY-SPLENDOURED CINEMA *(Selected articles)*

MORE OF AN INDIAN *(Novel)*

BLUNDERING IN WONDERLAND *(A partial memoir)*

MASKS AND FACES *(Stories)*

GODREJ: A HUNDRED YEARS 1897–1997, VOLUME II

GIVE ME A BOMBAY MERCHANT—ANYTIME!: THE LIFE OF SIR JAMSETJEE JEJEEBHOY

FINAL VICTORY: THE LIFE—AND DEATH—OF NAVAL PIROJSHA GODREJ

ABUNDANT LIVING, RESTLESS STRIVING: A MEMOIR

VIJITATMA: PIONEER–FOUNDER ARDESHIR GODREJ

COUNTING MY BLESSINGS: AN AUTOBIOGRAPHY *(Forthcoming)*

B.K. KARANJIA

LIFE'S FLAG IS NEVER FURLED

Godrej
A HUNDRED YEARS
1897-1997

VOLUME I

PENGUIN
VIKING

VIKING

Published by the Penguin Group
Penguin Books India Pvt. Ltd, 11 Community Centre, Panchsheel Park,
New Delhi 110 017, India
Penguin Group (USA) Inc., 375 Hudson Street, New York, New York 10014, USA
Penguin Group (Canada), 10 Alcorn Avenue, Toronto, Ontario, Canada M4V 3B2
(a division of Pearson Penguin Canada Inc.)
Penguin Books Ltd, 80 Strand, London WC2R 0RL, England
Penguin Ireland, 25 St Stephen's Green, Dublin 2, Ireland
(a division of Penguin Books Ltd)
Penguin Group (Australia), 250 Camberwell Road, Camberwell, Victoria 3124,
Australia (a division of Pearson Australia Group Pty Ltd)
Penguin Group (NZ), cnr Airborne and Rosedale Roads, Albany,
Auckland 1310, New Zealand (a division of Pearson New Zealand Ltd)
Penguin Group (South Africa) (Pty) Ltd, 24 Sturdee Avenue, Rosebank,
Johannesburg 2196, South Africa

Penguin Books Ltd, Registered Offices: 80 Strand, London WC2R 0RL, England

First published in Viking by Penguin Books India 1997

Copyright © B.K. Karanjia 1997

All rights reserved

10 9 8 7 6 5 4

Typeset in *Times New Roman* by SÜRYA, New Delhi
Printed at Chaman Offset Printers, Delhi

This book is sold subject to the condition that it shall not, by way of trade or otherwise, be lent, resold, hired out, or otherwise circulated without the publisher's prior written consent in any form of binding or cover other than that in which it is published and without a similar condition including this condition being imposed on the subsequent purchaser and without limiting the rights under copyright reserved above, no part of this publication may be reproduced, stored in or introduced into a retrieval system, or transmitted in any form or by any means (electronic, mechanical, photocopying, recording or otherwise), without the prior written permission of both the copyright owner and the above-mentioned publisher of this book.

To
Ardeshir B. Godrej
1868-1936

with whom the story began

*They are not dead; life's flag is never furled:
They passed from world to world.*

—Edwin Markham

CONTENTS

All in the Family	*xiii*
Manufacturing Flowers	*xviii*
Finding a Vocation	1
The Call of Swadeshi	21
Towards Self-Reliance	33
A Complexion Pure	44
Proudly 'Made in India'	53
Brother's Keeper	67
Blue-Printing a Dream	78
An Eden of Contentment	96
Curiosity-Breeding Joker	113
Superman PUF	128
Only the Best	135
A Way to Sell	150
Global Presence	159
Mr Environmentalist	174
Social Concerns	184
The Larger Citizenry	196
The Tragic Flaw	218
Afterword	232
Appendices	235
Bibliography	259
Index	261

Acknowledgements

There were many, within Godrej and outside, who contributed to compiling the material for this work. My heartfelt thanks to each one of them, more particularly to:

Sohrab P. Godrej, Soonuben N. Godrej and other members of the Godrej family for their wholehearted co-operation in making this book possible.

Kerse Naoroji and Kaikhusru Naoroji for invaluable assistance in defining industrial relations and exports, respectively.

Rustom Sanjana, former Sales Manager, Godrej & Boyce, for the fascinating anecdotes about the long (almost fifty) years he spent in the service of Godrej.

E.J. Kalwachia for sharing his reminiscences with me and for his constant encouragement and help.

K.A. Palia and P.E. Fouzdar for detailing the financial background of the Godrej enterprise.

K.R. Gokulam, Manager of Godrej Soaps, now retired, for his interesting reminiscences about the early struggles of Godrej Soaps Limited.

K.R. Hathi for scrupulously examining the manuscript and offering valuable suggestions.

P.D. Muncherji too for scrupulously examining the manuscript and for sparing us his diary with interesting details about the manufacturing processes of various Godrej products: locks, typewriters, refrigerators, machine tools beside others.

K.R. Krishnaswamy, Sohrab's secretary, for his co-operation at all stages of the writing, particularly his untiring efforts to put me in touch with all who matter in Godrej, and for his constant encouragement.

R.M. Majoo, Sundareswaran K. (Suresh) and Joan D'Souza in the Chairman's Office for their help in a hundred little ways.

Naoroji's secretary, C.S. Raje for his assistance in placing all the old files I required at my disposal and helping me trace some important documents.

Jamshyd's secretaries, Falguni Joshi and Pervin Patel, Burjor's secretary, Nancy Gonsalves, Adi's secretary, Marjorie Charles, and Priya Eshwaran of Pragati Kendra, for their willing help in locating and captioning the photographs.

Nariman Sarkari and Nader Shroff, both retired employees of Godrej, for their assistance in giving information about Pirojsha's and Naoroji's style of working.

S.S. Potdar of the Library, University of Bombay, for loaning us various books required for researching this project.

Gool Tata of the Parsi Punchayet, for making available the papers regarding Ardeshir Godrej's bequest of the Nasik land to the Punchayet.

Usha Mehta for giving us access to various letters written by Mahatma Gandhi.

Homai Modi of the Cama Oriental Institute for allowing us use of the Institute's library.

F.T. Khorakiwalla, Ex-Sheriff of Bombay (1992-93), and A.M. Qazi, Dy. Sheriff of Bombay.

I. Laxminarayan and M. Godfrey of the American Centre.

Acknowledgements

S.D. Choksey, Principal of the Udayachal Pre-Primary and Primary Schools and D.B.J. Jahina, Principal, Udayachal High School (now retired).

Percy Madon for his sincere efforts in tracing Ardeshir's will and the various Patents acquired by the Company.

Yohan Dadabhoy and Burjor Gandhi (who are handling the Godrej Trusts), B.N. Doongaji, Aspi Medhora, Gev Gandevia, C.R. Sawant, Kumaran Ambalagan.

My wife Abad for scrutinizing the manuscript and helping me to correct the proofs of this book as she has done for my previous books.

Dr R. Mahadevan, acknowledged as an expert, for making valuable suggestions which have contributed to the book's enrichment.

Last, but hardly the least, Rashna Ardesher, my talented and efficient secretary, for the patience and good humour with which she typed draft after draft of the manuscript, the eagerness with which she volunteered to help in researching for the book and her infectious enthusiasm for the project.

My very special thanks to David Davidar, Editor and Publisher, and Mrs Raj Kamini Mahadevan, Sr. Asst. Editor of Penguin Books India Pvt. Ltd., competent and conscientious publishers, who assess a writer's skills and then take him to the limit, making him give of his best.

ALL IN THE FAMILY

My acquaintance with Godrej goes back a long way. My father and Pirojsha Godrej were friends and, although they met but rarely, shared a deep mutual regard. Sohrab, Pirojsha's eldest son, used to come to some of the tea parties my mother, a redoubtable but endearing Victorian, was fond of giving. My real contact with Sohrab was when we jointly brought out a twelve-page supplement in the *Times of India* (24 September 1955), recording for the first time the early struggles of Godrej against the entrenched British interests and Godrej achievements in diverse fields.

As Sohrab and I were otherwise occupied during the day, we would meet late in the evenings at his Ridge Road residence. His recall was almost total, and I would diligently take down copious notes in my own brand of shorthand. Exhausted as he often was after a hard day's work, it was by sheer will-power that he sat through these exacting sessions, answering my innumerable questions, lasting up to midnight. On one or two occasions he dozed off, and I would remind him gently that it was late and time for me to leave. With the graciousness that is part of him, he would accompany me to the door, inquire if I had a car and admonish me to drive safely as the hour was late.

Sohrab stayed with his father. In the distinctive, elegantly furnished flat one sensed the presiding presence of Pirojsha's wife, long since dead, who was a remarkable woman and had been a formative influence when Sohrab was a child. On a couple of occasions when I showed up rather early, father and son invited me to share their simple meal. Uppermost in Pirojsha's mind was the industrial township then coming up at Vikhroli and he talked about his dreams and plans, the stakes of which were so high that he daren't fail. I listened fascinated when, with a sudden switch, he looked down at my plate and noticed that I was hardly eating. 'I think Burjor is shy,' he remarked smiling to Sohrab. How could I tell him that I wasn't shy at all, but awed to sit at the same table breaking bread with a man about whom my father had often spoken loftily?

The supplement was well-liked, and I joined Godrej as Publicity Manager. In those days, we executives used to sit in a large hall at Lalbaug, divided by a glass partition from the rest of the staff: Pirojsha at the head, sitting ramrod straight, a commanding presence, commanding respect. His youngest son Naval with his flair for mechanics that was akin to genius, sat on his right and Sohrab, on his left. His younger son Burjor, a scientist and research scholar of rare distinction, a 'Professor of Industry' as he was fondly called, presided over the soap factory, across the railway lines, at Delisle Road. Giving him companionship, for as long as he lived, was his wife Jai, a gifted teacher.

A frequent visitor at the Lalbaug office was Naval's wife Soonu, attractive in white, with a personality that truly sparkled. She was then engaged in helping to lay the foundations for what was to become a model school at Vikhroli. She concerned herself with the welfare of workers' wives and children, contributing to the *parivar* atmosphere that was sedulously cultivated.

The six years I spent at Godrej were happy ones. Yet, because of certain compulsions, I left to join the *Times of India* publication *Filmfare* as Editor. Naturally, the Godrejs were upset, Sohrab particularly so. I couldn't tell them how much it hurt me too; they had been so good to me.

But we continued to maintain excellent relations. I would meet Sohrab off and on at the Godrej Bhavan office. Incidentally, this office replaced a picturesque little building which had served as the Bombay sales office, with Sohrab's cousin Kerse Naoroji and his wife Jeannie residing on the top floor. Kerse was in charge of industrial relations at Lalbaug and later at Vikhroli.

Once when I was with Sohrab in Naval's chamber, a bright young boy barged in to whisper something in his daddy's ear. Sohrab introduced him as Jamshyd, Naval's son—a strapping young man today, self-confident, totally in control of the metal products company his father has left him. Those days I would often see Adi, Burjor's eldest son, much younger then and resplendently eligible, speeding around town. Small wonder he won the heart of the glamorous socialite and interior decorator Parmeshwar and married her. A 'go-ahead' man, he has made the struggling soap company a power to reckon with in the dog-eat-dog soap business. His younger brother Nadir I met, as it were, on the wings of poesy when Sohrab proudly showed me a poem, 'The Captain', Nadir had written in memory of Naval after his tragic death. It was a loving nephew's moving tribute to a great achiever. Nadir, married to Rati, a caring physician, ever-ready to help one and all, is co-Managing Director with Adi of Godrej Soaps.

As one grows older, the world grows smaller. Sohrab's sister Dosa, a girl of many accomplishments, married Kerse's elder brother Keku Naoroji, who had passed out from the

London School of Economics and was then an executive in Imperial Chemicals, but later took charge of Godrej exports. Dosa and my wife Abad became great friends, driving ambulances for the St John's Ambulance Brigade during the War, years. Keku's son Rishad is a naturalist and an environmentalist at heart who has specialized in raptors (birds of prey). Jamshyd's wife Pheroza, I was later to recall, used to be the lovely freckled little girl whom I knew of as the daughter of Phiroze Shroff, my schoolmate at St Xavier's for eight long years. Pheroza's fascinating speciality is modern Indian art and the work of British artists in India. She has edited and published some prestigious art publications.

A welcome addition to the family was Vijay Crishna, married to Naval's daughter Smita. Long years ago I had seen an impressive performance of his in a play whose title I can't recall now. He is in-charge of Godrej-GE Appliances. Smita's interests are in art and heritage.

The Godrej story doesn't stop with the third generation. Ushering in the fourth is Adi's daughter Tanya who is in-charge of the marketing of Godrej Soaps. It is a continuing story.

Behind its success is the story of strong, determined men and their devoted women, with the gift of vision, with contrasting and sometimes conflicting personalities, who have lived through triumph and tragedy. At the helm, helping in keeping the family together, is Sohrab, industrialist in spite of himself and gracious patriarch.

A family that lives together, as they say, stays together. The Godrej family has stayed together even though, with the family expanding, some of the younger members live separately. They have stayed together because they have a name to live up to, the name that is both a binding and an elevating force.

So the memories keep flooding in. But one memory

lingers—rankles. My last encounter in 1961 with Pirojsha, and how disappointed he was when I told him I had to leave Godrej. I was painfully conscious of causing hurt to one of the two men I have revered most in life (the other being Sir Rustom Masani, my mentor, greater in what he was than in anything he *did*, although he did more than most men). But there was no way I could help it.

But atonement is always possible. When God shuts one door, He opens another, so they say.

Let's enter the other door.

B.K. Karanjia

MANUFACTURING FLOWERS

It was in 1935, in the thick of the freedom struggle, that Pandit Jawaharlal Nehru, who was to become the country's first Prime Minister, visited the Godrej factory at Lalbaug, Parel.

Pandit Nehru's acquaintance with Godrej went back several years when, on visits to Paris, he had been meeting Pirojsha Godrej's elder brother Munchersha in his Paris office. Munchersha had lived in Paris for over half a century. It was Munchersha who invited Nehru to the factory.

Taken round the factory by Pirojsha and his youngest son Naoroji (Naval), along with Munchersha, Nehru was impressed by the range of manufacture from locks to safe-deposit vaults. 'I don't see any foreign technicians,' he remarked as he was leaving. He was told that all that he saw was done by Godrej themselves and that they didn't need any foreign technicians; Godrej were pioneers in developing their own technologies. He was also aware that apart from security and other steel equipment, Godrej had also manufactured high quality soaps from vegetable oils for the first time!

This variety of manufacture made a deep impression on

the Nehru family. Indira and Feroz wanted Godrej to do big things for the country after Independence. They had in mind a weighty project in which they wanted Godrej to manufacture instead of the public sector. Of course, Godrej had no problem regarding land. Indira fixed up a meeting for Sohrab with her father first thing in the morning when Panditji, according to her, would be in a good mood! It was a meeting with an interesting sidelight to it.

While Sohrab was discussing the issue, the Russian Ambassador also had an appointment to present Nehru with a horse and could not be kept waiting. Godrej ultimately could not take up the project because of lack of necessary facilities.

When, after the meeting at which Indira was also present and took a keen personal interest, Sohrab presented the Prime Minister with a bouquet, Nehru jestingly remarked: 'Don't tell me you manufacture flowers also!'

The Godrej Family Tree

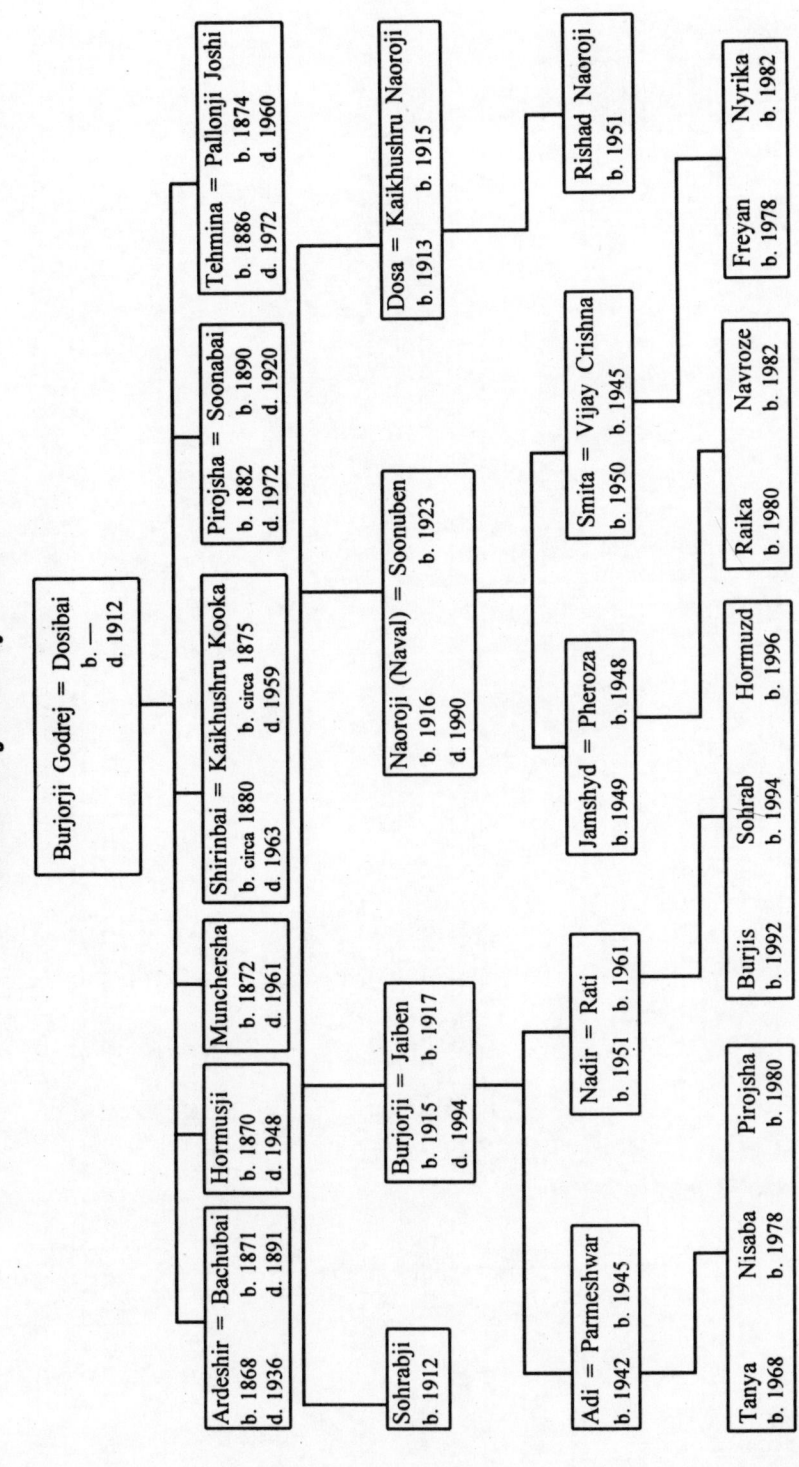

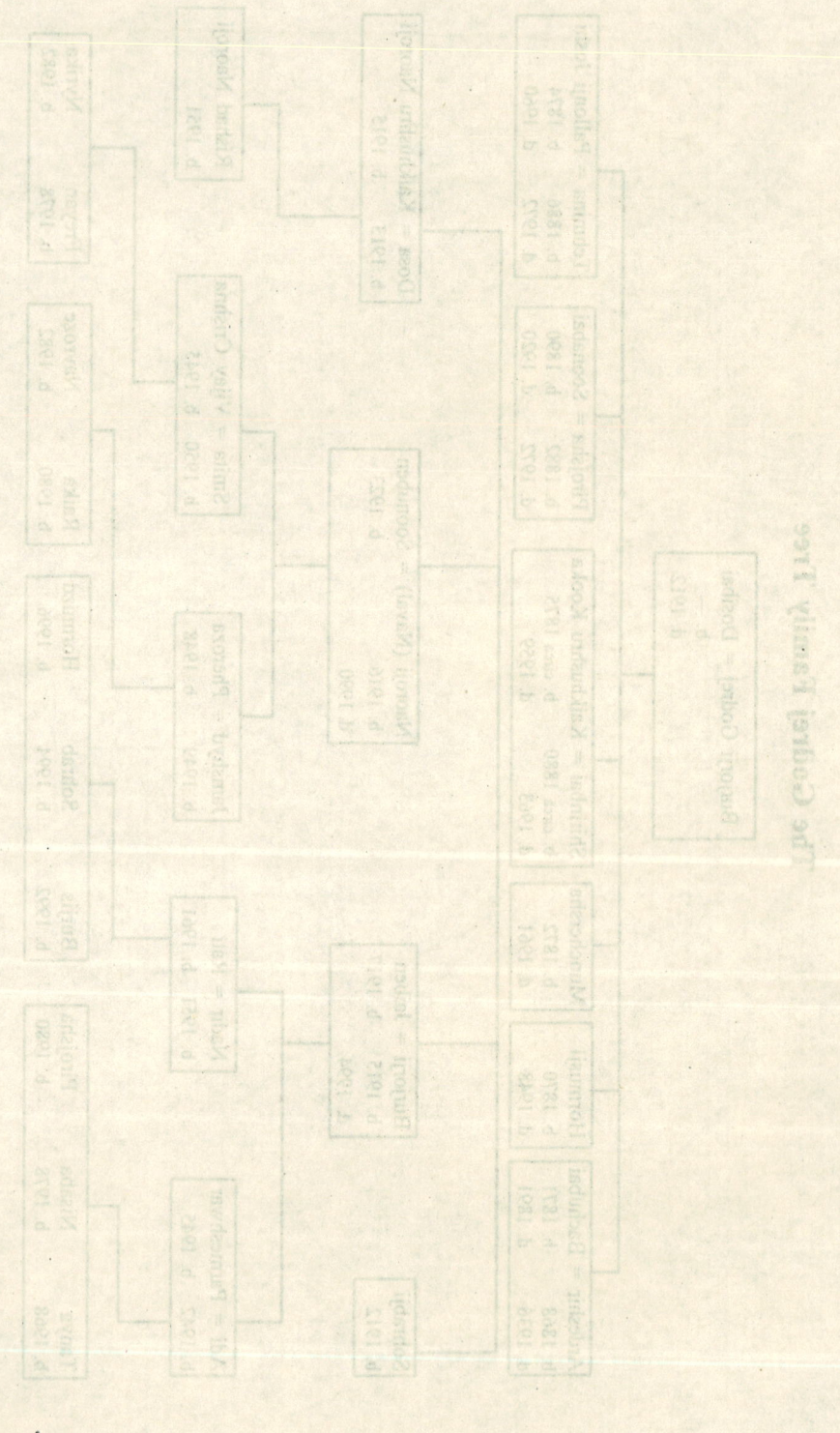

1
FINDING A VOCATION

The Godrej story begins not in Bombay, but in distant Zanzibar, in 1894, where young Ardeshir Burjorji Godrej, fresh from law studies in Bombay, had gone to argue a client's case on behalf of a well-known firm of solicitors.

Little is known about the case. But Ardeshir, being the man he was, must have mastered the brief. His future as an advocate depended on how he conducted his case. If he won, his fame would precede him to Bombay and more briefs would follow. If he failed—well then, he would have to begin all over again.

The case went well. Ardeshir conducted his arguments not with flamboyance but with calm and reasonableness, when, during the course of arguments, an unforeseen difficulty arose. The truth would have to be twisted in his client's favour, the sort of thing that the usual lawyer takes in his stride. But Ardeshir was an unusual man. He refused.

Those around him in the court and outside could not comprehend his stand. They tried to reason with this quiet man of solemn mien, bespectacled, in black *pheta* and white *dugla*, but found themselves up against true steel. They couldn't possibly have been aware that he was so highly principled that he had refused to accept the amount he had inherited, leaving it to be shared by his brothers and sisters.

Young Ardeshir returned to Bombay. Deep within him he was proud of the principled stand he had taken. He didn't know it then, but it was only the first of many similar stands he would be called upon to take in the course of his life. But he also realized now that he had damaged his career as a lawyer, perhaps beyond repair. Without any alternative means of livelihood, he was returning to a briefless future.

Nevertheless, Ardeshir didn't return empty-handed. He brought back a parrot, the unique African Grey. Unlike Flaubert, who used to always keep his stuffed green and pink Lulu on his writing-table, Ardeshir didn't bring the parrot with him for inspiration. Perhaps, in its plumage of riches, he found consolation.

Ardeshir was born on 26 March 1868, in Broach (Bharuch), to Burjorji and Dosibai Godrej. Burjorji was a businessman dealing in real estate. He owned some property in Saugar, Madhya Pradesh. Quiet and unassuming, Burjorji was rather ineffective. His wife Dosibai was the dominating influence in the family. The name Godrej was derived from Guderz, the name of an important tribe in Iran.

Ardeshir had come to Bombay some years earlier from

Broach. Bombay could not yet aspire to lay claim to be India's first city. But it was witness to far-reaching changes and influences.

The seven islets, that were later to become Bombay, were held in the seventeenth century by Portugal and were ceded to Britain as part of the Infanta's dowry. This irked the local Portuguese who stalled the transfer of the territory for four years. On the direct intervention of the Supreme Court of Goa, however, the promised islets were handed over to the new rulers in 1665. Three years later, in 1668, the Crown bestowed the islets to the Honourable East India Company 'to be held in free and common soccage, as the Manor of East Greenwich, at a farm-rent of 10 pounds payable on September 30 in each year.'

A contemporary writer described Bombay as it was then as seven islets in a cesspool. The sanitary arrangements were almost primitive. Sewers and drains discharged on the sands, the rocks served as latrines. Sickness raged. The city came to acquire notoriety as 'the morgue of India', 'a city of dearth and death', 'a charnel-house in which two monsoons were the age of a man'. On a morning, the despised and downtrodden 'halalkores' could be seen carrying baskets of night soil on their heads to a depot located amidst houses in a secluded locality. People in those days, taking the sight or sound of many an everyday object as an omen, would often say that to see a sweeper the first thing in the morning was most auspicious! In spite of the unhygienic conditions and several attacks on the islets by marauders, the spirit of determination persisted among the inhabitants. 'Out of all this scum there might arise another Carthage,' predicted Fryer way back in 1675. His hopes were shared by Gerald Aungier who became Governor of Bombay in 1669. Among his many achievements which included laying out a town plan, introducing law and order and establishing a Court of

Judicature, a mint, a small hospital and even a printing press, must be mentioned the importing of English ladies to marry the English settlers. Bombay 'is a city,' Aungier declared, 'which by God's assistance is intended to be built.'

Two factors helped the city to become what it is today: able British administrators who had the vision and the means to mobilize the resources required for translating that vision into reality; and innumerable Indians of all races and creeds who helped to implement and execute the bold plans being made for the city's development. The original seven islands (Bombay, Dongri, Mazgaon, Sewree, Sion, Mahim and Worli) were in 1709-10 gradually brought together into one. What began now has been called 'a great epic of reclamation' whereby the three Breaches between Sion and Dharavi, between Mahim and Dharavi and between Mahim and Worli were tackled by the year 1710. A little later, work was begun on the great Breach between Worli and Mahalaxmi and this was completed by about 1723.

A notable event in 1735 was the Bombay Council's decision to shift the Surat shipbuilding yard to Bombay. The Parsi foreman of the Surat yard, Lavji Nusserwanji Wadia, renowned for his shipbuilding skills, was brought to the city. It was at his insistence that the upper old Bombay dock was constructed in 1754. The construction of two or more docks followed in 1762 and 1765. Lavji served as master builder till 1774 when his scions carried on the tradition established by him of building ships universally acclaimed for their strength of construction and seaworthiness. It is rather ironical to recall that it was the Wadias who thus helped to maintain the Pax Britannica, carrying the flag of the Royal Navy across the seven seas to the farthest reaches of the British empire!

Gambling and excessive drinking used to be common vices on the island. The East India Company treated gambling as an offence, while unlicensed selling of liquor was punished with a Rs 25 fine. On the public demand for greater security, sundry regulations for better police management were laid down in December 1769. Two years later the Bhandari militia, divided into 48 officers and 400 men, were employed on regular police duty aided by night-guards and regular patrols.

Almost a century later, in 1771, William Hornby became Governor of Bombay. He encouraged building activity and a vellard was built between Mahalaxmi and Worli at a cost of Rs 1 lakh. This was bitterly opposed by the Company's penny-pinching directors, but Hornby went ahead nevertheless. This great piece of reclamation now known as Hornby Vellard effectively welded the eastern and western shores of the island into one area. It also set the pace for further reclamations during the Governorship of Sir Bartle Frere (1862-67) from Apollo Bunder to Colaba Church, from Custom House to Sewri and, on the western side, the great Backbay Reclamation between 1909 and 1918, extending from Colaba to the foot of Malabar Hill.

Architectural activities reached their zenith during Sir Bartle's governorship. Top British architects were commissioned to draw up the plans of new buildings in the highest traditions of Victorian Gothic architecture. The buildings begun then but completed later to become the city's proud heritage were the Secretariat, the University Library and Convocation Hall, the High Court, the Telegraph and Post Offices, all facing the sea. Other buildings executed in similar style were the Elphinstone College, the Victoria Museum, Elphinstone High School and the J.J. School of Art.

The dreaded bubonic plague broke out in Rajkot in 1896, and spread to Bombay, incidentally killing some servants working in the Godrej family. It is interesting to recall that a young barrister, Mohan Karamchand Gandhi, then on a brief visit to India from South Africa, was one of the two members of a hastily set up Plague Committee who showed willingness to visit the stricken quarters of the untouchables in Rajkot. But not until 1897 did the epidemic's ravages provoke the introduction of a necessary agency into the sphere of civic government—the City of Bombay Improvement Trust.

In other ways too, 1897 was a significant year. The picturesque palanquins carrying busy citizens from one part of the city to another had already been replaced by *palkis*, a simpler form of the palanquin, drawn by sweating hamals shouting *'Poise! Poise!'* (Step Aside! Step Aside!) for pedestrians to clear the way. The first automobile would reach the Indian roads in that year. Even in England, the country of India's rulers, motor vehicles were driven then with an attendant running ahead ringing a bell!

Queen Victoria's Diamond Jubilee celebrated in England in 1897, has been termed 'the most successful imperial pageant ever staged.' Several Maharajahs came from India courtesy Thomas Cook & Son who had won renown as 'Booking Clerk to the Empire' and had opened an office at Hornby Road in Bombay (P. Brandon). These Maharajahs were among the most exotic and extravagant of Cook's tourists, displaying a pomp and circumstance unusual even by the standards of royalty.

On a sadder note, the year 1897 marked Lokmanya Tilak's first arrest (the first arrest of a prominent national leader on charges of sedition) on 27 July. The trial was held in the High Court of Bombay. Large crowds, comprising mainly the working classes, collected every day to hear the proceedings of the case. And when Justice Strachey sentenced Tilak to 18 months' rigorous imprisonment on charges of sedition, there was a public outcry. Committed to Bombay's

Finding a Vocation

Dongri jail and treated like an ordinary criminal, having to cord coconut fibre for mats for long hours in unhygienic surroundings and on a meagre diet, his health failed and there was a general fear that he might die in jail. Only after the outbreak of plague in the city was he shifted from Bombay.

The office of the Sheriff of Bombay was endowed with even greater dignity and honour from this time on. Mr George Cotton belonging to the well-known business house of Greaves Cotton (later he was knighted) decided that he would not like to personally benefit from the Sheriff's fees, poundage, etc. Since then, the Sheriff of Bombay is entirely an honorary position. All the fees, poundage, etc. of the Sheriff of Bombay are credited directly to the government which has the entire responsibility of meeting the expenses of the establishment including the salaries of the Deputy Sheriff, the staff and the bailiffs. This was unlike the Sheriff of Calcutta who until 1950 enjoyed the pecuniary benefits of his office and the Sheriff of Madras who, in lieu of his salary, took all the fees averaging about Rs 400 a month plus a part of the establishment expenses. The dignity and importance attaching to this office has arisen from its customary and time-honoured treatment as a position representing the people despite the existence of other representative institutions. Ardeshir's nephew, Sohrab's appointment as Sheriff of Bombay, a century later in 1982, therefore was a recognition of Godrej's yeoman service to the public.

Cinema too came to India during the monsoon of 1896. The Bombay edition of the *Times of India* dated 7 July, carried an advertisement inviting its readers to reach Watson's Hotel, Kala Ghoda, at 7.00 p.m. to witness 'The Marvel of the Century, The Wonder of the World.'

The 1872 census had recorded the city's population as

six and a half lacs. Its beautiful spots like Malabar Hill, Breach Candy and Mahalaxmi were monopolized by the European and wealthy Indian population. Ardeshir with his younger brother Pirojsha and their parents were staying at Grant Road, full of greenery then, while the poorer classes herded in the city's ancient oarts and alleys.

Building activity saw an unprecedented spurt at the end of the nineteenth century. A large number of houses had already sprung up in the whole area between the sea and Girgaum Back Road. 'Houses are rising in all directions,' reported the *Times of India* correspondent, 'and what was some ten years ago merely a coconut plantation will, within the next half century, be as thoroughly urban as Mandvi and Khara Talao.'

Much has been written about the contribution of Parsis towards enriching the social, cultural and economic life of the city. Earliest among them was Sir Jamsetjee Jeejeebhoy who began life humbly by selling bottles, grew to be a millionaire and used his considerable wealth to establish hospitals and found the J.J. School of Arts. His wife, Lady Jamsetjee contributed handsomely to the construction of the causeway connecting Bandra and Mahim. A staunch advocate of introducing railways in India, Sir Jamsetjee was a founder-member of the Indian Railway Association which was formed at a meeting of Bombay's citizens held in the Town Hall on 3 July 1844. To be named, originally, the Bombay Great Eastern Railway, extended to cover the 21-mile route from Bombay to Thane, it was supplanted by the more ambitious scheme floated by one John Chapman for a railway to be named the Great Indian Peninsular (the 'r' was later dropped) that would cross the Indian plateau and reach Madras, Calcutta and Delhi. Sir Jamsetjee was one of the seven Indian members who, along with thirteen Europeans, constituted the Bombay Provisional Committee of the GIP.

This Committee later became the Bombay Board with ten founder-directors, and whose bas-reliefs adorn the facade of the magnificent Victoria Terminus Building.

Sir Jamsetjee was the first Indian baronet. Legend has it that when he drove about in the city in his two-horse carriage, he would sit between two bags of coins from which he distributed coins to beggars lining his route.

It was during this period that Sir Pherozeshah Mehta, who was to earn the title, The Lion of Bombay, established an independent newspaper, the *Bombay Chronicle*, and helped in founding the Central Bank of India. Another great Parsi, Jamsetji Tata, destined to become one of the country's greatest industrialists, established a textile mill known as the Empress Mills, giving his workers facilities unheard of till then like cheap housing, medical relief, etc. The year he died (1904), saw the fulfillment of a cherished dream, the completion of the majestic Taj Mahal Hotel in the same year. A lesser-known Parsi whose name deserves to be recalled nevertheless was Dr Bahadurjee who returned from England to Bombay by the *Oceana* on 10 November 1891 after doing yeoman service in England in the cause of the millhands and mill-owners of the leading cotton and textile industries. He countered in the *London Times* the singularly erroneous views of one Hult Hallett who had maligned the industries in its pages. The highest measure of his success, however, was that he was invited to speak on Indian factory labour before the members of the prestigious Manchester Chamber of Commerce. Unfortunately, owing to shortage of time, Bahadurjee could not accept the invitation.

The period also saw, under the stewardship of Sir James Ferguson and later Lord Reay, the establishment of the Victoria Jubilee Technical Institute where Ardeshir's younger brother Pirojsha got his training, and several hospitals including the St George's Hospital. An asylum for lepers was built at Matunga, as also the Victoria Train Terminus and the Merewether and Victoria Docks.

Another far-sighted governor, Mountstuart Elphinstone laid the foundations of an educational system in the city. Encouraged by this ardent advocate of both higher and vernacular education, the Bombay Native Education Society was founded in 1822, which established both English and Indian language schools. These efforts were helped by notable Indians who also came forward to contribute.

Women were, however, excluded from the system. In his biography *Dadabhai Naoroji: The Grand Old Man of India*, Rustom Masani recounts how in those early years, Dadabhai, with some friends, actually went to Parsi homes in the Fort area, and pleaded with parents to allow their daughters to be given education. The response was highly disappointing and even frustrating. Dadabhai would often be turned out of the house unceremoniously and bluntly told that Parsis did not want their daughters to be 'memsahibs'.

But progress in women's education could not be so easily halted in the face of other powerful impulses. In 1883, the Postmaster of Belgaum, which was then a part of the Bombay Presidency, Mr S. Khurshedji made an application for his daughter to be allowed to sit for the matriculation examination. The doors of the Bombay University being closed to women at the time, this application was turned down. Not to be deterred, Khurshedji wrote letters of appeal to the Governor of the Presidency as well as the Chancellor of the Bombay University, Sir James Ferguson. Khurshedji, who must have been quite a campaigner, also got several friends of his to write letters of appeal to these dignitaries. As a result of these efforts women came to be admitted to the University in 1883. Miss Cornelia Sohrabji became the first woman to graduate from the University, in the year 1888. She was later to become the first woman barrister—perhaps the first in the world.

Finding a Vocation

The influence of Annie Besant, notable social reformer and activist in Indian affairs, was also significant. In 1889 she became a member of the Theosophical Society and landed at Tuticorin, South India, in 1893. Widely publicized at this time was her vision of India: 'The India I would give my life to help in building is an India learned in the ancient philosophy, pulsing with an ancient religion, an India to which all other lands would look for spiritual life—where the life of all should be materially simple but intellectually noble and spiritually sublime.' This vision naturally included women. Besant established the Central Hindu School and College, which later became the nucleus of the Benares Hindu University. More than 40 national schools, for girls as well as boys, were established to nurture a sense of responsibility and self-sacrificing service in the minds of the young.

Later, inspired by her example, the businessman Jaganath Shankarshet established scholarships for school-leaving students. Ignoring the persisting opposition to the education of women, he encouraged the renowned missionary and educationist, Dr John Wilson to open a girls' school on premises which he made available for this purpose.

The city's first water supply system was set up about this time. Its pipelines ran from Vihar Lake, Tansa and, later, from Tulsi to the city and formed probably the most extensive system in Asia. When gas lamps were introduced in the city, several public-spirited citizens donated large ornamental lamps to the Municipality to be placed at prominent and central positions on the main roads. Thanks again to the generosity of the successful speculators of 1861-65, the city began to acquire some of its distinguishing features—the Rajabai Tower donated by the uncrowned king of Bombay in those days, Premchand Roychand in memory of his mother, and which was later to be the scene of a tragedy in Ardeshir's life, the Victoria and Albert Museum, the Sassoon Mechanics Institute, and the Gokuldas Tejpal Hospital. The donations anticipated today's traffic islands maintained by businessmen and industrialists. They were as varied as they were munificent—an ophthalmic hospital, a convocation hall and forty drinking fountains donated by Sir Cowasji Jehangir, an equestrian statue, Kala Ghoda, to commemorate the visit to Bombay of Edward, Prince of Wales, presented by Sir Albert Sassoon to the 'Townsmen of the Loyal City', and the largest market for wholesale textiles built by Mulji Jetha.

In the meantime, setting the seal on the city's phenomenal growth, the Bombay Municipal Corporation acquired its first coat of arms in 1877, with the motto 'Urbs Prima in Indis', and depicting a lion representing Great Britain, a leopard symbolizing India and three sailing ships representing Bombay. It wasn't till 78 years later, in 1955, that a new coat of arms was introduced with four panels representing the Government of India, a geared wheel symbolizing industry, three sailing ships in outline and a symbolized design of the Corporation Building. 'Urbs Prima in Indis' was replaced by a motto suggested by the then Chief Minister, B.G. Kher, 'Where there is righteousness, there is victory.' This new civic crest was unveiled by the ex-Mayor, S.K. Patil on 15 August 1955.

After what had happened at Zanzibar, Ardeshir was certain of one thing; he did not want to continue in the legal profession. He wasted no time brooding. What if one vocation was lost, there would be others. Ever since the founding of the Indian National Congress in 1887 there had been rumblings of political discontent. Concerned as Ardeshir was by the political enslavement of his country by the British, he came to be even more concerned with the economic degradation of his people. His achievement, to be fairly assessed, has to be seen in the broad context of the tragic decline of India's age-old industries under British rule. It brings into focus the originality and daring of his thinking and puts the extent of his contribution to Indian industry in its proper perspective.

T.B. Desai in his carefully researched *Economic History of India* shows how the neglect of India's beautiful handicrafts, the decline of the once prosperous and well-organized textile industry with only a quarter of the mill cloth needed being produced in the country, the balance coming mainly from Great Britain, and the replacement of Indian fabrics by cheaper machine-made British manufactures, caused considerable economic distress in the first half of the century. In Broach, for example, from where Ardeshir hailed, English cloth of superior quality could be obtained at a much lower price than the best *dhotis* and *haftas* locally available. Just before Ardeshir's birth, almost all varieties of cloth came to be imported. This followed the decline much earlier of the famed silk industry mainly because of the heavy taxes imposed by the rulers. To add to the woes of silk manufacturers, women began to show an increasing preference for Chinese silk.

Desai goes on to recount how as a consequence of the widespread use of European cloth by the Indian middle class, weavers and spinners in several centres lost their means of livelihood. Weavers among the Parsi community abandoned their calling altogether. The stark alternative was to change over to the English yarn or face unemployment and consequent loss of income. Deliberate underselling by the rulers led to the decline by 1820 of most indigenous goods, with the exception of certain fabrics. Levers, for example, wiped out the soap cottage industry, mainly in Bengal.

For the sugar industry it was the same sad story. There was a time when sugar was actually exported owing to its easy availability because of plentiful sugarcane in the country. But by 1907 sugar came to be imported from abroad to the extent of seven crore rupees a year. In this respect India suffered more than other countries because it stuck to old world, outdated methods of production.

Rise in fuel prices and the import of cheap steel sheets from Europe, Desai points out, put the Indian smelting industry at such a disadvantage that it ceased to exist by about 1850. It was replaced by English iron and steel, particularly for the making of weapons. Even in the seventeenth century, cannon were regularly purchased by Marathas from the Europeans, with only rough cannon balls being manufactured indigenously. Indian metal was no longer in demand, and the community of the Dhavads had to give up their calling altogether. Mints situated at various places had to be closed after the advent of British rule, as also several old ordinance factories. Artisans and unskilled workers in the armament industry also faced unemployment.

Paper used to be produced in the eighteenth century in western India, but with the import of better and cheaper foreign varieties, its demand ceased. European paper came to be preferred by the Indian ruling classes. The few indigenous paper production centres which survived were able to produce only negligible quantities.

Desai recalls how deep-sea trading vessels and warships used to be built in the old days in several shipbuilding yards in the country. Local carpenters, a Muslim community known as the Vadhas and the seafaring Bhandaris used to build the vessels. Parsi craftsmen excelled all other builders in imitating foreign ships. Surat shipbuilding declined, however, with the growing importance of Bombay as the chief port of western India. Thanks to the supply of fine teak, the availability of expert Parsi craftsmen and its fine docks, Bombay became an important shipbuilding centre in India.

These various factors led inevitably to the decline of urban industries in the first half of the nineteenth century. True, a few artisans acquired new skills and found new jobs as a result of the import of European articles, but this was only in very exceptional cases. Some blacksmiths in cities like Poona began repairing watches. Crafts declined. The saddle-makers who had prospered under Maratha rule, the one-time prosperous Jingars, began making wooden toys and occupying themselves in other less remunerative occupations. In Khandesh when the demand for gunpowder ceased after 1818, the workers turned to lime-making for a livelihood.

The East India Company's monopoly of salt and opium imposed an oppressive burden on India. The people were reduced to going without salt altogether or substituting an unwholesome product obtained from common earth impregnated with saline particles. Romesh Dutt in his *Economic History of India (Victorian Age)* recounts how Robert Bird who had served for thirty years in India as a judicial and revenue officer was asked by the Bombay Government if the salt tax was as oppressive as it was represented to be in a petition submitted by Rustomjee Viccajee and others to the Bombay Government. Bird stated that there was no doubt that it was a very severe duty indeed. He drew pointed attention to the searches for salt carried out in the palanquins transporting women across the frontier which had brought considerable disrepute to the Government. 'I would only say,' he added (Dutt quotes from the Commons's Fourth Report, 1853), 'that if they were not to be searched, we should have more Lot's wifes (sic) brought into the Western Provinces than you ever saw in the country; that every woman's palanquin would be filled with salt from top to bottom.'

Both Dutt and Desai agree that nothing more vividly illustrates the inequity of the economic drain to Great Britain as the land revenue. Cultivators paid this by selling a large portion of the produce of their land, keeping the barest minimum for their own consumption. In 1876-77 when the country was on the brink of one of the severest famines of the century, it was made to export a larger quantity of food grains than ever before! And even a province, devastated by famine, continued to export food to pay for the exacting land revenue. Dadabhai Naoroji in his classic *Poverty And UnBritish Rule in India* writes eloquently about how the exaction of land revenue, over and above the many other taxes, imposed a crippling burden on the Indian people: 'The Land Revenue did not rain from heaven. It formed part and parcel of the annual wealth from which the State Revenue is taken in a variety of different names—call it tax, rent, excise, duty, stamps, income-tax, and so on . . . It was the usual official fiction that the incidence of taxation in India was small as compared with that of this country (Great Britain). But when they considered the incidence of taxation they must consider not simply the amount paid in such taxation, but what it was compared with the capacity of the person who paid it. An elephant might with ease carry a great weight, whilst a quarter ounce, or a grain of wheat, might be sufficient to crush an ant . . . The fact was that the pressure of taxation in India, according to its means of paying, was nearly double that of wealthy England, and far more oppressive, as exacted from poverty.'

A voracious reader, Ardeshir must have pored through this contemporary classic on the subject, by Dadabhai Naoroji. Ardeshir's oft-quoted words, 'We are being fooled (by the British),' reflect the tenor of Dadabhai's writings. He could not but be conscious, as Dadabhai was, that in every sphere the interests of the rulers were put above the interests of his country. In the choice between railways and canals, to give but one example, the former were preferred because they helped Britain's trade with India. The canals, on the contrary, would have helped agriculture on which the vast majority of poor Indians depended. The railway rates were so arranged as to encourage the import of manufactured articles from England and the export of raw materials from India. There were cases, for instance, of lower rates for longer distances, in the case of raw materials going to the ports. The rate structure aimed similarly at discouraging the export of India's finished products. Worst of all, because the dividend on railways was guaranteed, there was waste and even corruption, resulting in a loss of forty million pounds by 1900 which was made up by taxes from India.

The British made vast fortunes from an unlawful monopoly of trade and industry. Indian merchant princes had no alternative but to close shop. Again, in the financing of foreign trade, Indian 'shroffs' were replaced by British exchange banks who favoured their own nationals. The profits of key sectors like railways, shipping and insurance went out of the country. Currency and exchange, fiscal policy and purchase of stores were manipulated to encourage imports of British manufactures. As a result millions of artisans lost their livelihood.

British factory products poured into India so that millions of Indian artisans lost their skills and livelihood and became labourers or fell back on land. The British also acquired a monopoly over indigo, tea and jute in India. The indigo cultivators and tea-workers were cruelly exploited. While Factory Acts were imposed in India from 1881, because of pressure from Lancashire, there was no regulation of working-conditions in plantations. Further, all import duties in India were removed by 1882, while an excise duty was put on products of India's cotton mills in 1894.

India's import and export figures dramatized the extent and nature of the drain. The total imports were about a hundred crore rupees annually and the total annual exports were about 150 crores. After taking into consideration the precious metals that came into the country to redress a part of the balance, a loss of 30 to 40 crores was still borne by India. The process was well-described by the Honourable Gopal Krishna Gokhale, scholar and patriot, while addressing an audience in Lucknow in 1907. 'Now, I will put a simple question to those present here, if a hundred rupees come into your house every month and a hundred and fifty rupees go out, will you be growing richer or poorer? And, if this process goes on year after year, decade after decade, what will be your position after a time?' He added: 'No country, not even the richest in the world, can stand such a bleeding as this.' Bleeding was, he admitted, a strong word, 'but it was first used with regard to this very process by a great English statesman—the late Lord Salisbury—who was Prime Minister of England for a long time and was before that Secretary of State for India.'

It wasn't only Indian industries, but agriculture too that had declined. Sixty-five to eighty per cent of the population depended on agriculture. The soil was becoming rapidly exhausted and the yield per acre had considerably declined. This was because agricultural science and modern agricultural implements were practically unknown in India, and the prevalent small holdings did not lend themselves to the use of advanced equipment.

Dadabhai's words and those of other distinguished nationalists were a clarion call to Ardeshir: 'Thus there was injustice and exploitation in every field. The result was unemployment of millions; plenty turning into poverty; the deadly famines with all their immediate and ultimate effects, famines more frequent, more widespread and more fatal than any known before in the history of India or of the world; the narrowing of the sources of national wealth, the almost exclusive dependence on agriculture and its further consequences; the loss of balance in the economy; the sharp increase in taxation expenditure and public debt. Agriculture and industry, trade and shipping, banking and currency, all the branches of the economy suffered.'

But what also impressed the extremely fair-minded Ardeshir was that while condemning the drain, Dadabhai handsomely acknowledged the British contribution to India's welfare. British rule offered many a priceless blessing to India. Among these were western education, peace, strong and effective government, wise laws and courts of justice with high standards. To these Dadabhai added irrigation works, a fine system of famine relief which, however, broke down on occasions, modern means of transport and communication and which resulted in the economic and political unity of India. Not that these works, however great, could ever make up for the loss in self-respect. Only self-reliance could instill this.

The situation seemed to Ardeshir, as it did to Dadabhai, to be intolerable and unforgivable. He would have agreed with the Poet Laureate of his age, the deep moans round with many voices: 'Come, my friends, 'tis not too late to seek a newer world.' Gone was even a trace of regret in his mind over what had happened at Zanzibar. In its place was a resolve to take up this tremendous challenge to break the British stranglehold and to dedicate his life henceforth to improve the plight of his countrymen by all the means at his command. He had lost a job, but found a vocation. A conviction stirred within him, that this was what destiny had ordained for him. His beloved country appeared to be caught in the tentacles of the British octopus. She had to be freed.

Once again, as so often in history, David found himself pitted against the mighty Goliath. Hopefully, David had a stone in his shepherd's sling.

2
THE CALL OF SWADESHI

At the time Ardeshir was engaged in fighting a legal case in East Africa, news came to him of his compatriot Mohandas Karamchand Gandhi who was waging what looked like a losing battle for the rights of Indians in South Africa. When Gandhi returned to India, Ardeshir met him along with other nationalist leaders and was deeply influenced by him.

While the two, who met frequently, shared an interest in winning freedom for the country, they differed on the methods to achieve it. Gandhi was waging a political battle, whereas Ardeshir believed firmly that, until and unless India became economically self-reliant, freedom would remain a distant dream. British goods sold in India at the expense of the Indian goods, at times of as good if not better quality, were forging the chains that kept the country subjugated. People were becoming hopelessly dependent on these foreign goods. The British had therefore to be beaten at their own game. Indian goods had to be manufactured in India that would be as good as the imported ones, and be cheaper.

Ardeshir's conviction was strengthened by his faith in India's traditional craftsmen. The wealth of the country's natural resources that was being continuously drained by the British rulers as forcefully described by Dadabhai Naoroji, had to be retained within the country and exploited for its own benefit. The trouble was, as Justice Mahadeo Govind Ranade took pains to point out, the industrial domination of one people by another attracts much less attention than the political domination by a foreign people. The industrial domination is less visible and operates in a more insidious, dangerous and far-reaching manner. Ardeshir was able to drive home this point with Gandhi when the struggle for independence was not making the expected headway. Ardeshir advised Gandhi, reflecting the nationalist ideas of Swadeshi then current, that the only way was not to depend on foreign goods. With their imports ceasing, the economy of the ruling country would be affected and India's economy correspondingly strengthened.

Swadeshi, in its truest and widest sense, could be the biggest single contributory factor towards the desired economic resurgence of the country and so to its political freedom. As enunciated by Ardeshir this concept did not mean merely boycotting British goods and buying Indian goods. It propagated the philosophy that every country, India or any other, had to choose its technology, production, consumption-habits and marketing-techniques depending on its resources and based on its genius. No country should coerce another to export its techniques, production and marketing systems. Underlining the uniqueness of each country, the concept was therefore universal in its application.

Another political leader of that era, Gokhale, felt the same way. 'The idea bears repetition,' he declared in 1907, 'that Swadeshism at its highest is not merely an industrial movement, but that it affects the whole life of the nation—that Swadeshism at its highest is a deep, passionate, fervent, all-embracing love of the motherland, and that this love seeks to show itself, not in one sphere of activity only, but in all: it invades the whole man, and it will not rest until it has raised the whole man.'

The Revd C.F. Andrews, a true friend of India, writing in the *Tribune*, Lahore, invested the movement with a spiritual purpose: 'True Swadeshi is a spirit and there are many of us who hope that this spiritual purpose, namely, the achievement of national self-consciousness, will become the fuller meaning of the word in future and that a man will not only be regarded as a true Swadeshi who purchases Indian goods, but also the man who breaks through denationalizing caste prejudices, who forsakes customs which separate Indian from Indian, who meets with and treats with his fellow-countrymen on equal and brotherly terms.' Andrews held the true goal of Swadeshi to be 'the motive of making all human life in this fair motherland healthier, happier, nobler, sweeter, purer.'

Ardeshir was further considerably encouraged in his belief and faith in Swadeshi by his friend and contemporary, Lokmanya B.G. Tilak, who organized the Paisa Fund to help the Swadeshi movement's activities in production, trade and consumption. Gandhi himself became a willing adherent of this concept and was gracious enough to admit to Ardeshir that his eyes 'opened too late.'

It was characteristic of Ardeshir to whom challenges

were the stuff of achievement that he should have begun by trying his manufacturing skills on a product that would test them to the utmost and could only be put to a highly specialized use. Of course, he was following in the glorious tradition of surgery going back to Charaka and Sushanta whose teachings are described in the *Charaka Samitha* and the *Sushrata Samitha*, from the second and fifth century respectively. The *Sushruta Samitha* describes about one hundred and twenty-one surgical instruments of various kinds that were in use way back then.

It was not too surprising that the idea of making surgical instruments in India fired Ardeshir's imagination, not that there was any demand for surgical instruments as such, the imported ones being sufficient to meet the existing demand, but because Ardeshir wanted to prove that even such highly sophisticated instruments could be made in India. He approached Merwanji Cama, a philanthrophic old gentleman owning several properties in the city. Merwanji, before he died, set apart cash and property of the value of Rs 25 lakhs to establish the Muncherji F. Cama Athornan Institute in memory of his father. This Institute affords education, especially religious, to the sons of the Parsi priestly class whose amelioration was always close to Merwanji's heart.

Merwanji had high regard for Ardeshir and readily gave him the few thousand rupees he needed. Ardeshir began by acquiring the necessary experience, repairing surgical instruments in 1895-96 for a well-known firm of chemists. He achieved such perfection that the firm of chemists was duly impressed. There was a hitch, however. The stranglehold of the British was such that 'Made In England' tagged on to a product automatically ensured its sales. Convinced that nobody would buy surgical instruments made by an Indian, the firm of chemists wanted to market them under a foreign name. Ardeshir found this insulting. Besides, it would defeat the very purpose for which he had spent long hours shaping and re-shaping these instruments. Fate decreed that Ardeshir would never become another William Ferguson (1782-1877) whose surgical instruments are still in use today.

Ardeshir was disappointed, but not disheartened. On the contrary the incident hardened his resolve to prove that India could do it. He felt God's nudge to try again and try something different. But first he went to his friend Cama to reassure him that he would return the loan as soon as he was able to. Cama, however, was not so much interested in the return of his loan as he was in the future of this eager, idealistic but seemingly unlucky young man in whom he discerned outstanding talent. With time this talent was to be recognized and to be amply rewarded. Gifted with a restless and innovative mind and the itch to inquire and experiment, Ardeshir was now to try and experiment with a wide variety of products. Indeed, a lifetime was to prove too short for all that he wanted to and indeed could have achieved.

Ardeshir's attention turned to what has unjustly been described as 'the lowly lock.' Considering that the history of lock-making goes back thousands of years and that it inspired many ingenious devices by inventors in as many countries, in man's unending search for absolute security, locks can hardly be described as lowly. The lock, too, like surgical instruments, goes back 4000 years, to the ruins of the palace at Khorsabad near Nineveh. The earliest known type of lock and, incidentally, the biggest in size, this lock was made of wood, with the bolt held in position by several loose, wooden pins which fitted into holes made in it. A long, wooden key with pins on it could be inserted into a slot in the bolt. These pins raised the loose, wooden pins to the height that would allow the bolt to be withdrawn.

Later, the Romans invented metal locks and keys. The system of security was provided by wards which were projections around the keyhole inside the lock to prevent the key from being rotated. This system was for hundreds of years the only method of ensuring that only the right key would rotate in the keyhole.

Various improvements in design and degree of security continued to be made by several renowned lock-makers like Barron, Bramah, Chubb and others. When Ardeshir arrived on the scene, a wide variety of locks existed. Locks which couldn't be blown open. Locks whose keys could be altered at will. Locks which could be opened or closed by several different keys, but could be unlocked by only the particular key which closed them. Locks devised to prevent the thief from exploring their insides or from detecting with a picket tool slight changes of resistance in the mechanism. Locks which could be opened with a code word and, believe it or not, locks which could shoot or stab intruders or seize their hands. Much later, electrical devices came to be used to manipulate combinations or make it possible to control locks from a distance.

A factor that encouraged Ardeshir to undertake lock-manufacture was that by the end of 1850, with the improvement in transport facilities, the limited spread of modern education, the rise in trade and the accumulation of capital due to conditions created by the American Civil War, western India's economy was well set towards industrial development on modern lines. The first attempt to start a weaving mill was made in 1845 by Jeejeebhoy Dadabhai, a Parsi merchant of Bombay. It was only in 1851, however, that Cowasji Nanabhoy Daver, son of a rich merchant who held the agencies of several English firms, founded the Bombay Spinning and Weaving Company as a joint-stock company. Its foundation was laid in 1854 and it commenced working in 1856 with seventeen thousand spindles and no looms. Within a decade, by 1865, there were ten cotton mills in the city working with twenty-five thousand spindles and three thousand three hundred and eighty looms.

Another Parsi, hailing from Navsari and whose name was to become a legend also came to Bombay in 1853. He was Jamsetji Tata who launched a private trading firm in Bombay with a capital of Rs 21,000. Jamsetji and his associates obtained a contract to furnish supplies required by the Expeditionery Force of General Napier in Abyssinia. The profits they reaped from this venture were large enough to launch Jamsetji on a career in textiles. He bought an old oil mill in partnership with a few friends, converted it into a textile mill and made it a going concern only to sell it a couple of years later. Bombay was then known as the 'cottonpolis' of India. Jamsetji planned to set up his new mill at the very spot the cotton came from, Nagpur. The company floated in 1874 with a capital of Rs 1,500,000 came to be named the Empress Mills.

In this milieu, Ardeshir made a small beginning by hiring a tiny shed beside the Bombay Gas Works at Lalbaug, at Rs 20/-a month and started manufacture on 7 May 1897. He could have done little else, even had he had a capital of more than a few thousand rupees, because industrialization as we know it was just starting. As Prof Divekar points out in the *Cambridge Economic History of India*, till the middle of the nineteenth century, the *karkhanas* of the Maratha rulers were only storage-places or, at best in a few cases, workplaces where craftsmen worked in their traditional way. The prevailing economic and social situation, as also education, which still had a strong theological bias and no scientific content, were not conducive conditions for the emergence of the factory system. While European products were being used on a large scale by the population, there was little or no curiosity about European techniques of production. European capitalists too hardly took any initiative in starting factories mainly because of lack of governmental encouragement and lack of transport facilities.

All this was changing and Ardeshir was to play a crucial role in this process. He purchased the necessary implements and materials and banded together a group of skilled workers from Gujarat and Malabar to establish a workshop in the shed. Ardeshir's younger brother Pirojsha, fresh from the Victoria Jubilee Technical Institute, became his willing assistant some time later.

Ardeshir had three brothers, Hormusji, Munchersha and Pirojsha, and two sisters Shirinbai and Tehmina. Pirojsha was the only one to join the business. Hormusji, elder to him, was not at all interested. His interests were in literature and the arts. Munchersha's interests too lay elsewhere. He joined the firm of Tatas and opened a branch for them in Kobe, Japan, which he did so successfully that they asked him to open a similar branch in Paris where R.D. Tata accompanied him. Later, Tatas withdrew from Paris, but Munchersha enamoured of the City of Lights stayed behind. He was hardly the typical tourist, much more like a Frenchman in his respect for Paris. He started his own business in precious stones and pearls, and selling cars.

One of Munchersha's major interests in his capacity as President of 'L Association Sociale et Commerciale Hindoue' was to entertain Indians visiting Paris. Pandit Nehru was one of them. Rabindranath Tagore was another. A tea party was arranged for the latter by Munchersha in June 1921 to enable him to meet Indian residents in Paris. In the course of his speech he made the announcement of a scholarship of 20,000 francs to be offered by two Indian gentlemen to an Indian student for the study of social sciences and industry in France. He also announced that Sir Rabindranath Tagore had been requested to select the student. Munchersha requested the poet to convey a message to India, that Indians in Paris were in full sympathy with their compatriots' efforts and sincerely shared their toils and troubles in the task of national awakening. Among the speakers on this occasion was the renowned Prof Benoy Kumar Sarkar who stressed the importance of assimilating the essential and useful elements of French culture which could be of great service in building up Greater India.

Munchersha had an interesting friend, Burjorji Padshah, who accompanied him to Paris. Padshah was closely linked to the Tatas and, along with Ardeshir Billimoria and Nawroji Saklatvala, worked tirelessly towards the establishment of the TISCO and Hydro concerns. On his retirement Padshah found it cheaper, instead of residing in Bombay, to stay permanently on a P & O liner travelling between India and Australia.

But to return to the lock-making business. There were other lock-makers scattered over the country at Aligarh, Howrah and elsewhere, but these operated mostly by hand. The technique of production was crude, the process mainly labour-intensive. First, patterns were prepared for each of the lock components. Then, with the help of these patterns, moulds were made with sand mixtures. Next, casting was done by pouring molten brass into the moulds. All these processes were done by hand with simple tools. Filing, polishing, fixing, cutting, welding, fitting and the final adjustment of the lock were also done by hand. Ardeshir realized that the labour costs involved could only be reduced if any or all of the above processes could be mechanized. He was determined to use modern methods with modern machinery. His factory, when fully equipped, would cost him eighty thousand rupees.

This machinery was worked by a 40 hp steam-engine.

Thus, in 1897, Godrej & Boyce Mfg. Co. Ltd., was set up. It was later incorporated with limited liability on 3 March 1932 under the Indian Companies Act 1913.

Queries have often been raised about the 'Boyce' in the metal products company's name. Boyce was actually Mehrwanji Cama's nephew. When Ardeshir went to Mehrwanji to repay the loan he had taken from him to start his business, Mehrwanji refused to accept it but suggested instead that Boyce be taken in the business. This was done, but Boyce soon lost interest. His name was retained, however, as a legal obligation.

Work began with the manufacture of high-security locks, named Anchor Brand, in 1897. Several ingenious ways were devised to make these locks 'absolutely unpickable', reflecting how Ardeshir's extremely security-conscious mind worked. The patent Gordian locks incorporated in safes highlight this. The Gordian lock was provided with a distinct pair of keys; the No. 1 key was for opening and securing the lock in the usual way. The No. 2 key was meant to be used in case the No. 1 key was lost. The No.1 key could not open the lock by itself; the No. 2 key had to be used first and then the No. 1. The No. 2 key could not by itself either open or secure the safe. In other words, the No. 2 key was only a counter-check to the No. 1 key. These locks and the eight-lever locks were displayed at twelve exhibitions in various parts of the country and secured the highest awards in each case.

The Detector locks, as its name implies, were meant to apprise its owner of attempts to open the safe in his absence. When a key approaching the true key was turned in this lock in the opening direction, the bolt got fixed and could not be thrown back afterwards with the true key. Thus interference was detected. When this happened, the right key had first to be turned in the closing direction. This would release the bolt and the lock would open in the usual way. Ardeshir went on to warn potential buyers that the price of a lock did not depend solely on the number of levers. A well-made four-lever lock would not yield to any but its proper key. Another having eight or ten levers, but carelessly made, could be opened with a dozen different keys. It all depended on the amount of labour put in to secure unpickability.

Ardeshir learnt as he went along. He supervised every detail of the lock-making process, devising new methods to defy the lock-breaker. In a booklet published by him in 1911, Ardeshir could claim 'the work is done on modern methods, with the aid of modern machinery with which the factory is equipped throughout at a very large outlay. We do not buy our locks or any safe parts readymade but we manufacture all our requirements ourselves. We have a large number of specially trained lock-makers having over fifteen years' practice. This enables us to make our locks as accurately as those by the best European makers. Our keys are all deep-forged and machine-cut and not filed out by hand. We cut the keys first and make the locks to fit the keys. This makes our locks absolutely unpickable and ensures long wear.'

The variety and intricacy of lock-making fascinated Ardeshir. For high-quality padlocks or safe locks, the fitting clearances required to be maintained were within a thousandth of an inch, whereas the vital components themselves were prepared in special machines to dimensional tolerances of the order of 5/10,000th of an inch and less. The process of manufacture also was far more elaborate than of the tumbler padlocks. First, the levers were prepared. Then the bottom was fitted to the shackle. Next, the levers were inserted according to the number of the key, with the keyhole fitted. Then the top was fitted, with the nails hammered in. Finally, the front and back brass plates were provided. Such locks were cent per cent unpickable and any of them selected at random would respond to but one key, its own, from mountains of other keys that might be tried.

Godrej locks were not only as good as the imported variety, they effected marked improvements in the latter. In all locks made hitherto, European or American, the levers depended for their proper working on springs attached to them. Such locks were liable to give trouble or totally refuse to yield to the key when for some reason the levers sometimes stuck to one another, or when one of the numerous springs broke. Ardeshir was the first to invent and put on the market a lever lock without springs. Hitherto, many users had sometimes encountered a lock that defied all efforts of the skilled lock-maker to open it, leaving them no choice but to break open a valuable safe or strong room. Even the best safe-makers' products were not free from being liable to such mishaps. The Godrej patent springless lock, as its name implies, had no springs attached to its levers and therefore was not subject to any such disorders. This was the earliest of the thirty-six Godrej patented inventions.

The sales of these locks exceeded even Ardeshir's expectations. Even today, a hundred years after Ardeshir started making them, locks continue to be a profitable business line, constituting 10 per cent of the Godrej turnover. The name Godrej has come to acquire a proud place in the long and romantic history of lock-making.

But Ardeshir could not sit back content. The quest for self-reliance would not allow it. His restless nature forbade it. He had arrived—but he would have agreed with the poet that it is better to travel hopefully than to arrive. The foundation laid by him with such loving concern had to be built upon. Fresh fields of endeavour remained to be explored.

3
TOWARDS SELF-RELIANCE

From locks to safes—the logical line of succession. This brings to mind the story of the Turkish shopkeeper. This shopkeeper was preparing to lock up and go home one day when a friend brought him a gift of two melons. For lack of a better place to keep them for the night, he put them in his safe. Only next morning did he realize how very lucky he was, for his shop had caught fire in the night and the juice from the melons had saved the valuables in the safe from being burnt to ashes.

This is said to be the origin of the device, whereby, in the event of fire, a moisture-generating compound is released in a safe. This fire-resistant quality, besides its being burglar-resistant, is one of the strongest selling-points of a safe.

But we are getting ahead of our story. Leaving the lock business in the responsible hands of his brother Pirojsha, Ardeshir travelled to England, France and Germany in 1906 with the primary aim of visiting the factories making security equipment in these countries. He wanted to see for himself their methods for manufacturing security equipment, the machinery and materials they used, their marketing and publicity techniques. He had already improved on imported locks. He wanted to see for himself whether he could do the same with safes. The search for security was the origin of the demand for safes. There were a few scattered safe-manufacturers in the country, but they were no match to the British manufacturers, Chubb and Milners. Ardeshir was able to prove that the fire-, fall- and burglar-resisting qualities of his safes were superior to the foreign ones. World-famous British security equipment manufacturers had established more or less a monopoly of sales in India. None of the few scattered Indian manufacturers of safes could even dare dream of competing with these giants. None except Ardeshir. God nudged him again.

The small shed at Lalbaug in which Ardeshir had begun had now grown into a factory in the real sense of the word. On one side was a fair-sized shed housing the lock department where as many as five to six hundred skilled workers assembled the machine-made components of a large variety of locks and latches. At another, even bigger shed for security equipment, tough steel plates were subjected to the tortures of flattening rolls, heavy plate-bending machines and high temperature electric arc-welding before they emerged into pre-designed structures of high mechanical strength to form a modern safe. The bodies of fire-resistant safes were lined with a special, fire-resistant and moisture-generating compound.

During his visit abroad and from certain happenings in Bombay itself, Ardeshir shrewdly laid his finger on certain weaknesses of the foreign safes bearing the names of well-known manufacturers. The *Scientific American* of 26 May 1908 carried a trenchant article describing the havoc wrought on so-called fireproof safes manufactured by European and American manufacturers: 'It is sad to have to say that the San Francisco fire has demonstrated the worthlessness of many safes and vaults guaranteed by the manufacturers to be proof against burglars and fire. The manufacturers, dealers and agents have in many instances been shown to have sold fireproof safes that were of little more value than wooden boxes and the fireproof composition with which they are lined might as well have been sawdust. It is to be sincerely hoped that the manufacturers of and dealers in these worst (sic) than worthless devices may be put out of business for all time.' On this Ardeshir had this comment to make: 'After reading the above it will be a surprise to know that safes of certain well-known European makers are actually lined with sawdust to a very great extent.'

Another weakness noticed by Ardeshir was that in foreign safes the backs were attached to the bodies by means of angle-bars, which made it possible for the back to be removed by forcing the rivets. This led Ardeshir to incorporate three very important patented inventions in his safes, the Patent Door Frame, the Double-Plate Doors and the Lock-Case. The first improvement entailed bending the back edges of the body into flanges and placing the back in position from the front and riveting it to the flanges so that it could not be detached by forcing the rivets. As regards the Double-Plate Doors, Ardeshir was aware that several unscrupulous foreign safe-makers were sending articles to India that looked like safes but were so made that they could be broken open by any one in five or ten minutes with no other tools but a small hammer and a punch. In Godrej safes, therefore, the door plates were made of two separate sheets and the Lock-Case and other vital parts were attached to the inner plate, all the joints being thus protected by the outer plate and covering them so as to put them out of reach of the burglar's tools. The Lock-Case too was constructed so that once locked the door was perfectly secure against any attempt at forcing it open with levers, wedges or other means. The shooting-bolt mechanism was controlled by an eight-lever double-control Gordian lock, and the inside drawer fitted with an unpickable six-lever lock.

Ardeshir cleared the prevailing misconception that the heavier the safe, the more secure it was. He stressed that it was the design, not the weight, that made all the difference. The 16-corner bend of Godrej safes made them fire-, fall- and burglar-resistant. For the 16-corner bend, one single sheet was folded to form the four sides of the safe and this sheet had sixteen bends. The back plate was welded and the front door was fitted subsequently. This gave extra rigidity to the sides of the safe.

Ardeshir himself had occasion to demonstrate the breaking open of a European safe belonging to Dhanjibhai Batliwalla, a wealthy mill-agent of Bombay. In three minutes flat the safe was broken open in the presence of the owner and a friend. Ardeshir's renown as a safe-maker was once again called into play, but this time in the contrary role as safe-breaker by one Mr Bawla who had bought a well-known European maker's safe at a very high price. Ardeshir was able to do so in ten minutes. 'Instances like these could be cited indefinitely,' claimed Ardeshir. 'Even our cheapest safes could not possibly be so contemptuously treated even by the best of cracksmen equipped with the best of tools.'

An even more dramatic test was done at the residence of a well-known citizen of Bombay, Mr Lallubhai Samaldas. In Ardeshir's own words, 'Lallubhai is a millionaire and occasionally leaves large amounts of cash in his safes, so he decided to satisfy himself by practical test whether Godrej's safes were really worthy of their good name. Arrangement was made with three professional safe-breakers to break open the safe on a fixed day and I [Mr Godrej] was advised of it. On the appointed day the safe was handed over to the tender mercies of the three men in the presence of Lallubhai, his assistant and me [Mr Godrej]. The work was of course not subject to any embarrassing limitations of time or noise usually attending burglars' operations and the men had a reputation to gain, so they hammered away with hearty goodwill for three hours and at the end of that time they threw up their tools in despair declaring that in the three hours they had made almost no headway and that the safe was beyond their skill and strength.'

Ardeshir established rigid standards to determine the fire-resisting quality of a safe—the quality of retaining efficiency not for a short period but indefinitely; the ingredients should not react chemically with one another; they should have no corrosive action on iron or steel; they should be prepared to give off their water of crystallization long before being heated to a temperature that would 'injure' paper. Significantly, no other safe-maker had the courage to submit his mixture to such chemical tests. Prof Shanial, M.A., Professor of Chemistry, Queen's College, Banaras, after a prolonged examination of the mixture prepared by Ardeshir, reported that it satisfactorily fulfilled all these conditions. Ardeshir was awarded the highest prize in this regard.

The fire-resisting quality of Godrej safes was proved beyond a shadow of doubt by an elaborate test conducted in the presence of John Wallace, C.E., Editor of the *Indian*

Textile Journal. The safe was placed in an open space adjoining the Godrej factory. Mr Wallace put into the safe a strip of pinewood to which were attached pieces of linen, calico, flannel and silk; also a small coil of pure tin electric fuse-wire, a ten-rupee currency note, a sheet of foolscap paper, several newspapers and a wooden box lacquered on the exterior and containing a piece of wax.

A fire was lighted all around the safe till the outer plates became red hot. A pile of red-hot embers was put on the top so that five of the six sides were exposed to the fire. After almost four hours the safe was sluiced with buckets of water which produced the effect of a fire-hose.

On opening the safe, it was found that neither the strip of pinewood nor the tin fuse-wire showed any sign of having been affected by the heat. Except for a slight discoloration, the textile samples were unharmed, as also was the ten-rupee currency-note. As far as the wooden box was concerned, the wax had melted but the lacquer remained. An astonished John Wallace happily concluded, 'I may therefore conclude that books, documents, valuable instruments, and jewellery of gold, silver or gems would have been undamaged had they been in the safe during the test.'

Testimonials to the fire- and burglar-resistant qualities of Godrej safes kept pouring in. Some of these make interesting reading. The one from Nusserwanji & Co., dated 7 September 1904, stated: 'Our office peon who was dismissed some time ago had, as he admitted in his trial, possessed himself of the safe key and paid a number of nightly visits to our office, making attempts to open the safe. This he could not do owing to our being in the habit, since the key was lost, of re-locking the safe with the check key you supply for preventing fraudulent use of lost keys. We congratulate you on such excellent contrivance of your safe-locks. The peon we may add has been sentenced to two months' rigorous imprisonment by Mr Dracup.'

K.S. Dubash & Co. (17 November 1914) affirmed: 'On entering my room after the fire I found everything completely burnt and reduced to ashes. Seeing the state of the room I was very doubtful as to whether I would recover my books, papers and cash box which were in one of your safes which was also in the room, but on opening the safe to my surprise and the astonishment of those with me everything was found absolutely intact and there were no traces of the intense heat having penetrated the safe.'

Chatarbhuj Kalidas stated: "I congratulate you on the behaviour of your safe when its fire-resisting capacity was put to a test in the recent fire in Luxmidas Khimji's cloth market. Of the hundreds of other shops in the market that were gutted the fire was nowhere more severe than in my shop and in spite of that currency notes for Rs 3,000 that were in the safe showed no sign of having passed through such a severe trial.'

Gorhdandas V. Patel's testimonial (28 November 1914) said: 'I had in my use a Godrej's safe when my house in Girgaum Back Road was on fire some days ago. Everything in my room was completely burnt up and the severity of the fire was greatest near where your safe was lying. It contained currency notes, valuable papers, some gold ornaments and a packet of loose pearls. The safe being Godrej's we were confident the papers would be found intact, but some of us had doubt about the safety of the pearls. On opening the safe we were all agreeably surprised to see that the pearls were perfectly safe and as lustrous as before the fire.'

In the Dharamtolla films fire—the most devastating conflagration ever to occur considering the damage it did—currency notes, diamonds, pearls and other valuables kept in Godrej safes emerged unscathed. As one of the victims of the Dharamtolla fire, A. Ghani Z. Abedin, wrote to Ardeshir on 8 April 1925: 'We have very great pleasure to inform you that we had one of your safes, C quality, in our cloth shop at 6, Dharamtolla Street. On the top flat of our shop was the store of films belonging to Messrs J.F. Madan & Co. The store caught fire on the night of 2nd April and completely destroyed and reduced to ashes our shop and its contents. Your safe was subjected to the severest test, being under flames from beginning to end. On the 5th April when the safe was broken open, everything in it to our astonishment, currency notes, diamonds, pearls, gold and silver ornaments to the extent of thousands of rupees came out absolutely intact. Neither any paper nor the thin silk cloth containing jewellery was injured or damaged in the slightest way nor any gold or silver was melted though the heat round the safe was very fierce and above the safe celluloid films were burning with terrific fury . . .' From then on banks, business houses and other business institutions, switched over to Godrej for their requirements of safe and other security products.

Godrej safes passed test after test, although the supreme test was to come some years after Ardeshir passed away, in 1944, during the wartime ammunition explosion in the Bombay docks. The fires lasted for days, and the loss was tremendous. After the terrific explosion, Godrej safes in more or less battered condition, but with their contents intact, were brought to Lalbaug to be opened. To give but one example, Godrej safes saved five and a half lakh rupees for the Mandvi Branch of the Union Bank, which acknowledged the fact in heartfelt gratitude.

Ardeshir could proudly claim that HIM the Queen Empress used a Godrej safe throughout her tour of India in 1912. Among other distinguished institutions that relied on Godrej safes were His Majesty's Mint, the coin-vaults at the Currency Office, Bombay, the Greater Indian Peninsular

(GIP), Bombay Baroda and Central India (BBCI) and other railways, the Imperial Bank of India and banks throughout the country, the States of Hyderabad, Mysore, Kashmir, Baroda, besides Bombay. Godrej became 'guardians of the nation's wealth.' There were customers who, dissatisfied by the security offered by the foreign safes, turned in desperation to Godrej safes. Sir Sassoon J. David, Bart, after a thorough inquiry into how other safes had behaved during recent city fires, decided to replace all such safes with seven bought from Godrej. The Government of India, after several experiences with safes of other makers, installed 910 burglar-resistant safes. The Savings Banks in India and Burma ordered 400 safes after a severe competitive test by fire in Calcutta by the Director-General of Posts and Telegraphs in July 1912.

Ardeshir was emboldened by his astounding success to publicly offer a prize worth double the value of the safe of any foreign make to those who could compete successfully with a Godrej safe in a fire test. In issuing this challenge, Ardeshir was following the example set by the famous lock-maker Joseph Bramah in England. So confident was Bramah of the security of his lock that he exhibited one in his London shop and offered a reward of £ 200 to the first person who could break it open. For over fifty years it remained unpicked until 1851 when a skilled American locksmith, A.C. Hobbs, succeeded and claimed the reward. Nobody, however, came forward to take advantage of Ardeshir's offer.

For those who did not need or could not afford a regular safe, there were specially designed Godrej safe-cabinets; coffers, which were built like a safe from strong steel plates with special armour over the locking device. Coffers could be embedded in walls. There were also Godrej cash and jewel boxes which could be fitted to a counter, desk, shelf or in a cupboard.

If, later, Pirojsha took pride in any one aspect of security engineering, it was in being entrusted with the building of almost all safe-deposits and strong rooms in India. Hundreds of such safe-deposit vaults were built and equipped by Godrej for banks and safe-deposit concerns, both in India and abroad. Indeed 92 per cent of security equipment in the country was by Godrej. This included the equipment supplied to the Imperial Bank of India, now the State Bank of India, in 32 centers.

The vital part of a safe-deposit vault is the main vault-door. Thought and ingenuity were lavished by Pirojsha on its design and construction. Although the one feature of this door that never fails to impress the layman is its massivity and evident strength, it is built with the precision of a fine machine tool, to micrometer standards. In the Godrej vault doors nothing is left to chance. If attempts are made to dislodge the lock with explosives, a fool-proof mechanism built into the locking mechanism closes the door. So staggering is the figure of possible combinations of these locks that burglars may fiddle with them for months without hope of hitting upon the right combination.

Such was Ardeshir's inventive genius that Godrej were the recipient of several Certificates of 'Registration of Designs and Patents' from the patent office 'in pursuance of and subject to the provisions of the Indian Patents and Designs Act, 1911 and the Indian Patents and Designs Rules, 1933'. Later, the strongest vaults were without exception built by Godrej on their patented methods of reinforcement (patent numbers 21573, 22501 and 46302).

Ardeshir was now on sure ground. The quality of safes manufactured by him were of world standard. Time was when not only Indian safe-makers but Indians generally believed that they would never be able to compete with British safe-makers. The position was now reversed and

Ardeshir could proudly claim that it was the British safe-makers who could not now dare to compete with their Indian counterparts. He went on to explain why. Foreign safe-makers had to pay for the excessively dear European labour (six to ten times as dear as Indian labour). The price they charged had to provide for the big profits claimed by European makers, the packing expenses, high railway-charges, freight and import duties, the expense of loading and unloading, insurance, dock dues, customs-duties, cart and loading hire to godowns, dealer's profits and in some cases the importer's commission. Ardeshir conceded that foreign makers could buy their plates a little cheaper. But this advantage was trivial, seen against the disadvantage of the thirty per cent added cost due to the factors enumerated above. 'When', said Ardeshir 'the high cost of European labour is also considered along with this, it will be easy to understand that, quality for quality, two of our safes can be bought for the price of one foreign safe.'

It is noteworthy that in the meantime, the foreign firm which once held the monopoly of security equipment sales in India, quietly transferred its sales operations to Australia. Sohrab, Pirojsha's son, recalls how the firm's representative approached him with the suggestion that they be given a share in the business in India. 'What about giving us a share in your UK business?' Sohrab retorted.

Ardeshir could now be proud that at least in this one field of security equipment, India had become self-sufficient and totally self-reliant. Swadeshi was a concept whose time had come.

The concept was becoming a power.

4

A Complexion Pure

> *Get thee a skin of exquisite texture, of a soft and delicate bloom, and a complexion pure and clear...*
> —Yoga Sutra

Copy for a soap advertisement today? No, a line from the *Yoga Sutra* dating back to the second century AD. Soap, the commonest of articles of everyday use, taken for granted and dismissed lightly, though wrongly, can yet be a possible measure of a nation's modernity and manners. Soap can tell a story of health habits and, what is more, can be a guide to the purchasing power of a people. The German chemist, Justus von Liebig, declared early in the nineteenth century that the quantity of soap consumed by a nation was an accurate measure of its wealth and civilization. The annual per capita consumption of soap in America and on the continent varies from twenty to twenty-five pounds. In India it is between ten and twelve pounds. But if it is any consolation, the consumption is lower still in China.

Having taken a giant step forward in achieving total self-reliance in security engineering, one would think that Ardeshir would have sat back content to consolidate his gains. But it wasn't in Ardeshir's nature ever to sit back. Gains as such, in a monetary sense, meant little or nothing to him. He wanted just enough for his needs, and his needs were spartan. He didn't care about money, in fact he was careless about money because he hadn't anybody to leave it to. A dedicated pioneer, he was restless unless he was trying out new things, exploring yet newer avenues to self-reliance as if seeking to capture some mysterious inner vision. There was some satisfaction in knowing that an industry now existed that hadn't been there before. But, in his youth, Ardeshir had seen too many industries collapse under foreign rule. A single industry wasn't enough for him. He decided to also undertake the manufacture of soap.

Soap, still, is a far cry from security equipment. But it was characteristic of Ardeshir, an industrialist who was very much an intellectual, to try his hand at something that had a long and romantic history behind it. Long before soap manufacture was known to India, Indians were using their own cleansing agents like soap suds for washing and gram flour for bathing purposes. In 1879, for the first time, an English concern undertook soap manufacture at Meerut. Ardeshir couldn't have been unaware that his distinguished contemporary, Sir Pherozeshah Mehta, also an ardent advocate of Swadeshi, had, along with friends like Kashinath Trimbak Telang, launched a soap factory in 1916-17. The enterprise had come to an untimely end with Pherozeshah remarking that 'it was a case of self-sacrifice in a good cause.' But Ardeshir, obsessed as he was with the pursuit of self-reliance by the production of high-quality goods, would only try something that he was confident of improving upon. In soap, as it happened, he effected not only an improvement, but an almost total transformation.

The origin of soap is lost in antiquity. No one knows how it came to be discovered, though there are naturally many stories. One of the better-known, maybe apocryphal, attributions has it that the poor among the Romans made sacrifices to their gods at crude altars outside Rome, on Sapo Hill. Fat, from the sacrificial animals, and ash accumulated at these altars. Rain washed these basic ingredients of soap into the clay soil. Women found it more convenient to clean with this soapy clay. So sapo clay, researchers say, was the origin of soap and the word 'sapo' itself has come to stay in various forms in many languages.

It is said that a full-fledged soap factory was found in the ruins of Pompeii. According to Pliny the Elder, the Phoenicians prepared soap in 600 BC by boiling goat tallow and causticized woodash and which was used sometimes for barter with the Gauls. Soap is said to have been widely known in the Roman Empire. It was the Celts who named the concoction made from animal fats and plantash as 'saipo', from which the word soap is said to be derived. The importance of soap for washing and cleaning was, however, recognized only in the second century AD. Prior to that soap had been used as a form of medicine. The Greek physician Galen (AD c.130-c.200) mentioned soap not only as a medicine but as a means of cleansing the body. Similarly, the eighth century Arab savant, Jabir ben Hayyan, also

A Complexion Pure

mentions soap as a cleansing agent.

There are fascinating incidents connected with the early manufacture of soap. The product was so little used in Central Europe that a box of soap presented to the Duchess of Juelich in 1549 caused a sensation. Again in 1672 when A. Leo, a German, sent Lady von Schleinitz a parcel of soap from Italy, he accompanied it with a detailed description of how to make use of the unfamiliar contents. In London, in the thirteenth and fourteenth centuries, soap-makers at Cheapside had to pay a duty on all the soap they produced. After the Napoleonic Wars this duty rose as high as three pence per pound. Soap-boiling pans were actually fitted with lids that were locked every night by government officials to prevent production under cover of darkness. Only in 1853 was this high tax finally abolished, causing, it is said, a loss to the State of over 1,000,000 pounds.

In America soap-making was a household art with few industrial developments until after about 1800. The process and extent of soap manufacture was revolutionized during the first half of the nineteenth century as a result of M.E. Chevreul's classical research on the constitution of oils and fats and of the introduction of the Leblanc process (invented in 1791) for the manufacture of soda from brine. The method of producing soap by boiling with open steam was introduced at the end of the nineteenth century. With the development of large-scale manufacturing operations, the industry rapidly became able to process individual kettles of soap containing from 1,00,000 to 1,000,000 lb. per charge.

It wasn't until the early twentieth century that India saw the development of the soap industry on modern lines. In 1906, the Indian National Congress, at the instigation of Lokmanya Tilak, Ardeshir Godrej and others, administered the Swadeshi vow in respect of soap. Ten years later the governments of Mysore and Madras started independent soap factories. Two years later, in 1918, Ardeshir came out with a washing-soap bar which, unlike the washing bars then in use, did not shrink out of shape and cleansed better with its rich and creamy lather.

The Swadeshi vow was necessitated by the foreign soaps then flooding the Indian market, bearing exotic names like Vinolia White Rose Soap and Regina Peroxide Soap; also world-famous brands like Lux, advertized as 'the beauty soap of the film stars', Pears glycerine soap, Windsor, Cuticura 'ideal for baby's tender skin' and others. On the other hand, in several parts of the country, soap was a cottage industry. But the soap made lacked the necessary stability and tended to become mushy after a little use. The first modern soap factory in India was established in Meerut in 1897 under the name of the North-West Soap Company. Some of the other major soap factories established in the early years of this century were, apart from Godrej Soaps, the Bombay Soap Factory, Hindustan Lever, Swastik Oil Mills, East Asiatic Co., Government Soap Factory at Bangalore, Calcutta Chemicals and Kusum Products. Significantly the import of soaps dropped from Rs 2 crores in 1920-21 to Rs 18 lakhs in 1940-41!

Competition was bitter between the foreign soap-makers who were favoured by the British rulers and their counterparts in India struggling to make their voice heard. It would take another fifteen years before the latter formed the Indian Soap and Toiletry Makers Association (ISTMA) to speak with authority and conviction on the problems agitating them. In the meantime, quietly, in his unpretentious factory at Delisle Road, Ardeshir was conducting an experiment in soap manufacture that would lead to a scientific discovery of the first order and bring world renown to its inventor.

Ardeshir loved to experiment. He noticed that in making soap one had to choose between two necessary evils, either

A Complexion Pure

to tolerate an excess of sodium chloride or caustic soda. He solved this problem admirably by making a small quantity of soap separately and making fatty acids therefrom by acidulation for neutralizing the free alkali. A good toilet soap had to be neutral, and this process proved efficient and successful.

Ardeshir went on to experiment with the idea of making stable toilet soaps from vegetable oils instead of animal fats as was the accepted practice in most countries since the beginning of soap manufacture. The soap experts expressed doubts whether this could be done, but were proved wrong when in 1920 he produced the first toilet soap to be made purely from vegetable oils and sold commercially. Economically, it was a sound proposition because plentiful supplies of vegetable oils were then available within the country. Socially, too, the experiment was blessed because it respected religious sentiments by replacing animal fats from which foreign soaps were made. To drive his point home, Ardeshir displayed horrifying pictures of animals—the fat of which was being used in a cleansing agent like soap!

An old staff member recalls the angry exchange of letters between Ardeshir and a rival soap-maker in the columns of the now defunct *Bombay Chronicle*. When matters came to a head, Ardeshir angrily sent in a drawing of a pig, with an arrow piercing it, to suggest that till then soaps were made out of its flesh. Fortunately, the Editor put an end to the controversy. But the point was made. The eyes of the orthodox Hindu community were opened.

It is significant that the first vegetable-oil soap marketed by Ardeshir after many years of research was named 'No. 2'. When this soap was introduced, experiments were still being conducted, and when these were completed the resultant 'No. 1' soap with a lingering rose perfume proved to be better in more ways than one. Many people used this soap for years after it was introduced in 1922. No. 2 soap continued to be sold side by side with No. 1. Later, in the early eighties the manufacture of both No. 1 and No. 2 was stopped. Ardeshir was once asked why he introduced the 'No. 2' soap first and then the 'No. 1'. Shrewdly, showing a rare sense of marketing, he replied: 'If people find No. 2 so good, they'll believe No. 1 to be even better!'

Paeans of praise were showered on Ardeshir. Typical of the sentiments expressed was that of Rabindranath Tagore: 'I know of no foreign soap better than Godrej, and I have made it a point to use Godrej soaps'; Dr Annie Besant: 'Godrej soaps are the best I have ever used and I am recommending them to my friends'; Dr M.A. Ansari: 'I have great pleasure in testifying to the most excellent qualities of Godrej soaps. I have used them now for the last ten years and have found them better than the best soaps manufactured in Europe or, for that matter, any other country'; and more recently C. Rajagopalachari, 'Godrej was a name that I learned when young to respect, not on account of steel safes, but on account of the soap that so completely equalled the then most famous.'

The richest tribute came from Mahatma Gandhi. Approached by another soap-maker for his blessings, he replied: 'I hold my brother Godrej in such high regard and he is of such a charitable disposition that if your enterprise is likely to harm him in any way, I regret very much I cannot give you my blessings.' A facsimile of this, written in Gandhiji's own hand, in Gujarati, on a postcard, is a prized possession of the Godrej family.

Equally gratifying was the response abroad. The most scientifically advanced nations in Europe, including Germany, naturally got interested in toilet soaps manufactured exclusively from vegetable oils and imported them. Notable among the several highly favourable reactions was that of

A Complexion Pure

Herr Carl Luzurtze, a German skin specialist: 'I have devoted years of study to the functions of the human skin. I have tested by personal use and chemical experiment your vegetable toilet soaps and I unhesitatingly give them a place of honour as health and beauty soaps. As a hair wash they can rank with the best of soaps and their daily use should form an item of every woman's toilet and even of the sterner sex . . .'

The ingredients used in 'No. 1' were essentially costly. Ardeshir's aim, followed by his successors, was to put quality soaps within the reach of everyone. Hence, a soap named 'Turkish Bath' was introduced in 1926 and sold in a box of one dozen. It was one of the lowest costing, good-quality toilet soaps on the market, ideal for families which bought their cakes by the dozen and thereby making it still cheaper. These soaps were unlike the moisture-laden washing soaps (thirty-three per cent water, whereas the quantum should be only ten per cent), which were then extensively used as bath soaps under a mistaken sense of economy.

Ardeshir who in himself constituted a one-man market research unit realized that even 'Turkish Bath' did not solve the problem wholly. It did not cater to the tastes of all. Accordingly, other soaps were later introduced from time to time, the most important of which was 'Vatni'. A popular priced soap, 'Vatni' was scientifically better than other soaps in the same price class. Known to users as India's own soap, this green soap with its distinguishing green and white wrapper had a delightful fragrance. More importantly, 'Vatni' did not turn mushy but remained fresh and fragrant to the last wafer.

Among other toilet soaps introduced were Godrej 'Sandal' which was comparatively cheaper than other sandal soaps. Shaving soaps were introduced in 1932 but soap petals and washing-soap grains made their appearance only around 1950.

While soap flakes were mainly for use on delicate fabrics, the soap grains served as an all-purpose washing soap. The high quality of washing-soap grains was borne out by the remarks in the Government Test Certificate, which said, 'The sample represents an almost dehydrated soap in the form of soft creamish colour grains coarse and fine, possessing a faint, agreeable odour. In respect of composition, it conforms to specifications and represents a high-class washing soap.' Godrej bars proved to be superior to other washing-soap bars, in that they did not shrink out of shape and their rich and creamy lather cleansed better. A washing-soap powder later introduced as 'Dip' contained Optical Brightener for the brighter washing of textiles.

Locks, safes, security equipment—a wide variety of soaps—but that wasn't yet the end of the line for Ardeshir.

5
PROUDLY 'MADE IN INDIA'

There come moments in the life of a nation when it covers in a brief span the track of centuries. India in the early twentieth century was at such a point of time in its history.

It was a great time to be alive. A time to dream great dreams. There was a tremendous upsurge of activity everywhere. India's underdeveloped economy was undergoing a rapid transformation, as if the energies of the entire nation were bent by one common urge, not only to be free, but to eradicate the vestiges of age-old poverty and misery of the masses.

It also happens in the life of nations that the hour brings forth the men to shape its future—like Dadabhai Naoroji,

Jamshetji Tata, Pherozeshah Mehta, Wadia, Gokhale, Ranade, Ardeshir Godrej, among others.

Safes and soaps make at first sight a strange combination. But not when you take into account the other even more different but equally colourful products Ardeshir was now to set his heart upon. Both the safe and soap businesses were doing well. So the safe business was left to his brother, Pirojsha's care. He turned to new enterprises. Ideas, with the excitement of wings, stirred in his capacious mind. To experiment was a joy to him. He found in the course of his day-to-day work that Indian inks were not up to the mark. This urged him on to start experimenting with ink-making, the results of which he gave away. He made toffees from papaya and tried his hand at perfume manufacture. He experimented with vegetable dyes and even published a booklet on the subject. Unfortunately, this is out of print. His nephew Sohrab recalls how on one occasion in his childhood when they were about to eat biscuits—of course British-made and most attractively packaged—Ardeshir threw the lot out of the window—to the great disappointment of the children. He admonished them that they should think of eating biscuits only after they were made in India, adding that, anyway, home-made chapatis were healthier. But his approach was always positive. He took the initiative to launch a modest baking and confectionery concern which, had he lived longer, would have expanded into a pioneering industry in India. After his death his friends and colleagues Nadirshaw Kawasji, Sir Hormusji Dinshaw and others took upon themselves the responsibility of carrying on his work. The concern was converted into the charitable Godrej Memorial Institute with the aim of employing jobless Parsi youth and providing them training in baking and confectionery. About twenty-two to thirty young men were employed.

These latest activities must have puzzled his associates and family members who could not quite comprehend why he was trying new enterprises instead of consolidating and developing the already successful ones. But he was following a chosen path, attuned to a deeper wisdom. His foresight and clarity of thinking become evident in what he next set out to do. He saw the basic need and a great future for the processing and canning industry and straightaway bought a large tract of land, the largest in India, about 600 acres—425 in Pimpalgaon and 156 in Mashrul in Nasik—for vineyards. It was a matter of regret for him that youth, particularly of his community, weren't at all interested in the countryside. He agreed wholeheartedly with Gandhi about the importance of village uplift, and developing the rural areas. The degradation brought about by neglect of the countryside in which the vast majority of people lived in squalor touched him deeply.

There were other considerations too that prompted Ardeshir to try his hand at promoting the processing and canning industries. India was the largest producer of fruit after Brazil and America and of vegetables after China. India had an enormous livestock population, a long coastline of 7,500 kms., a rapidly expanding economic zone, 28,000 kms. of rivers and 3,000,000 hectares of reservoirs of freshwater lakes. There were in addition 1.4 million hectares of potential water area which meant a huge potential of fish and marine catch of which not even half was exploited.

This huge potential was utterly wasted in India. Even today, fifty years after Ardeshir visualized the possibilities, India is able to process only one per cent of the fruit and vegetables that are produced (amounting to 84,000 tonnes on an average) as against Brazil which processes seventy per cent of its output, Malaysia ninety-three per cent and the Philippines seventy-eight per cent. We are the biggest producers in the world of mangoes with alphonso mangoes holding pride of place, yet it is Brazil which beats us in mango exports to Europe. There is of course a simpler explanation as to why, despite Nature's abundant gifts, we perform so poorly in exploiting them—uncoordinated effort, unscientific planning, lack of imagination and casual operation.

By putting all his marvellous talents and those of his co-workers in clear focus, being obsessed as was his wont and emerging as the leader in the field, Ardeshir could have realized this potential had he lived longer. But it was not to be. Even in his lifetime he was hindered by dishonest middlemen and others who took advantage of his gullibility to cheat him.

After Ardeshir's death in 1936, the executors and trustees of his Will (he had willed the vineyards to the Parsi Punchayet) obtained a High Court decree and handed over the two farms to the Parsi Punchayet. They tried to run the farms, with the help of an advisory committee. Their aim was to get Parsi youngsters to apprentice themselves in farming, with a view to establishing a settlement. But the odds were against them. The farms were too far off from Bombay for administrative purposes. As Shapur Desai says in *History of the Parsi Punchayet*, while the Mashrul farm was desert-dry, the one at Pimpalgaon had a surfeit of water. This yielded sufficient produce, but because it was the height of the Second World War, railway wagons and trucks were not available to transport it to Bombay.

Ultimately, the Punchayet sold the farms to Nusserwanji Hormusji Dinshaw on the understanding that he would continue to employ Parsis. 'Sad to say,' comments Desai, 'the Pimpalgaon farm is now under water as the government has built a dam there. And so the idea of a Parsi agricultural settlement now lies deep under water, perhaps for ever.'

Fate dealt the cards evenly—fortune in business, misfortune in life. Tragedy struck Ardeshir immediately after his marriage when on 21 April 1891 his young wife Bachubai, still in her teens, accompanied by her cousin Pirojbai Sorabjee Kamdin, went up the Rajabai Tower for a bird's-eye view of the city. They were followed up the stairs by a ruffian whose threatening demeanour so alarmed the girls that, panic-stricken, with no way to escape, they jumped off the railing to their death in the University gardens 200 feet below.

The event caused a sensation in the city. There was an outcry in the Press. Typical of the sense of outrage and commiseration were these words of J.R.B. Jeejeebhoy in his *Bribery & Corruption in Early Bombay*: 'They (the two girls) loved the name of honour more than they feared death. It was a glorious immolation, the triumph of the soul over the flesh, for which the annals of Bombay seek for any similarity in vain.'

The miscreant who happened to be the son of a well-known millionaire was caught. But he narrowly escaped imprisonment and infamy by the usual means. 'Money was then, as now,' comments Jeejeebhoy 'a compensation for taking stains out of [a] character.'

In memory of the two ladies who met with such a tragic and untimely end, a block was built and furnished as part of the Bahadurji Sanatorium at Deolali. The sum of Rs 9,628 was donated by the Committee of the Rajabai Tower Tragedy Fund for this purpose.

But what of Ardeshir? He was heartbroken. Tragedy drives some men to despair, it ennobles others. Behind Ardeshir's great works, one glimpses, as in a glass, darkly, the image of an extraordinary man. Glimpses, because little is known of the man apart from what he achieved. He doesn't seem to have had much of a personal life. He had no children. He never spoke about his loss. It was almost as if he didn't want anybody to share his burden: Not for him the seductive surrender to self-pity. He didn't seem interested in bringing the miscreant to justice, nor did he appear disappointed when he got off scot-free. His reaction, or rather the lack of it, appeared strange, as if, in his deepest being, he believed as the saints do that beyond sin is the forgiveness of sin. By all accounts he was a lonely man, given to plain living and high thinking, grown lonelier, who left his house at eight in the morning and didn't return till nine in the evening, so that even his brothers and his brother's children hardly got to know him.

A recluse, who inhabited a solitude and always kept his distance, he inspired awe rather than affection. When he entered a room, family members and friends would stop talking out of respect for him. He exuded the confidence of one who had the measure of his task. But he showed no pride in his achievements, and seemed not to consider himself in any way an exceptional human being. He was only doing his duty as an Indian, doing his best for India.

Ardeshir wasn't demonstrative by nature, nor even communicative. He was, however, fond of children, for he showered great affection on his brother Pirojsha's children, particularly on Dosa who was greatly attached to him, more perhaps than to her own father. His nephew Burjor, fondly recalls the advice Ardeshir gave him as he was leaving for further education in Germany. 'When I went to Germany, he came to the ship to see me off. He told me to take advantage of the trip and learn something in Germany that nobody else in India knew. And that is what I did and that is what has helped make me what I am.'

Ardeshir held a high opinion of Germany and the Germans, perhaps because Germany was known in those days as the fatherland of technology. Henry Ford says in his *Today And Tomorrow* that, before the First World War, Germany was far more advanced in metallurgy than America.

He believed in deeds, not words. He wasted no time in

railing against the British. Rather, he utilized the time to prove that what the British could do, Indians could do as well, if not better. 'We are being fooled,' was all he would murmur. While, like Dadabhai Naoroji, he admired the good qualities of the British and their contribution to India, he felt they had no business to be in India and to exploit it. But there was never any rancour in his dealings with the British. Rather, they were enlivened by a puckish sense of humour carefully hidden behind his serious demeanour, and his austere ways. A British friend remarked in the course of conversation: 'You know, Mr Godrej, we British are today on top of the world.' Quick came Ardeshir's retort: 'Well, I'm glad to hear that because, as you know, the world goes round, and what's up has got to come down.'

Great men have their weaknesses, too. Ardeshir was a poor judge of men. Prone to be gullible, particularly in matters of money, business associates, even friends and relatives, sometimes took advantage of him. Of course, this wasn't always so, as this incident suggests. A friend of Ardeshir's, Shivlal Shah, ran a ghee business at Porbunder. In 1918, owing to the semi-famine conditions prevailing there, ghee prices soared and Shivlal was in need of funds to continue in business. He sent a telegram to Ardeshir in Bombay, explaining his plight. Ardeshir asked him to come down to Bombay and meet him on an appointed day at the J.B. Petit Library at noon. Shivlal arrived on the stroke of 12.00 and found Ardeshir already waiting for him. Before he could even broach the subject of a loan, much to his surprise Ardeshir handed over a blank, signed cheque asking him to fill in the amount he needed. Shivlal put down the figure of Rs 30,000, gave him a receipt and the deal was concluded.

Whenever Shivlal was in Bombay, Ardeshir would take him for a drive in the car Pirojsha had placed at his disposal. They would go to Mahim, which was undeveloped then and had plenty of trees all around. They would enjoy themselves, eating Mahim halwa, a delicacy for which Bombay was famous, and washing it down with toddy. Shivlal recalls Ardeshir often talking to him about his experiments with vegetable oils for making soap. One evening, just before Ardeshir was confined to bed for a long illness, they were sitting at Chowpatty enjoying the fresh sea breeze and exchanging reminiscences, when Ardeshir talked about a grape plantation project at Nasik that he was working on. It was to be their last meeting. Shivlal's son, Navinchandra, recalls vividly how some days later when his father saw Ardeshir's photo on the front page of the *Times of India* with the announcement of his death, he wept like a child. Never before, Navinchandra says, had he seen his father weep like that.

But all who scrounged for money weren't like Shivlal. Ardeshir couldn't always have been unaware, shrewd as he was in business affairs, that he was being taken advantage of. Perhaps with his deep humanity he pitied the need that made them take advantage of him. If his weakness was a trusting nature, an over-willingness to see the good in people, it was one he accepted because it grew out of his great strength, his generosity of heart towards his fellow men. He might perhaps have defended himself by noting that thinking well of people sometimes made them behave better than they otherwise would. Ardeshir believed in the essential goodness of the human heart, even though he had spent his entire youth suffering the wounds of heartless rivals and mindless rulers.

Ardeshir died in January, 1936. It was only at his funeral that people were made aware of what his right hand had been giving without the left hand ever knowing. A large number of the very poor, not necessarily Parsis, came to pay their last respects. They came in droves, the deprived and the despairing, grieving that a source of sustenance had been snatched from them.

Ardeshir believed in simple, unostentatious living. He shared half of the household expenses. He would take public transport or walk to his destination, using a car only late in life at Pirojsha's insistence. A man of considerable culture and a voracious reader, particularly of books on literature and philosophy, he would spend all the time he could spare from his work at the J.N. Petit Library on (the then) Hornby Road or browsing at the Mazda Book Stores (which he had set up) on Medows Street. Well-versed in Persian, Omar Khayyam was his favourite poet, which isn't surprising since Khayyam who claimed his pleasures to be 'a book of verse, a glass of wine and Thou beside me in the wilderness' was also a mathematician of note, of the same rank as Pascal.

Ardeshir's acquaintances included some of the greatest names of that stormy era—Gandhi, Rabindranath Tagore and Lokmanya Tilak. In fact, he was one of the pall-bearers at Tilak's funeral. He never took advantage of their friendship—didn't feel the need for it.

Ardeshir was religious. Every morning he spent a few moments at the Vatchagandhi Agiary on Hughes Road. But he was truly religious in the sense that he lived his religion, particularly in the practice of philanthropy. In 1921 he donated three lakh rupees (now over three crores) to the Tilak Swaraj Fund, incurring in the process the wrath of the British rulers, who even issued a secret circular prohibiting Government departments from purchasing Godrej products.

Given the times, it was certainly a daring thing to do. Ardeshir's gesture received the warm applause of Mahatma Gandhi who wrote: 'Mr Godrej of the safe fame has eclipsed all donations to the Tilak Swaraj Fund with his announcement of three lakhs of rupees. His donations to public purposes have been hitherto quite unknown. But he was induced to appreciate the necessity this time of a public announcement.

I tender my congratulations to Mr Godrej and the whole Parsi community. I wish also to testify that, during the collection week in Bombay, not a day has passed without Parsi donations. Parsi ladies and gentlemen are also making door to door collections . . .' (*Collected Works of Mahatma Gandhi*.)

Referring to the secret circular issued by the British in 1921, Gandhi went on to say: 'This provoked a secret circular from the Government to the effect that no Godrej safe should be ordered for any of its departments, which used to go in for numbers of them in the past. Because Mr Godrej contributed to the Tilak Swaraj Fund, the "just" Government has boycotted his safes. How should the people deal with such a malicious and vindictive Government, if not by resorting to non-cooperation with it?' The Mahatma emphasized that Ardeshir had done something which far exceeded the charity efforts of other individuals: 'No other single individual has given so much. True, the entire amount is not available in cash today, but it is as secure as if offered in gold. He has earmarked the sum for two of the purest items in our programme, banishing liquor and 'Antyaj' uplift. Money was earmarked for the latter cause on his insistence. For myself, I would have preferred to employ only Hindus' money for this work. It is for them to carry out this particular reform. But how could I stand in the way of this friend who offered what he did in utter sincerity of heart? With the receipt of this amount, I believe the total contribution by Parsis, so far as my information goes, will easily come to not less than four lakhs, leaving out the value of the gifts promised by some of them. We cannot thank Shri Godrej and the Parsi community sufficiently.'

Ardeshir did not believe that wealth ought to be inherited, nor that it should be bequeathed. On his death he donated his vineyards to the Parsi Punchayet. Pirojsha had to buy the steel products business, no doubt at a concessional rate by paying three and a half lakhs. Ardeshir went a step ahead of Andrew Carnegie who propagated the gospel of the trusteeship of wealth. Carnegie left the residue of his fortune to his wife and upon her death to his only child, Margaret. Ardeshir gave away everything, living up to his friend and mentor Gandhi's precept: 'A trustee has no heir but the public.'

For Ardeshir, Swadeshi was the breath of Swaraj. His claim to greatness lies in that in his relentless quest for self-reliance, he gave a brave new dimension to the Swadeshi concept. Swadeshi meant different things to the British rulers and to their subjects. Lord Minto, looking askance at the boycott [British goods] movement, pleaded with Indians to cultivate 'honest Swadeshism' by which he meant non-political Swadeshism. He understood by it the movement for the promotion of the arts and industries of the country consistently with the Open Door in trade and commerce—that is, he wanted Swadeshi to operate within the limits of the free trade policy. Honest Swadeshism, was, according to him, economic Swadeshism. But, as Bipin Chander Pal pointed out, 'every tyro in political economy knows that there can be no economics divorced from politics. Economics and politics are organically related to one another.'

True, England herself was at that time following a policy of free trade. But only out of expediency. As Gokhale pointed out, for centuries England had followed a policy of protection, whereby she had built up her vast, industrial system. But half a century before Gokhale, with protection having fulfilled its purpose, England decided to give up the old policy and to adopt free trade, mainly to set right the abuses to which protection had given rise. England depended on foreign countries for most of her raw materials, and she supplied manufactured articles practically to the whole world: 'It was therefore to the advantage of England that there should be no import or export duties, as one result of such duties was to add to the cost of articles supplied to foreign countries.'

Forcing this policy of free trade upon a country like India, faced by circumstances like the absence of skills or enterprise of the West and unfamiliar with the recent developments of steam and machinery, would lead to two disastrous consequences—it would reduce India to the level of an agricultural country merely producing raw materials; it would cause its industries to perish as a result of the exposure to external competition. This was England's policy not only towards India but other colonies as well. America surmounted these consequences by shaking off England's dominion altogether. Ireland too struggled to do the same, but did not quite succeed. The worst sufferer was India.

The only solution therefore was to boycott British goods. Ardeshir was fully in agreement with this. But the plea for boycott was accompanied by a corollary with which Ardeshir totally and emphatically disagreed. Not only Gokhale but other political leaders of that era believed that, in the beginning, Indian goods were bound to be somewhat inferior in quality and higher in price. 'It is by ensuring the consumption of indigenous articles in their early stage,' argued Gokhale, 'when their quality is inferior or their price is higher, or when they labour under both these disadvantages, that we can do for our industries what protectionist governments have done for theirs by means of State Protection.' Sumit Sarkar in *The Swadeshi Movement in Bengal* says that this sentiment became a part of the movement 'that indigenous goods should be preferred by consumers even if they were more expensive than and inferior in quality to their imported substitutes, and that it was the patriotic duty of men with capital to pioneer such industries even though profits might be minimal or non-existent.'

Ardeshir considered sentiments such as 'good enough for India' as giving evidence of a defeatist mentality. As a businessman he considered it an unsound policy to expect people with capital to invest in industries which by producing inferior goods would endanger their capital. It would be even more wrong, pleas of patriotism notwithstanding, to expect consumers to spend their hard-earned money on inferior goods when superior ones were available. Above all, it was insulting to Indians as a whole to assume that, all difficulties and obstructions notwithstanding, they would not be able to produce goods as good as, if not better—and cheaper—than their foreign counterparts. Ardeshir didn't argue the point. He didn't need to. His towering achievements in security engineering and the manufacture of soap, where foreign competition was very fierce, were a sufficient rebuttal.

So broad was his outlook and deep his faith in his country that, had he lived, he would not have been surprised at the vast development projects of free India. He would have joined whole-heartedly in the great adventure of building a new India. He did not live to see the consummation of all that he had been striving for, the end of British rule!

Self-confidence leading to self-sufficiency. Self-reliance bringing about self-respect. . . . This was the path Ardeshir trod, paving it with glory. The shine of success was like an aura about him. He was generally admired, even revered, especially by the poor. He had few friends, but he was never really alone. He had 'great allies', his 'friends' were 'exultations, agonies, and love, and man's unconquerable mind.' He was able to achieve a synthesis between Carlyle's concept of work and Khalil Gibran's more modern one. Work, to him, was worship. But work, in relation to those who worked for, or rather, with him, was love made visible.

His mission was his life. The mission became the man who, before passing on, lent a certain greatness to the name he bore, which those coming after would have to live up to.

Ardeshir fulfilled the one criterion of greatness laid down by that great British thinker, Isaiah Berlin: 'To call someone great is to claim that he has intentionally taken a large step— one far beyond the normal capacities of man—in satisfying or materially affecting central human interests.'

Ardeshir did not have greatness thrust upon him. He became great because he had it in him. As Dryden sang of another figure in history, 'he was great ere fortune made him so.'

6
BROTHER'S KEEPER

No two brothers could have been as alike and yet so different as Ardeshir and Pirojsha. Both believed passionately in making the country self-reliant. Both swore by Swadeshi as the means to attain Swaraj. Both lived simply and thought richly, and felt deeply for the poor and the deprived. Both showed care and concern for their fellow-workers and, above everything, a profound respect for their customers. Both looked beyond their own to the national interests.

Ardeshir was very much an introvert, Pirojsha more outgoing. Ardeshir was a man of few words, Pirojsha didn't mince words—in fact, was quite outspoken. They didn't always agree. On the contrary there were strong differences of opinion between them, so much so that there was a time when Pirojsha would attend the factory later, only after his elder brother had left. But as far as their work was concerned, their thinking and temperaments complemented each other's, for the industry's and the country's greater good. It fell to Pirojsha's eldest son Sohrab, because of Pirojsha's concern in spite of these differences, to look after Ardeshir's creature comforts and ensure that he was never inconvenienced.

Ardeshir did not care for money in itself, but for a cause—self-respect through self-reliance. Pirojsha showed a greater sense of responsibility in showing that money used properly can do a lot of good. Money, to him, was for consolidation and expansion, for greater employment and bigger benefits to workers.

At the time of Ardeshir's death in 1936 both the companies, Godrej & Boyce Mfg. Co. Ltd. and Godrej Soaps Ltd. were well-established. Records extant reveal that for the calendar year 1935, sales of safes and cupboards accounted to Rs 10,12,328 and employees' salaries and wages to Rs 3,39,135. In 1936 the sale of safes and cupboards rose to Rs 12,03,770 and of salaries and wages to Rs 4,02,946. Similarly, the total turnover and net profit of Godrej Soaps showed a steady rise as under:

Financial Year	Total Turnover	Net Profit
	Rs	Rs
1929	2,15,846	41,834
1930	3,73,710	62,409
1931	5,50,266	99,810
1937	6,04,644	44,996

The number of employees in Godrej & Boyce was approximately a thousand but since a chemical industry requires comparatively less labour, Godrej Soaps had a strength of about five hundred.

Pirojsha who had done his schooling at the New High School and had subsequently joined the Victoria Jubilee Technical Institute, joined the business in 1906. He was twenty-four years old then. When Ardeshir died in 1936, Pirojsha was fifty-four.

The clock had moved ahead since Ardeshir died. Taking stock and consolidating, rather than establishing fresh enterprises as before, was now the need of the hour. Fate, for once, dealt the cards right. If Ardeshir had an obsession and was a visionary, Pirojsha was hard-headed and practical, pre-eminently a consolidator. One could take over the business smoothly from the other.

No doubt, to consolidate means to make or become secure and strong, to combine or to merge or take root. But consolidation does not preclude expansion; sometimes it is the prelude to it. It makes expansion inevitable and necessary. Pirojsha did not seek out new parameters, but within the broad parameters laid down by Ardeshir, he developed an impressive array of new lines, showing in the process a remarkable business acumen developed by a careful study of the country's needs and consumer preferences.

Ardeshir had moved restlessly from locks, safes, and soaps to biscuits and confectionery, canning and processing, but Pirojsha focussed on tending and nurturing these growing and already thriving industries. He too was obsessive in his quest for quality, making it the watchword of his manufacturing policy rather than a mere catchword. He made quality achievement the prime organizational objective, keeping in view profits too. Valuing the customer as a person, he valued customer needs. More than individual brilliance, he also valued teamwork and cohesiveness. Over the years he created a climate of openness within the organization by providing his workers not only job security but welfare measures that were way ahead of the times. These included more leisure hours and greater purchasing power to labour. This gave the organization a cutting-edge over rivals.

Security engineering pioneered by Ardeshir provided several offshoots which were now carefully exploited. The development of manufacturing technology made it possible for safe-deposit vaults to be made in 1935, followed by steel cupboards. Later, steel furniture was developed into an industry by itself. Fashioned from sheet and tubular steel, it reflected the swift progress and change which industrial science was bringing into homes, offices, factories and hospitals. Steel cupboards for the home were designed and manufactured for the first time ever, anywhere. Library stacks were a boon to the rapidly multiplying libraries, and steel shelving and easily arrangeable partitions cut warehousing expenses. The steel window and door industry added a touch of elegance to the home and office.

Pirojsha exemplified the new spirit in modern industrial outlook. Profits were religiously ploughed back into the business, taxes were paid to the State.

It was Pirojsha's direction that made Godrej policy develop along sound ethical lines. Service to the consumer was the keynote of this policy. It found expression in the marketing of standardised products, manufactured strictly according to specifications, at the lowest possible prices, even in boom periods and assured after-sales service. There are instances where Godrej brought down the price level to one-third of the prices of imported articles.

Small wonder Godrej became a household word and has continued to be so. This was true in a very literal sense, as can be seen from Raj Mehta and Russell W. Belk's study in 1991 on the favourite possessions of Indians and Indian immigrants to the United States, the findings of which were published in the *Journal of Consumer Research*. According to this survey, the second most frequently cited possession, especially by females in India, (as opposed to Indian immigrants, women and men) was the Godrej steel cupboard. This cupboard was presented to the bride at marriage by her parents or in-laws. If not, it was usually the first major purchase the young couple made. Formerly an upper-class status symbol, the product trickled down to the lower and middle classes as well. This cupboard ranked next in importance only to a family shrine, a family idol, or a guru's photo and ranked higher in importance than status symbols like the television, the VCR and the music system, etc.

It was also significant that except for this cupboard, no other piece of furniture was cited in the survey. The emotional attachment this product was able to evoke was brought out in the words of Mrs Rao, a respondent, 'Recently for the first time in my life, I lost the key to the Godrej. I cried for two days. We then had to get a locksmith to open the Godrej. The duplicate key was inside the Godrej. It was the most horrible feeling. Some outsider was going to lay his hands on my cupboard. The feeling I got was very similar to (the) feeling one gets when someone hurts your children. This Godrej has been with us since we were married. It has traveled everywhere with us. Now our children have gone and settled elsewhere; only the Godrej has remained with us.' Similarly, another respondent Mrs Mehta recalled that their cupboard had been with the family all through her married life. As with Mrs Rao, the cupboard became 'like a child to her.'

How Pirojsha adhered to service-after-sales was strikingly demonstrated exactly half a century ago in 1946. On hearing from a customer that liquid was oozing from the inside of his safe, Pirojsha had reason to suspect that the moisture-generating and fire-resisting compound supplied by a manufacturer of international repute was faulty, that water should generate only during a fire. This defect could be and was rectified, but only by getting back not only that safe but hundreds of others from all over the country even though the owners were reluctant, on Pirojsha's initiative and at his expense, completely changing the composition, and carefully packing and returning the safes to their delighted owners— all involving heavy unexpected expenditure through no fault of Godrej. The compound had not been tested because the supplier was a company of international repute. By taking this step Pirojsha ensured future security for all these safes, should any be caught in a fire. More important, it built enormous customer goodwill.

In 1956, Godrej began to manufacture steel doors and windows, angle irons and shelves, steel backs and sides, steel partitions, popularly known as 'Multiflex' for factories, warehouses, offices and for use in kitchens. This was followed by machine tools (1957). Later still, in 1961 another industrial product, forklift trucks, was manufactured, and in 1965 the steel foundry started functioning. In 1976 the Space Age made its demands and the Process Equipment Division was formed. With the coming of the electronic age in 1979, electronic typewriters were made (1984) followed by dot matrix printers and CAD/CAM systems, and fax machines (1992).

Godrej also catered to the needs of leading hospitals. Scientifically designed, Godrej hospital equipment included a full range of articles for wards, theatres and other departments. These included the Fowler and the Cardiac-position beds; neat, hygienic lockers, elaborately-fitted operation and examination tables, instrument cabinets, etc. For decades many state, municipal and railway hospitals, mill and works hospitals, public and private hospitals all over the country, as well as nursing homes and research institutes were served by such equipment. The oven-baked, scratchless enamel gave Godrej hospital equipment a unique, long-lasting finish in gleaming (non-yellowing) white. This line was later discontinued, along with steel windows and doors, largely because of the continuing steel shortage.

Steel furniture and equipment are prone to rust, especially in the coastal climate. To ensure a durable finish, leaving the equipment looking as good as new for many years, every piece of steel was subjected to thorough anti-rust treatment in huge steam-heated pickling and phosphetising tanks. Only a manufacturer with a reputation to maintain and with adequate resources would be conscientious in carrying out this important anti-rust treatment which is both elaborate and expensive. First, the sheets were immersed or 'pickled' in a steam-heated sulphuric acid bath, then rinsed in hot water to wash out the acid, and given a hot hydroxide bath to neutralise any remaining acid. Once again they were washed, given a protective phosphate coating and finally painted. A more rigorous method of thoroughly cleansing steel surfaces, used for heavy articles such as safes, was sand-blasting, whereby the surface to be cleansed was exposed to an intensive spray of sand or sharp steel shots under pressure.

The engineering unit came to be ranked as a full-fledged large-scale, secondary industrial plant of national importance in the early thirties. Pandit Nehru visited the plant in 1935. Its products comprised a major section of the overall secondary processing industry, which played a vital role in the economic development of the country. Way back in 1954 the industry used a little more than thirty per cent of the country's entire output of finished steel. The total offtake was 3,82,000 tons which represented the highest in the security and furniture industries. The unit was run on a modern assembly-line basis with its products subjected to strict quality control. The factories were continuously modernised. By consuming, among others, the output of the post-1947, new government-sponsored steel plants, the Godrej fabricating capacity came to form a link between heavy industry and the ultimate consumer as more and more products were turned out at progressively decreasing costs.

Godrej were thus able to rise to the occasion when called upon to manufacture 17 lakh ballot-boxes, in record time, for free India's first elections, in 1956, a momentous event in the history of democracy. Ballot-boxes, incidentally, were the first product to be manufactured at Vikhroli. The Chief Election Commissioner, realizing the impossibility of manufacturing so many individual keys, demanded a design that would have no external lock, being sealed, and besides was tamperproof and waterproof. After working at a furious pace on no less than 70 different models, Godrej came up with a suitable combination at the extremely reasonable price of Rs 5/- a piece. Orders from different states were executed at record speed and the 'election specials', as the wagons loaded with the ballot-boxes came to be called, were despatched round the clock from the Godrej Vikhroli railway siding to the country's remotest corners—and all this without in any way interrupting the normal manufacturing programme.

A cardinal principle of Ardeshir's policy had been to show Indians the way to do things for themselves. Pirojsha too rigidly adhered to this policy which thereby saved the country crores of rupees. No protection or financial assistance was ever claimed from the government. It was a spontaneous effort motivated by the desire to develop India's resources and to help put the country on the industrial map of the world.

It wasn't easy going for Pirojsha any more than it had been for Ardeshir, particularly in the rapidly growing soap industry which was struggling for survival against the unequal competition from the formidable multinational Lever Brothers. But Pirojsha went ahead regardless, in the conviction that

Ardeshir B. Godrej, the gifted pioneer. Visionary-founder of Godrej

Pirojsha B. Godrej. Pirojsha, seen here as a young man in a *pheta*, consolidated the Godrej enterprise

Soonabai Pirojsha Godrej

Soonabai Pirojsha Godrej's grave at Mussoorie

Sohrabji P. Godrej

Burjorji P. Godrej

Naoroji P. Godrej

Dosa Naoroji Godrej

Pirojsha B. Godrej with his English physician Dr Wilson in 1957

Pirojsha B. Godrej speaking at the 1965 Diwali function at Pirojshanagar. (Left to right): The late N.D. Sahukar, Adi Godrej and Soonuben Godrej

The three brothers, Burjorji, Sohrabji and Naoroji engrossed in a serious discussion

Soonuben and Naoroji on their visit to the Godrej dealer in Madurai

Jaiben and Burjorji at the wedding reception of their son Nadir Burjorji Godrej with Rati on 19 January 1991

At Vikhroli in 1966, (from left to right): Burjorji, Adi, Cooverbai Vakil (aunty), Soonuben, Parmeshwar, Naoroji and Jaiben

Burjorji P. Godrej with his sons Nadir (on his right) and Adi (on his left)

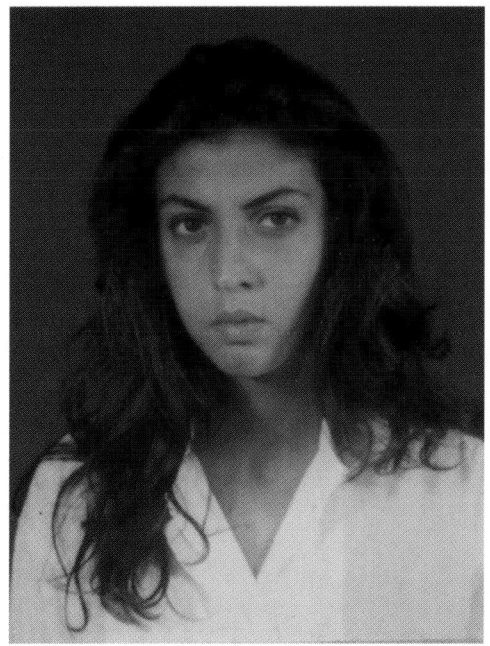

Tanya, elder daughter of Adi and Parmeshwar

Adi and Parmeshwar with children, Pirojsha and Nisaba

Nadir B. Godrej watering and sapling planted by him at the Valia Plant

Smita and Vijay Crishna

At the wedding of Nadir Burjorji Godrej and Dr Rati Vaghaiwalla at their residence on 19 January 1991 (from left to right): Adi Godrej, Vijay Crishna, Mrs Soonuben Godrej, Mrs Pheroza J. Godrej, Dosa Naoroji, K.N. Naoroji, Burjorji P. Godrej, and Jamshyd N. Godrej. (Seated): Sohrabji P. Godrej, Nadir B. Godrej, Dr Rati Godrej and Jaiben Burjorji Godrej

Jamshyd N. Godrej with (centre) S. Viji, Brakes India Ltd. and Dr Manmohan Singh, former Finance Minister of India and (right) Dr Pran Talwar, Vice-Chairman and Managing Director of Talbros Automotive Components Ltd., at the inauguration of the Auto Expo, New Delhi, 7 December 1993

Jamshyd and Pheroza Godrej with ex-President Bush, Bombay, 27 November 1995

Pirojsha at his estate he purchased at Vikhroli

Jamshyd's children (left) Raika and Navroze with Smita's children (right) Freyan and Nyrika at 40-D Ridge Road

The Old Dadiseth House which became Godrej Bhavan

Godrej Bhavan standing tall at 4A Home Street, Fort

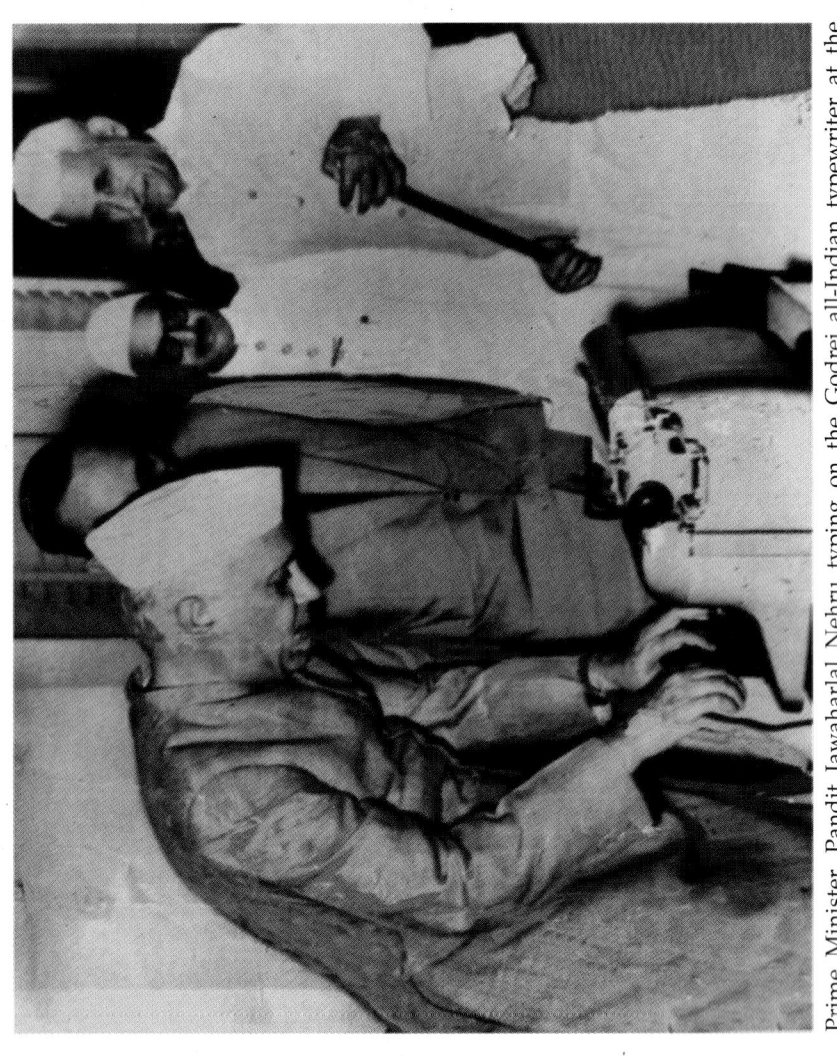

Prime Minister, Pandit Jawaharlal Nehru typing on the Godrej all-Indian typewriter at the Avadi Congress in Madras

quality tells, quality survives. In this he exemplified a virtue that he possessed to a greater degree than Ardeshir. This was the quality of perseverance, the hinge of all virtues. He had the further advantage Ardeshir never had—three sons Sohrab, Burjor and Naval (and a daughter Dosa) who worked shoulder to shoulder with him. Later, Burjor's and Naval's children too carried the torch, in what was to become a big and remarkable undertaking run by a closely knit family. Close-knit, but never aloof: they mingled and continue to mingle freely with their workers. Always approachable, they have been able to instill in their workers a sense of belonging. The Godrej *parivar* was and is a real, living thing.

After his return from Switzerland where he had to be for health reasons, Sohrab the eldest who had graduated in science from St Xavier's College took over the business promotion of Godrej products. More specifically he handled the firm's publicity and public relations, helping to make Godrej a household word and its characteristic logo (based, it is said, on Pirojsha's signature) the hallmark of quality. Evelyn Wood of the advertising agency, J. Walter Thompson, completely won Pirojsha's confidence with his quick understanding of the complex structure of Godrej safes. The relationship with Thompson's (now Hindustan Thompson) has continued to this day. The slogan 'Godrej for Safe and Clean Service' appeared as a by-line in all press advertising. In fact, till the early sixties, Godrej handled the creative publicity, for steel as well as soap products, with a full-fledged Publicity Department at the Lalbaug head office. Later, in the mid-sixties, with an additional workload and new media of advertising (particularly films and television), the work was distributed among several leading advertising agencies.

Trade missions are the cornerstone of exporting. Sohrab was a member of trade delegations to various countries. This fanned his keenness for travel, just one among his many interests. He became one of the most widely travelled of Indian businessmen, visiting as many as 160 countries, including Antarctica. Initially, he went on business travels, for he had to acquaint himself with knowledge of local market conditions and the practicalities of doing business, whether the company's products and services were likely to find a market in the country being visited, and to what extent, and whether insurance cover would be obtained on the commercial and political risks of particular destinations. Good promotion material had to be prepared and sent in advance of his visits for distribution.

With increased production Godrej expected to further their export markets in neighbouring countries. The quality and prices of both the steel and soap products came gradually to be appreciated the world over. But great shortage of steel then was a major impediment. The greatest barriers, however, as Sohrab discovered, were created by other Governments. They remained a problem for the Government in India to surmount.

Pirojsha had made it clear to Sohrab's younger brother Burjor even before the latter left in 1933 for higher education in Germany that he would have to look after the soap factory which had now grown into a unique large-scale factory (across the railway line from Lalbaug, at Delisle Road) with the very latest equipment and to which a well-equipped research laboratory was attached. Burjor calls himself 'a pucca Indo-German as I obtained all my three degrees, the Bachelor's, the Master's and the Doctorate at the Technical University of Berlin.' The last was the most difficult and the most prestigious, entitling him to put 'Dr Ing.' before his name.

Emphasis was laid on progressively improving qualities at decreasing costs. Consumer preferences were carefully studied and a wide variety of soaps emerged to meet these tastes. Powder soap, suitable for all types of garments, was introduced. But the greatest achievement was the introduction in India of toiletries containing G-11 or Hexachlorophene, the newest wonder germicide which found a place in the US Pharmacopoeia after exhaustive research and tests. Godrej Soaps, under Burjor's inspired direction, prospered mainly because of research. Research was a tonic to him. His motto: 'Only the best is good enough for me. And that brings prosperity if the research is capable.'

The man on the spot, when Burjor was studying in Germany and Sohrab hadn't yet returned from Switzerland, was Naval, the youngest and, because of his mechanical bent of mind, closest to Pirojsha. Immediately after schooling, he was put to work at the bottom at the Lalbaug factory, learning the nuts and bolts of every stage of manufacture and buttressing practical experience by devouring trade manuals to keep abreast of every technological development that pertained to steel manufacture, also acquiring business acumen in the process.

Naval steered Godrej through the challenging years to achieve an enviable sophistication in product range and uncompromising quality. He expanded the business to make Godrej one of the largest private-owned companies and among the most respected ones.

Their sister, Dosa, was fond of social work. She became an active member of the St John's Ambulance Brigade and rendered sterling service as an ambulance driver during the War and by working in hospitals.

The first wholly independent charge Pirojsha gave Naval was of the indigenous manual typewriter. But that's a great story that needs to be told separately.

7

BLUE-PRINTING A DREAM

What would you say of a man who, planning an industrial township, plants trees before laying the foundation of the factory buildings?

That he was a lover of nature? That he was deeply concerned about the environment? That he wanted a congenial atmosphere for his thousands of workers?

His workers were Pirojsha's major concern, next only to his customers. Considering human relations the first responsibility of management, he was far ahead of government legislation in the labour benefits he provided. Long before labour laws became the order, he introduced such benefits as holidays with pay, provident fund, bonus, gratuity, medical and canteen facilities. Small wonder that in their long history Godrej have been singularly free from labour trouble. They believe in healthy trade-unionism, and on the solitary occasion in the fifties when due to outside interference and for narrow political gains, adjudication did take place, the verdict proved that Godrej were on the right track. In fact, relations with workers were so close and cordial that Pirojsha and, later, Naval knew each worker by his name.

Pirojsha was fortunate in having talented managers who had his absolute trust and who gave him total loyalty. At the Lalbaug factory they used to sit together, Pirojsha at the head, Sohrab and Naval on either side of him, in a large hall separated by a glass partition from the rest of the staff. These managers were worthy men, each remarkable in his own way. None of them had weighty degrees in management. They learnt the hard way by example and experience, imbibed Pirojsha's deep-rooted belief in fairplay in all business dealings, helped him consolidate his gains and in the process developed a business philosophy that was ahead of the time and uniquely Godrej's.

Topmost among these trusted men was Khurshed Bardy. He wore a worried and rather harassed look and seemed to be always in a tearing hurry. He had a high-pitched voice which when he was excited about something became quite squeaky. This, and his manner of drawing back his lips and twitching his neck made him the butt of staff jokes and the object of mimicry at staff functions at which, in fairness to him, he would laugh the loudest of all. But this appearance of a lovable eccentric belied the fact that he was a financial wizard, with all the facts and figures at his fingertips, and which won him grudging respect from the sales-tax and income-tax authorities against whom he could always hold his own.

Bardy was easily irritated particularly when staff members

approached him for advances and he would zealously turn down their requests. But later, being soft-hearted and sensitive, he would make discreet enquiries through his assistants as to whether the applicant's need was genuine or not. If it was, he would invariably sanction the advance. One morning a staff member, constantly short of money, approached Bardy for a loan to pay for his dentures. Going through the man's file, Bardy chanced upon a medical certificate which stated that the man had pyorrhea. Enraged, he summoned the applicant, pointed out the discrepancy, accused him of dishonesty and asked him to forthwith submit his resignation. Later, he came to know, turning the pages of the same file, that the man's wife had long been suffering from cancer. Promptly, he sent for the man and in his presence tore up the resignation letter.

Like Pirojsha, Naval too respected Bardy's judgment on financial matters. When the company's head office shifted from Lalbaug to Godrej Bhavan in the Fort, Naval had to go through Bardy's room to reach his own. Invariably he would pause to question Bardy about the day-to-day financial position.

An extrovert in many ways, with flashes of temper, Bardy never harboured any prejudice or enemity towards the staff. His humour was broad and hearty, verging on the slapstick. Senior staff members recall an occassion when in an unusually gay mood, Bardy danced with Mr Narayanan, the Godrej Trivandrum dealer, on the garden roof-top of Godrej Bhavan at a cocktails and dinner party hosted for dealers. Small wonder he received a standing ovation from the guests.

The passing years saw Bardy devote more time to social and charitable concerns. He became a trustee of the Pirojsha Godrej Public Foundation, a trustee of the Kappavala Agiary, a trustee of the Elphinstone Cricket Club, a senior functionary of the Masonic Lodge, and an avid fund-gatherer for his beloved school, the Byramjee Jeejeebhoy School.

His life was long. His labour continuous for over fifty years in the service of Godrej. His social circle was wide and varied. In sad contrast, his passing away was unexpected and untimely in Malaysia, with only his son Aspi (the present Director of Godrej Malaysia) by his side. So attached was Aspi to his father that he gave expression to the following verse in memory:

> Beloved of all and berated by none.
> Restless at times with the remains well spun.
> For good designs and closer functions fit.
> Solid of affection and replete with wit.
>
> An animated soul which working out its way
> Fretted with pygmy body to decay,
> Till death overcame that animated clay.

Equally respected was Nariman Sahukar, the company's General Manager. Comfortably built, bald, with a strong nose and stern features, he needed only a toga to pass off as a Roman senator. A strict disciplinarian, he insisted on regular attendance. The office hours were from 9.00 a.m. to 5.00 p.m. and, so promptly at 9.15 a.m., the staff muster would be placed on his table. Latecomers had to face him. *'Kem, aaje konni paydast ma gayatha?'* he would taunt them: 'Well, whose funeral did you attend today?' They would slink off as fast as they could. But on one occasion a rather hot-blooded young man working in the publicity department retorted: 'Why must it only be a funeral? Couldn't it be an accident or having to take someone to hospital?' Sahukar gave him his implacable glare and told him to go to his seat, muttering: 'Making excuses, *sala*, for late-coming. But at 5.00 sharp they rush out like racehorses at the starting-point!'

In case anyone reported late for duty, he was compelled to face the consequences and pay the penalty. Five minutes late, a red circle was put against the employee's name in the muster on the date. Half an hour late, the employee was compelled to take half-day casual leave, though many sat down to work. Twenty-four such late attendances in a year, and the employee had to forego his annual increment, which would only be restored three months later at the Management's discretion. Such were the rules of the time, which continue to exist even today.

But seriously, Sahukar was the ideal bureaucrat who, unlike the popular perception of his tribe, got things done instead of inventing obstacles. His friendly contacts with the powers that be helped to get quotas of steel which was often in short supply. Known for his strictness, he was as much capable of dressing-down a reluctant worker as of expressing genuine appreciation for work well done. He suffered from rheumatism, but never spoke about it. An active member of the All India Manufacturers' Organisation, he left his impress upon that prestigious organisation.

Above all, Sahukar was a great communicator. He considered letter-writing an art—and a sure means to success. In September 1971, he issued an interesting circular to all members of the staff and dealers all over India: 'As correspondents we tend to be preoccupied in shooting out letters without too much thought to the environment of the recipients of our letters. In large organizations the morning mail will consist of several welcome letters, but in addition there will be a lot of trash and semi-trash. That is why Executives in large business houses usually have in addition to a large waste-paper basket, a large bottom drawer.'

The waste paper basket is understandable, but what about the bottom drawer? In it go letters that are badly written, do not convey what exactly is wanted and require re-reading.

Letters, according to Sahukar, should be prompt, well thought-out and adopt a friendly tone. The very first sentence should rouse the receiver's interest. A personal approach always helps. Possible objections by the recipient need to be anticipated. The letter should present a neat, tidy appearance and avoid typographical or grammatical mistakes. Finally, brevity is the soul of good letter-writing.

Concluding, Sahukar stated: 'Make better business letters your motto every day. Not only will you steadily improve your effectiveness as a correspondent, but you will also have the satisfaction of earning greater profit and goodwill for your Company.'

Then there was or, rather, is Rustom Sanjana, a surviving member of the old brigade. By dint of undoubted merit and hard work over a period spanning half a century, he came to head the sales organization of which he became the driving force, keeping his army of salesmen always on their toes. His fetish was tidiness—the first thing he did every morning was to set his table in order, putting all the stationery items in their proper places. This characteristic was noticeable in the way he talked and in everything he did—neat, straightforward, accurate and to the point. He was outspoken, sometimes uncomfortably so, and this quality above all his other qualities, won him respect. And then there was his humour—his constant awareness of the funny side of life. His jokes often enlivened a hard day.

In marked contrast was Jehan Dastoor, Works Manager and also In-charge, Electrical Department. He served Godrej for forty long years. A silent worker, he seldom spoke, but sometimes when he did, he could be quite caustic. His staffers remember him as a strict but fair boss, who sometimes carried his fairness to extremes, taking the side of the staff of other departments rather than his own.

Another executive fondly remembered, now settled in

Australia, was Hirji Lentin, a brilliant engineer in charge of refrigerators. Then there was Savak Desai, Chief Engineer, in charge of capital goods purchases. He was an avid reader of technical magazines and whenever he read about some latest development in a different part of the world, he would bring it to Naval's attention. Characteristic of the man, his serious disposition and searching mind, was his hobby—chess. Every afternoon in the lunch room after a quick bite, he would play a game of chess with another executive Nariman Panthaky, in-charge of costing. Finally, there was M.J. Jal, Sales Manager of steel windows and doors, a line that was subsequently discontinued, and two stalwarts Ratansha and Savaksha Udwadia.

One cannot afford to forget—in fact one cannot possibly forget—the tall, bearded, genial Kerse Naoroji, the living link for over half a century between management and labour. Kerse was the sort of man who would brook no nonsense and was at the same time the epitome of tact. He could employ the iron fist and the velvet glove with equal ease, depending on which the occasion demanded. All this—and an excellent sailor too, Naval's constant, devoted companion on his many voyages.

This man who could withstand the fury of the seas could surely stand four-square against the *hai-hais* and *gaalis* of his workers when, on a rare occasion in Godrej history, there was labour trouble. 'Shout and scream as much as you want,' he told the infuriated workers on that May morning in 1972, opposite the entrance to the Machine Tool Plant 9 in Vikhroli, 'but the Management is not going to be cowed down by your unreasonable demands.'

Here was a man, who knew that 'when the going gets tough, the tough get going'.

In Godrej Soaps there was K.R. Gokulam, Burjor's right-hand man. His loyalty to the company and personally to Burjor was equalled only by his high administrative skills.

Exuding confidence, he kept smiling through the company's years of struggle. One never saw him lose his cool, whatever the provocation.

An ex-officer in the Indian Army, Gokulam was largely responsible for implementing the Company's policy of having no compromises so far as dishonesty and discipline were concerned. Among his many achievements were the introduction of a productivity scheme and an expansion scheme in which a lot of liaison work in various governmental agencies was involved.

Gokulam was a member of the Bombay Management Association, the Bombay Productivity Council, the Indian Chemical Manufacturers' Association and Secretary of the Western Zonal Council of the Indian Soap and Toiletries Makers' Association. He was also an active member of various co-operative institutions either in the capacity of Chairman or Secretary for several years.

Then, there was V.N. Gogate, Senior Vice-President and Secretary of Godrej Soaps, now a Board member. Mild, soft-spoken, benevolent, he was a sort of father-figure to his staff. He had passed the Chartered Accountancy examination which then as now was considered a great achievement. Gifted with an elephantine memory, he recalled the names of all his school friends, kept in touch with them throughout his life and went out of his way to find suitable employment for them. He is a man of great integrity and enjoys the trust of the Godrejs.

A close friend of Pirojsha's who stood by him in the giant Godrej undertaking at Vikhroli was Kekhushru Navroji Katrak who ran an ancient architect's firm Merwanji Bana and Company in an ancient building (still standing in Dalal Street). Four days a week, for many years, a Godrej car would come in the morning to take Kekhushru to Vikhroli. In the afternoons he would return to his office and work till late.

Kekhushru was a remarkable man. His son-in-law, the well-known music critic S.K. Ookerjee, recalls him as a wizard at figures, meticulous in his methods of work and superlatively cautious in everything he did. He was in his day a keen tennis player. He also played bridge and chess and won a prize in a chess competition on board ship en route to the USA for cancer surgery. He used to go boating with Pirojsha—on a rowing boat on weekdays and a sailing boat on weekends. So loyal was he to the Godrej family that he refused to use any soap, shampoo or eau-de-cologne other than Godrej's.

'Kekhushru had undergone almost a dozen surgeries,' recalls Ookerjee 'and lived for much of his later life with one kidney, one eye and no stomach. By sheer will-power he reached the age of eighty-four finally succumbing to the disease.'

'Kekhushru was extremely abstemious and totally against liquor. He had kept, safely in his cupboard, a bottle of Henessy brandy for a possible medical emergency, but it was not opened in his lifetime. It was an ironical situation when, late one night, the police came to his house and almost arrested him because they had found that liquor was being brewed in that ancient office of his after office hours!'

Another friend who stood by Pirojsha through thick and thin was Dinshaw Daji, a great solicitor, who gave excellent advice not only on legal, but family matters too.

Invaluable service was also provided by Kersey Movdawalla who was attached to Kerse Naoroji in the personnel department. He supervised housing for the workers and was responsible for starting a Scouts Movement in the colony. He died in 1972, the same year as Pirojsha.

The Godrej story would not be complete without reference to the auditors Kalyaniwalla & Mistry, Chartered Accountants, and particularly to its founder Maneck Mistry who was known as Boty.

The Godrej accountant Khurshed Bardy and Boty used to play cricket as schoolboys. When Boty returned from London in 1928 after having qualified as an incorporated accountant, Bardy requested Pirojsha to give Boty an opportunity to prove himself. Fortunately, Pirojsha had also heard of Boty from his friends, the Sidhwas, who were Boty's maternal uncles. Boty was selected as Auditor of Godrej Soaps Limited.

A close association developed. The Godrejs were keen, in their pursuit of self-reliance to develop Indian industries, but all the foreign banks, mostly British, were not interested in financing them. Boty took the initiative in approaching the Central Bank of India from whom Pirojsha received the first major loan. Subsequently, Godrej went on to become the largest account-holder of the Central Bank of India.

As Godrej grew, Kalyaniwalla & Mistry continuously rendered advice on matters relating to taxation, accountancy, corporate laws and finance.

The major problem for Godrej was liquidity to meet liabilities under the Income Tax Act (as high as 93 per cent), the Wealth Tax Act (as high as 8 per cent every year on total wealth) and the Expenditure Tax Act. The major worry was Estate Duty, which was as high as 85 per cent. It was Kalyaniwalla & Mistry who suggested to Godrej to give a large chunk to charity and still maintain control. This was how the Godrej Foundation was formed. Senior members of the family became its first trustees, the only outsider being Boty. Till today the family has continued with this decision, to donate 32 per cent of its income to charity.

The association with Kalyaniwalla & Mistry still continues. After the death of Boty Mistry in 1972, his appointed partner Fali Sarkari has continued to audit and advise the Company to this day.

Says Chairman Sohrab Godrej: 'One of our active well-wishers was the genial and very knowledgeable Maneck Mistry heading this firm. A thoroughness in his preparation and zeal for promoting national industries, including of course Godrej, was a landmark in the history of this Company.'

Writing about Pirojsha one realizes how impossible it is to contain or compartmentalize greatness. He was now to show that he too was a visionary, in fact one of the great visionaries of his time. Among the factors responsible for this, was Pirojsha's deep concern as a humanist with the problem of industrial slums and the degradation to which they could lead. He had read hardly any books on management, but instinctively, with unerring insight, he was conscious that working in a modern well-laid-out factory in pleasant surroundings and with amenities would make work less arduous and more rewarding.

Lalbaug left no room for large-scale expansion. In the late forties, there were all indications that India would soon be free and freedom would open up undreamt of opportunities and create unforeseen demands for growth. There was no alternative to reduce congestion but to shift the factory to new and vast grounds. With his characteristic energy, Pirojsha set to work. He bought a tract of land in Vikhroli village at a public auction. There were several pockets of settlers in the neighbouring areas whom he bought off one after the other, paying more in the process than he had done for the original piece of land. Considering today's prices, what he paid was a pittance, yet he had to sell his shares and almost everything he had to defray the cost, besides taking loans.

He did this against the advice of friends and well-wishers who sincerely believed he was throwing money away and being unmindful of his children. Other people, suffering from the dole mentality, wrote in the press that Pirojsha could have better utilized the amount spent to provide relief to the poor in the community! But Pirojsha went ahead regardless. His prescience told him he was right. His vision of India's industrial future couldn't be confined to a Parel back lane.

Acquiring the lands at Vikhroli was a rather tortuous process. The lands were originally purchased through the Court Receiver in the late forties, passed by the High Court Order of 15 April 1943. The entire village of Vikhroli under Kowl was handed over from Nathaniel Hornby to Faramji Kavasji Banaji on 7 July 1835, and later sold to Amrutlal Amarchand, who was a predecessor in title, by an order dated 18 October 1919. On 18 January 1943 an auction was held before the Commissioner for sale of the village of Vikhroli in which Naval was declared the highest bidder. Later, the High Court confirmed the sale in his favour and handed over possession of the village through the Court Receiver to Naval in July 1943.

Naval, a Director and Nominee of Godrej & Boyce Mfg. Co. Pvt. Ltd., handed over the lands to the Company which was recorded by the letter received from the Collector of Thane dated 7 January 1948 confirming that the Government had accorded sanction of transfer of land in Vikhroli to Godrej & Boyce Mfg. Co. Pvt. Ltd. Naval along with his brother-in-law Kaikhushroo Naoroji who had bought over the rights, title and interest of Sutedars in the village of Vikhroli also transferred and assigned to Godrej & Boyce the rights purchased by them.

On Sundays, accompanied by his architects, engineers and others, Pirojsha would go to Vikhroli to acquaint himself thoroughly with his newly acquired possession. Standing tall, his white hair ruffled in the breeze, he would gaze at the vast marshy expanse, seeing in his mind's eye the lay of the land taking on the contours of his dream. Nobody who saw the humble shed being built to enable the architects and engineers to operate, standing forlorn in the vastness, could have visualized the transformation of the wilderness into an industrial garden township: an Eden of productivity and economic contentment, an attraction that would become the pride of the country. Nobody, that is, except the father who had a dream, who had a son to blue-print that dream.

After ensuring clearance of the whole area, the work began. Giant excavators, bulldozers and a fleet of heavily laden trucks sprawled all over the land like giant foraging insects. They bulldozed the hillocks into flat land, quarried, built the roads, filled the creeks, raised immense factory sheds along with comfortable, modern (fully self-contained and well-ventilated) generously subsidized houses, with balconies (and with regular water-supply) for the workers. Both sheds and houses are in a garden setting with long avenues of Ashoka trees, beds of bougainvillea and hundreds of crotons, flowering plants, manicured lawns and gurgling fountains giving it the aspect of a botanical garden. Characteristically, as much attention was paid to the design of the residential quarters as to the manufacturing plants. The four big modern structures—5 acres each—that were ready by 1960 have now grown into nineteen plants. Year after year, more and more flats were constructed, growing from three hundred and four in 1955 to one thousand five hundred and eighty-nine today.

When the factory shifted in the early fifties to Vikhroli the existing, somewhat unsophisticated manual process of Godrej Storwel production was replaced by a completely mechanized unit. Assembly-line production presupposes technological efficiency of a high order which Godrej had acquired the hard way. Godrej made their own dies and punches in addition to jigs and fixtures which were principally required to fabricate the parts of their products. With their up-to-date Toolroom they took up die-making which is a job requiring high skills and precision, and accuracy to 1/1000th of an inch.

Godrej were keen to manufacture bicycles also. As ill-luck would have it, the ship carrying the equipment for the entire plant was torpedoed when the War broke out in 1939. Godrej were left with a huge consignment of bicycle chains which had arrived by an earlier ship. These were later sold to Hind Cycles.

The large-scale multipurpose Godrej plant soon began to have repercussions over a wide economic field, with many indirect beneficiaries. Godrej used and continues to use the production of a large number of industries like steel and power, materials like paint, packing wood, cement and paper and non-ferrous metals and services like banking, insurance and transport. The screw industry, for example, benefits by the use at Godrej of billions of screws each year. In turn, Godrej supplies materials to other industries. Steel tubing, for instance, goes into the manufacture of Indian bicycles, besides several other uses.

But the shift to Vikhroli was important for another reason. It enabled Pirojsha to give further shape to his ideas of worker safety and welfare. With a view to preventing accidents and making the workers safety-conscious, a Safety Committee was formed for each plant with a Central Safety Committee to review their working. These committees functioned as channels of communication between management and workers. Films on safety were shown from time to time.

Family-planning was Pirojsha's abiding concern, next only to providing education for workers' children. He realized that economic development depends on the balanced and planned use of existing human, capital and natural resources. A population growing out of proportion to other factors in the productivity equation creates a vicious circle of lower income, drop in savings, less capital, less investment—all of which act as a brake on development. In carrying this message to the workers, his son Naval found a sincere helpmate in Soonuben Dastoor (daughter of Dinshaw and Gulbai Dastoor) whom he had married on 16 January 1947. Dastoor was the agent in Karachi for the Central Bank of India. Finding that her husband left home at 8.00 every morning and did not return till 8.00 in the evening, she wanted to do something to relieve his burden as well as occupy her time. With her active help, a Welfare Centre—Pragati Kendra—was opened at Vikhroli on 15 August 1955 with Pirojsha unfurling the national flag. A family-planning centre followed in 1957. In the initial stages only advice and contraceptives at concessional rates were given. As the results were not too encouraging, the emphasis was subsequently shifted to sterilization. In 1962, a family-planning exhibition was organized to bring about greater awareness among employees and residents. With the co-operation and support of Dr G.M. Phadke, a vasectomy centre was opened with several residents volunteering to undergo the operation. In 1965, when the IUCD was experimented upon in India, a research centre was launched with the help of Dr R.P. Soonawala and the Ford Foundation.

Volunteers were trained from among the workers to go door to door to propagate family-planning. The angle was not how family-planning would help the country, but how it would benefit the workers themselves and thereby the country. No financial incentives were offered to those who underwent vasectomy and tubectomy operations; good schooling and housing themselves proved to be incentives. Arrangements were made with the plant-in-charge to offer out-of-pocket expenses to workers who practised family-planning. No education was granted in the Udayachal School to the fourth child of a couple. Each and every one of the approximately seven thousand employees was covered by the family-planning programme through concerted efforts. Up-to-date detailed records are maintained of employees with the number of children, age and the planning method adopted. The Pragati Kendra too organized exhibitions, entertainment programmes, film shows and talks to bring home the importance of planning the families in their own and the country's interest. The co-operation of union workers and their wives was also enlisted. The hard work paid off in the long run with two children per family becoming the accepted norm.

A representative of the Ford Foundation on a visit to Vikhroli expressed surprise and concern that so much attention was given to this aspect. Soonuben was able to convince him that India's case was different from America's, and that family-planning was a dire need lying at the root of most problems in India. On another occasion, a union leader took it upon himself to go and complain to the then Home Minister of Maharashtra, who promptly dashed off a letter to Godrej that too much attention to family-planning would be tantamount to interference with personal freedom and that it would distract children from their studies. Godrej wrote back that this in no way interfered with workers' personal freedom, that persuasion and education were employed and not force, and that to learn about family-planning was for the national good and beginning with children was the best way to serve that good. Nothing more was heard from the Minister concerned.

A notable achievement, whose consequences were going to be far-reaching, was the provision of education for workers' children. On his routine visits to the company, Pirojsha was disturbed by the plight of these children who, having nothing else to do, were just whiling away their time in the streets. He discussed this with Naval who then broached the idea of a school for them with the noted educationist, the late Mrs Cooverbai Vakil, Auntie to Indira Gandhi, who happened to be a family friend. A prodigy of Shantiniketan, she brought its inherent love for nature and fine arts to the proposed school and came familiarly to be known as 'Auntie'. Associated with her in this venture was another well-known educationist Jyotsnaben Mehta who brought her long experience to bear on the project. Started at Bal Mandir in a grain store in the Godrej welfare centre with a handful of children, it grew into a magnificent edifice in black stone, in an idyllic setting of roads lined with gulmohurs and copper pods, lush green lawns, cooing pigeons and birds on the wing. More importantly, its innovative and almost revolutionary methods of teaching children would make it a model school, a trail-blazer in the field of education. Not only bricks and mortar went into the school's construction, but also much concern and much love. The school opened on 15 August 1955.

Pragati Kendra, being the nucleus of all Godrej's welfare activities, has been in the forefront working with the employees and their families, providing valuable counselling, concentrating on developmental programmes of both women and children and creating awareness about environmental concerns. In addition to adult literacy, the Kendra provides training in gainful spare-time occupations like caning chairs, polishing chair-frames, batik, pottery-making and so on. To help supplement the income of the families of employees, orders are secured by the Kendra from the company and work is distributed among the colony housewives.

The Kendra works hand-in-hand along with 'Upchargraha' towards curative as well as preventive aspects of health.

Employees are covered under the company's medical benefit scheme. Health care includes a variety of facilities like preventive measures, a dental clinic, physiotherapy, a pathological laboratory, a psychiatric clinic and yoga and gymnasium classes. The immunization programme in Godrej is the best in Maharashtra, perhaps in the whole of India.

The Pragati Kendra has also been involved in a cleanliness campaign to drive home the message of 'Clean and Green Pirojshanagar'. This was done through home visits, poster campaigns, interaction with the Mumbai Municipal Corporation and public education. Programmes were organized on the occasion of 'Vanamahotsav' and World Environment Day. A Nature Club was also initiated. Courses on Ikebana and bonsai were also organized.

The Pragati Kendra team have adopted as their motto Robert C. Savage's memorable lines:

Today I found
Life's greatest problem
I Discovered it in the Mirror
It is I!!

A Scouts and Girl Guides Movement was started for the children of the Godrej colony in 1964. There is also a well-trained unit of Home Guards for Civil Defence. By intensifying programmes for better living, including family planning, the Godrej endeavour is to inculcate social and national consciousness among their workers.

The facilities provided at Vikhroli grew out of Pirojsha's conviction, shared by Naval and other family members, to look after the workers in the best manner possible, to enable them in turn to give of their best. Burjor's wife Jai proved to be a gifted teacher, much loved by her students. Naval's wife Soonuben continues to this day to supervise all aspects of welfare work.

8
AN EDEN OF CONTENTMENT

'Great things are done,' wrote William Blake, 'when men and mountains meet. This is not done by jostling in the street.' In the Godrej story, instead of 'mountains', there were acres upon acres of marshy land extending as far as the eye could reach. And the 'jostling' was not in the street, but in newspapers and on public platforms, by well-intentioned busybodies in the Parsi community who felt that the money spent on buying this waste land could have been better utilized for relief of the poor.

But Pirojsha went ahead, regardless, like another pioneer before him, none other than Jamsetji Tata. When in 1898 Jamsetji set aside fourteen of his buildings and four landed properties in Bombay, amounting in value then to thirty lakh rupees, for a university of science, he was criticized by fellow-Parsis for diverting the community's wealth instead of utilizing it to provide shelter, food and clothing to Parsis in need. How wrong Jamsetji's and Pirojsha's critics were is proved by the fact that Jamsetji's dream university was one day (years after his death) to grow into the prestigious Indian Institute of Science, Bangalore, and in Pirojsha's case, into the industrial garden township Pirojshanagar, which became 'an Eden of productivity and economic contentment.'

Pirojshanagar is an industrial garden township in which as much attention is paid to the design of the residential quarters as to the spacious, airy manufacturing plants. Large open spaces have been left, thousands of trees planted and flower-beds laid, to make the environment healthy and happy for the multitude of workers. Not only the workers: the future of their children is provided for by educating them, in the fullest sense of character-building and allround development, at the Udayachal schools, which are looked upon as model schools in scholastic circles for the results achieved, with the weaker children getting special coaching and, as seen in the previous chapter, at the Pragati Kendra. Sports and cultural activities are encouraged.

The advantages the schools provide are only possible because the numbers are manageable, thanks to the successful family-planning programmes inducing parents to limit their families and children since overpopulation leads inevitably to environment degredation, and to care for and look after the environment.

In fact, glancing through the remarks in the Visitor's Book at Pirojshanagar, what becomes apparent is that the social concerns of Godrej have impressed visitors more than anything else.

'Facilities for the workers seem to be the prime objective of management—a rare thing elsewhere.'
—*Joe Appish, Roving Ambassador for the Ghana Government.*

'One of the finest factories I've ever seen, especially in regard to the welfare, education and housing of the workers.'
—*Tan Toh Hong, M.P. Malaysia.*

'If more of our industrialists were as progressive and forward-looking as the Godrejs, it would be all to the good.'
—*Subhash Dhar, Planning Advisor, United Nations, New York.*

'I am absolutely amazed. I admit that one would find very few enterprises so favourably disposed in France.'
—*Jean Coutenay, Journalist, France.*

'Godrej are a leader in industry—known to every citizen of this vast country. Godrej are or have become a leader in conservation of nature.'
—*Kisan Mehta, Municipal Counciller, Municipal Corporation of Greater Bombay.*

'A most impressive example of enlightened capitalism.'
—*Vijay Joshi, Economic Advisor, Ministry of Finance.*

'An Industrial Wonderland.'
—*Malati Srivastava, Secretary, Breach Candy Hospital, Bombay.*

Pirojsha might not have heard of Thomas J. Watson Sr. who founded the world computer giant, IBM, in 1914.

An Eden of Contentment

Instinctively, exemplifying the new spirit in modern industrial outlook, he sensed and put into practice the three value commitments Watson had laid down—that the individual worker must be respected, that the customer must be given the best possible product and service, and that excellent and superior performance must consistently be pursued. These time-enduring, time-honoured principles, still upheld by IBM, were kept alive by Pirojsha in his own characteristic way, not so much by conscious organizational intervention as by a clear and positive vision of development of the organization, percolating down from the top to the lowest worker.

Pirojsha was a man of strong instincts, and his instincts were more often than not the right ones. Sensing the changing mores of the working-classes in the new India that was being built, he provided his workers with benefits like holidays with pay, provident fund, gratuity, benefits which, it is a matter of record, anticipated labour legislation. He knew, as most of us do, that a happy contented worker is a productive worker. Yet it would be the gravest injustice to a man of extraordinary vision and great humanity to attribute all that he did for his workers to mercenary motives, to a so-called 'profit strategy' which in any case would have been self-defeating.

Because he cared for his workers, knew most of them by name and was aware of their contribution and sympathetic to their needs, it wouldn't even have occurred to him to manipulate and manoeuvre them merely for material ends. He had strong genuine convictions, instilled into him by Ardeshir, about the nobility of the Swadeshi concept and the sort of institution they were trying to build. Industrialization was an article of faith with him, meant to promote jobs, decent living standards for employees and a fair deal to consumers. Hence, housing, education, health care, family-planning and environmental considerations were integrated into his industrial activities through profits ploughed back into the business consistently.

Just as he did his best for his workers, he expected them to give of their best. When on occasions they did not, he would fly off the handle. In many ways he was larger than life. So were his outbursts of rage, which fortunately were rare. He could be terrifyingly blunt when the occasion demanded. 'First deserve, than desire!' he would roar at a disgruntled worker who came asking for a raise. Great men are known not to suffer fools gladly. Sometimes Pirojsha took time off to point out to a fool the extent of his foolishness. He despised laziness, and the indiscriminate charity that leads to sloth. Each man, he believed, had the birthright to be given an opportunity to prove his worth.

Pirojsha wasn't a born leader of men. He acquired the qualities of leadership as he went along, so that by the time he was in his fifties, his career graph provided an anatomy of leadership. In the early days he would personally examine, say, each Storwel before it left the factory to see for himself that its locking arrangement, its finish, everything about it was as it should be. He would study the bills of purchases by his workers at the office grain-store to find out their preferences, what they could or could not afford. Often he would question them whether they had noticed any shortcomings in the company's products or had any suggestions to make about them. Endowed with an eye for detail, he would keep a diary and note down the day-to-day sales details. The cement-concrete foundations of the Vikhroli plant needed to be watered continuously for twenty-one days so that they would become strong enough to last for years. Pirojsha would maintain a daily record of this watering so that it was done thoroughly.

An Eden of Contentment

An incident about Pirojsha's uncanny eye for detail stands out. When they were still in Lalbaug, it was usual for Pirojsha to go on a tour of the factories at four o'clock every afternoon, carrying an umbrella. On one occasion, he noticed a large number of safes lined up ready for despatch to destinations throughout the country. He stood for a long time eyeing a particular safe and then summoned the supervisor to enquire whether these safes had been checked before delivery. The supervisor nodded 'yes'. Pirojsha then sent for the worker who had actually done the checking. He asked him the same question and got the same answer. Without another word, Pirojsha took out a ten rupee note, folded it carefully, then went up to the safe he had been eyeing and inserted it between the door and the body. Tongue-tied, the supervisor and the worker hung their heads. In a fit of temper, Pirojsha hit the worker with his umbrella, ordered him to remove the defective safe and warned him that if such a thing happened again, he would lose his job.

On another occasion when steel furniture was being successfully manufactured by Godrej, the General Manager, Nariman Sahukar, and the Sales Manager, Rustom Sanjana, went up to Pirojsha with the suggestion that now that this furniture was being manufactured in India, they should approach the government to put a ban on the import of furniture. 'But why?' asked Pirojsha. 'Let us compete with them. Competition is good. If there is no competition, we will become complacent.'

Two other attributes thus marked him out for greatness. Apart from his attention to detail, these were his sound instincts which enabled him to see beyond the obvious and the temporary, and his tremendous perseverance to see things through to the end. Life, he knew, was not a hundred yard dash, but a long-distance championship. He was clear about what he wanted to achieve. Respecting specialization, he never interfered with operating decisions based on it. He delegated authority, allowed people sufficient freedom to operate and egged them on to succeed. Surrounded, as we have seen, by talented and loyal managers, he went out of his way to always acknowledge their contribution to his success, although for him his workers came first.

Independent by nature, Pirojsha had great respect for individual dignity. He disliked an overbearing attitude as much as he did servility. One of the earliest lessons Sohrab recalls being taught was: Treat everyone with respect and courtesy, but never say 'Sir' to anybody.

Above all, in the true spirit of leadership and with remarkable foresight, Pirojsha created the conditions that would enable Godrej to survive him. His leadership style provided the direction and communicated the vision which bound people together for a common objective. He built adaptive structures of the kind that could generate ideals and sustain them. With his foresight and skills, he was able to steer and lead people, to develop a proper focus for the future and a definite plan of action which he shared with his sons and communicated to his managers and workers.

A far-sighted man, he consistently harped on the 'requirements of our country' and the strategic role that industry played in economic development. Although old in years, his outlook remained as modern and fresh as that of his sons, and he was ever receptive to new and daring ideas. He believed in the common man, and in the realization of his vision of a self-reliant and prosperous people. He cautioned, however, that India with its size and teeming population, required inputs of immense effort for fulfilling the critical task of industrialization. Taking upon himself the trusteeship of the country and the peoples' welfare, he devoted his life in selflessly contributing towards the realization of this noble goal.

An Eden of Contentment

Kerse Naoroji who successfully looked after the company's labour-relations for fifty years from 1943 onwards and continues to do so in an advisory capacity even after retirement, recalls Pirojsha telling him again and again that his workers were his greatest asset. During the Depression when Pirojsha was faced with the alternative of closing down the company or persuading his workers to accept a voluntary cut in their salaries, several workers themselves came forward to accept the latter alternative. Pirojsha never forgot this gesture. Within the year, with conditions improving, their salaries were restored, with increments added, and they were looked after even after retirement.

Pirojsha's faith in his workers was amply reciprocated by them, sometimes in unusual but touching ways. On the occasion of Burjor's wedding on 15 April 1941, the staff members 'with our hearts full of gratitude and affection' offered Pirojsha a token of their feelings in the form of a beautifully engraved casket. In the accompanying address, the staff members stated: 'It is a matter of no small gratification to us that whereas only a decade ago hardly a few hundred men worked on this edifice, today it has come to employ, shelter and sustain such a vast body of men.' They were referring to the two generous measures that had been adopted just recently—the provident fund and annual leave on full wages 'even to the lowliest workmen.' They concluded by praising 'the untiring hard work and unceasing devotion to duty of his three sons which must be a source of joyous pride to a father's heart.'

The culture-building process in Godrej, under Pirojsha, was organic as well as evolutionary. Ameeta Madhok, a human resource development consultant, speaking about changing company cultures quotes an analogy provided by a consultant friend in the 'Ascent' supplement to the *Times of India*. The change is likened to *samudramanthan*, the evolution of the world according to Hindu mythology where God churned up the seas, yielding on one hand the *amrit* which consisted of peace, beauty, harmony and the good things in life and the *vish* or poison on the other. While it is true that in an organization *vish* and *amrit* coexist, it is upto the processes of change to churn the organization's culture in order to polarize the two. The nectar can then be harnessed to fuel the vibrancy of the culture. The poison must, however, be dealt with in a constructive manner, so that its destructive effects can be nullified. Only thus can synergy be achieved.

That Godrej achieved this synergy in fair measure is proved by the fact that in their long history they were singularly free of labour trouble. Pirojsha welcomed the formation of unions, provided they comprised the workers themselves: he was totally, resolutely against outside interference. It was only once that the *vish* was thrown up, leading to a strike for narrow political reasons. The first strike was on 20 June 1972, followed by another one on 24 June, 1972. Then there was a lock-out from 26 June to 12 July, 1972. It was like a nightmare for Pirojsha. Knowing how sensitive he was about this subject, Kerse with Naval's help tried to hide from Pirojsha its ugliest features, the riots, and even the occasional killings. To him his workers had always been partners in a great enterprise. They were part of his *parivar*. He had given of his trust to them, and when that trust was betrayed, he felt deeply hurt. Kerse, along with several retired employees, believes that he carried the hurt to his dying day. He passed away just six months later.

Sometimes it happened that the workers' wives showed greater appreciation of what the management was doing for them, particularly in welfare activities, than their husbands. A limit of three children per family, later reduced to two, was laid down as the norm for admission to the Godrej school. When on one occasion, the workers gheraoed the

An Eden of Contentment

Godrejs at their residence demanding that all their children should be admitted, it was the wives who supported the management.

Pirojsha had the innate humility to make light of his achievements. He would disclaim any credit for himself, saying that it should really go to his brother, Ardeshir, the founder. Reading about American and Japanese industries in *Fortune*, he would often say that the achievements of Godrej in India were minor compared to those of the developed countries.

As a young man, Pirojsha was fond of sports, particularly swimming and rowing. He had tremendous physical stamina. The story goes that he would swim from Apollo Bunder across the bay to Gharapuri (Elephanta Caves). Among his other pleasures was to attend with his family, shows of touring Italian opera companies who would perform at the Royal Opera House and the Excelsior Cinema in Bombay. He thus initiated his children into an understanding and appreciation of Western classical music. He was also fond of Indian classical music.

Reading was his other hobby. He enjoyed reading Herbert Spencer. Perhaps, the writer who influenced him most was Charles Darwin, though his favourite was another Charles, the great novelist Dickens. Darwin's *The Origin of Species* inspired Pirojsha's realization of man's impact, as a biological species, on the environment and the need for mankind to reform its ways and control its growth in order to survive in the long run. As for Dickens, his moving portrayal of the degradation of the poor and deprived struck a sympathetic chord in Pirojsha. The dingy, smelly slums through which he would drive every morning on his way to the Lalbaug factory brought to mind 'the Dickensian rookeries pullulating with life, pedestrians and horse-drawn drays dodging one another in the criss-crossing alleys, the sweepers with their brushes and pans, the raucous laughter issuing from crowded ale-shops, the pungent odours of onions and sausages frying.' In Dickens, Pirojsha recognized a radical crusader against the wrongs suffered by the poor in the slums, the courts, the prisons and factories of Victorian England.

Throughout his life Pirojsha felt deeply for the poor. He was practical enough to descend from the lofty concept of the trusteeship of wealth in which he implicitly believed and which he scrupulously practiced, and would distribute five and ten rupee notes to the poor lining the narrow lane to Lalbaug for them to be able to meet their immediate needs. In the pre-Vikhroli days he was known, when made aware of a worker's straitened circumstances, to pay his rent arrears or his medical bills.

Often the price of greatness is loneliness. Like Ardeshir, but to a lesser extent, Pirojsha too was a lonely man, and like his elder brother, he too had his share of tragedy. He was married to Soonabai whose father Pestonjee Dinshaw Dastoor was a pioneer cricketer (included in the first Parsi team to play in England) and the proud head of a Karachi bank. Pestonjee's father was the high priest who, according to a family legend, travelled from Baroda to Bombay in a bullock-cart bringing the *atash* (sacred fire) with him.

Pirojsha loved Soonabai deeply. She bore him four children, but died unexpectedly in 1920, at the young age of thirty, of the Asian flu then raging. A little later, in November 1926, her brother Maneck, who also was a well-known cricketer was killed in a motor-cycle accident on McLeod Road in Karachi. While trying to avoid collision with a Makrani pedestrian, the motor cycle swerved and braked. Maneck was pitched off and sustained fatal head injuries. He was just thirty.

An Eden of Contentment

Pirojsha not being a communicative man even with his family members, his wife would often intercede with him on behalf of his children. She was a quiet, gentle person, spreading sweetness and light, and of a strong character. She was fond of Western music and of playing the violin, and looked after the house as only a caring woman can, with, in Milton's words, 'those thousand decencies that daily flow, from all her words and actions.' The sons, particularly Sohrab the eldest who is in some ways the most sensitive, have fond memories of her. Her untimely death left a void in their lives that was never quite filled. She lies buried at Mussoorie, in the Christian cemetry, in land bought by Pirojsha. Hers is the first of eight graves in the Parsi cemetry.

After Soonabai's untimely demise, it fell to their maternal grandmother Veerbaiji who lived at Karachi to come down to Bombay and to take over as mother for about seven years. After Maneck's tragic accident, however, Veerbaiji did not feel like leaving Karachi. She was a very good housekeeper besides being an excellent cook. Again, the house was bereft of a woman's touch.

For Pirojsha his wife's death was a terrible blow. He survived it, but the loss seemed to have transformed him in subtle ways. Like any well-to-do middle class family man, he had been fond of simple pleasures like swimming, sailing, going on weekends to Versova, and going on picnics. But after her death he lost interest in everything except his favourite karkhana. The karkhana became his dream, his passion, his obsession, his very life. Sohrab recalls an amusing incident in this connection. The well-known educationist, Cooverbai Vakil, who had helped in founding the Udayachal School, and was a highly refined and cultured lady was staying with the Godrejs for a period of time. She would join Pirojsha and others at mealtimes at which the talk would centre on the karkhana. One day she suddenly stopped doing so, and when Sohrab enquired why, she said: 'Oh, I'm fed up of eating steel at meals!'

There were those around Pirojsha, including some family members, who criticized him as having a one-track mind. But then, the dividing-line between a one-track mind and single-mindedness, born of single-heartedness, is thin as a razor's edge. His single-mindedness, amounting almost to the obsession of a prophetic vision but reined in by discipline, achieved a quality of greatness that was dramatic. All great men have this quality—great thinkers, great leaders, great scientists, writers, artists and musicians.

Seeing that their father was losing interest in things that had meant a lot to him, as if he were losing interest in life itself, Sohrab and Burjor (Naval was just over three years old when his mother died) were concerned. The thought of a stepmother particularly worried Sohrab who had been close to his mother. One day, seeing Pirojsha relaxed and quiet, reading the morning newspaper, Sohrab picked up the courage to broach the subject of his not having married again. It was one of those rare moments when the mask dropped from his father's face. He became pensive. His eyes shadowed. Quietly, as if speaking to himself, he said in Gujarati, 'There is no room in my life for another woman.' Nothing more was ever said on the subject.

Nothing was said, but the power of life to transmute a person's needs as life itself changed was implied and understood. To a man like Pirojsha, people's ready consolations, of there being other women and other enchantments, were anathema. There could be no other woman but the woman he loved, no other enchantment. As novelist and essayist Charles Morgan philosophizes, life is not lived by forgetting or substitution, but by remembrance and transmutation and so freed, death being not a change of

An Eden of Contentment

state but merely of lodging, 'an incident in a continuous immortality.'

Pirojsha had always taken calculated risks. For instance, he made a lot of money investing in Tata shares which helped him to buy Godrej & Boyce Mfg. Co. Pvt. Ltd. from his brother. But he still needed money for expanding the business. He had always been a proud man and asking for loans irked him. Sohrab would accompany him on such occasions. Sohrab recalls one particular meeting with a rich businessman who was into money-lending. Naturally, the latter put certain questions which any businessman would. After the interview Sohrab could make out from Pirojsha's face that he was terribly hurt, as if the questions had cast doubt not on his business plans but on his credentials.

Before her untimely death Soonabai had always interceded with Pirojsha on behalf of her sons. With her going Sohrab found him becoming increasingly difficult, for his father was becoming impatient of opposition, insistent that things should be done his way, adamant and obstinate. Of course, Sohrab recalls him always having been a bit of a dictator and his relationship with him, born of fear, as being a strained one. But it must be added as the years passed, Pirojsha did mellow down somewhat, and in turn, as Sohrab grew to share his deep concerns about population explosion and environmental degradation, their relationship warmed and became quite cordial. A fair assessment has to take into account these weaknesses or excesses, depending on how one looks at them, as the flip side of Pirojsha's greatness.

If he could take calculated risks, he was also by nature exceedingly cautious. When during the War there was the threat of a Japanese invasion, he built an air-raid shelter at 40-D Ridge Road. He took the added precaution of acquiring alternative accommodation at Thana. To safeguard a few documents of value, he had a *tijori* (safe) specially built with so many secret compartments and locks that, had the Japanese invaders been confronted by it, it would have taxed their ingenuity to the utmost!

One day, without any fuss as if he were announcing an item from the morning newspaper, he told Sohrab, 'Take me to the cancer hospital.' Pirojsha had had two major illnesses—mastoid and herpes—but cancer? Sohrab was shocked beyond words. He rushed his father to Dr Jussawala who, after several tests, confirmed the diagnosis—cancer of the throat. He told Sohrab that a family member should take his father for treatment to London without any delay. Naval wanted to accompany him to London for this purpose. But Pirojsha's first concern, as always, was his karkhana. Who would look after the karkhana if all of them left? Ultimately, a family member, an uncle, Soonuben's father, and Dr Aspi Golwala accompanied Pirojsha.

This was the third major illness in Pirojsha's life. The cancer was controlled after the prescribed chemotherapy. Only a white patch on his throat betrayed the ordeal he had been through. Back in Bombay, he continued to attend office, undergoing periodic check-ups at the Tata Cancer Hospital, with Sohrab accompanying him each time. He never complained of discomfort or pain, but took it in his stride.

Ultimately, what took him wasn't cancer but old age.

The death of a pioneer creates an emptiness that is seldom filled. Pirojsha died on 1 December 1972 and the next afternoon was laid to rest in the smallest *bungli*, the only one available on that day, at Doongervadi. But the crowd of mourners he drew was perhaps the biggest seen on these sanctified grounds, overflowing into the neighbouring bunglis and the open spaces around. A thousand grief-stricken faces, trying hard to fight back the tears; by contrast his face, drained of blood, was calm, even serene. Small wonder, too, for how many of those present could claim at the end, 'I dreamt great dreams, I knew great fulfillment?'

The prayers over, the mourners followed him in pairs, holding handkerchiefs according to ancient custom, up the garden path towards the White Towers. The pebbles crunched under their dragging feet, the black birds of death circled perilously low, winged shadows. A sad procession which he, prostrate, still led.

When just outside the Towers, they uncovered that well-loved, white-haired face for the last time, the wrench was painful. Memories crowded in of small beginnings and great ends, of early doubts and discrimination, of dogged persistence and ultimate triumph, of a glory that was and was now departing.

Pirojsha was not only a father-figure to his family and relatives, friends and admirers, his thousands of employees. He was a father-figure in Indian industry. History would no doubt place him among the great pioneers of industrial India, along with his brother Ardeshir. Pirojsha was a *sethia* in the finest sense of the word, a true representative of his great community. All the same, he had no time for its petty squabbles and pointless controversies. For him, his work was paramount. Steel and soap were his breath and beat.

In truth, he had achieved more than is given to most men to achieve. 'He never sold the truth to serve the hour/Nor pattered with eternal God for power . . .' Those who came to pay their last respects could not reconcile themselves to see him lying supine on that cold marble slab. They had grown so used to seeing him day after day, even after his illness almost to his dying day at the ripe age of 90, sitting at his desk, erect, alert, dressed in a simple Parsi cream-coloured dugla and a pair of white cotton trousers that, on him, were the livery of greatness.

But now instead of the giant machines throbbing away to an industrial future, they heard the peacock's startled cry, bringing them rudely back to the place and the time, inevitable and final. Yet, as the soft-footed *khandhias* lifted his bier to their shoulders and with bowed heads the mourners made way, all present knew in their innermost heart that the machines would continue to thunder to their destined future.

For the house he built has many pillars.

9

CURIOSITY-BREEDING JOKER

On Pirojsha's death in 1972, control of both Godrej and Boyce Manufacturing Co. Ltd. and Godrej Soaps passed smoothly, in the spirit of continuity he had fostered, to his three sons. Naval, the youngest, was in the process of proving that India could produce its own typewriters and refrigerators, which he was later to establish as market leaders, helping the country to move towards achievement of its goal of hi-tech electronics.

Burjor, elder to him by a year and a half, in-charge of Godrej Soaps, had in some ways a harder task, faced as he was by the unequal, and to Godrej, somewhat unfair competition—if necessary, they could underprice Godrej out of the market—from the giant multinational, Lever Brothers. Godrej Soaps passed through hard days. But Burjor, gifted in research, remained undaunted and persevered. With the acquisition of the rights for G-11, a germicidal chemical compound, in India, no soap before or after had a stronger selling-point, and his company soon became the leader in the premium toilet-soap market.

Sohrab, the eldest, who was appointed Chairman, further extended the company's public relations, reaching out to national and international concerns like family-planning and environmental degradation. One of Sohrab's main interests was scientific management, and, having travelled widely, he felt the need of enhancing exports. He was interested in the export promotion of Indian products and manufactures including the Godrej ones. A man in his time plays many parts. Sohrab plays more parts than most men or, rather, he deliberately underplays them in what has come to be recognized as the classic Godrej tradition.

Naval loved challenges, and the manufacture of a high-precision job like the typewriter was one such. There was, besides, the growing demand in the country for typewriters. Foreign typewriter manufacturers like Remington and Halda had hitherto met this demand and had established themselves in the country. Naval decided to meet this challenge head-on.

The manufacture of the Godrej all-Indian typewriter is of significance in India's industrial history. When prime minister Nehru typed on it for the first time on the occasion of the Avadi Congress, Madras, the nation received the message that India was taking its place among the few highly industrialized countries of Europe and America capable of typewriter manufacture. India was the first such in Asia.

Godrej had actually conceived the idea of typewriter

manufacture as early as 1942, but due to restrictions before Independence and War-time conditions, it was not possible to implement the idea then. The real start for manufacture of the toolings and insulation of machinery for typewriter production was made in 1951, and by the year 1953, typewriters started rolling off the assembly-line.

Typewriter manufacture necessitated the training in up-to-date factories of a nucleus of specialized workmen for manufacture as well as servicing at reasonable rates, through a network of centres throughout the country.

Although today the typewriter, manual or electronic, is an indispensable adjunct of modern life, the high-skill and specialized nature of its manufacture is seldom if at all realized. For, in addition to the usual turning, drilling, tapping, riveting and punching jobs, typewriter manufacture involves the making of over a hundred and fifty varieties of screws with special threads, not to speak of a whole series of specialized jobs like die-casting, spring-coiling, rack-cutting, gang-milling and heat-treating. Steel, iron, aluminium, brass, rubber, plastic and many other materials go into its making.

These specialized processes in turn call for highly specialized machines like special milling machines and type-bar segments, carriage guides and mounting frames; die-casting machines for main frames, top plates and spool covers; automatic rack-cutting machines for carriage racks, tabular stop and margin stop bars; multiple spindle drilling and tapping machines for key lever mounting, carriage and plates and other components which require precision drilling.

These component pieces number no less than 1800. To bring them to their present high degree of serviceability, has taken almost a century of world-wide experimentation.

Way back on 7 January 1749, an English engineer Henry Mill, applied for a patent which the then reigning Queen

Anne was pleased to grant for 'an artificial machine, enabling one to print or transcribe letters, one after the other just as when writing by hand.' But, according to the records of the British Patent Office, Mill's machine never reached the stage of manufacture.

Almost a century later in 1829, a patent for a similar machine was granted, this time in Detroit, to one William Austin Burt. Ill-luck seemed to dog this new-fangled invention. After years of painstaking labour, a single model was built according to the specifications of the patent—only to be destroyed by fire in the Washington Patent Office in 1836.

It was a Frenchman, Xavier Progin, to whom a French patent was granted in 1833, who reached the first milestone in typewriter manufacture. His machine, which can be called the prototype of our present type-bar machines, was called the Ktypographic machine or pen. The feature distinguishing this from earlier models was an assembly of bars with types, each type striking upon a common centre. The next important advance, longitudinal movement of a cylinder or platen to effect letter-spacing, was made by an American Charles Thurber of Worcester, Massachusetts, to whom an American patent was granted in 1843.

Other devices like the paper cylinder, line-spacing and carriage-return mechanism, the escapement which causes the letter spacing, arrangement of type-bars so as to strike the paper at a common centre, printing through an inked ribbon and the position of the different characters of the keyboard conforming almost exactly to the arrangement now known as 'Universal', were all embodied for the first time in the typewriter manufacture in 1867 by three citizens of Milwaukee, Christopher Latham Sholes, Carlos Gidden and Samuel Saule. Their product was marketed in 1874.

The world's first practicable typewriter bore striking similarities in outward appearance to the sewing-machine. It

Curiosity-Breeding Joker

was ornamented with floral designs and mounted on a sewing-machine stand, with a treadle geared to the carriage to effect a mechanical return. The world, however, was strangely indifferent to this new invention. Only 1,200 machines were sold in the first seven years! The total proceeds from patents amounted only to $ 12,000 so that the inventor Sholes died almost in penury.

The new-fangled machine excited interest in unexpected quarters. Mark Twain, for instance, secretly owned this 'curiosity-breeding little joker,' with which he wrote *Life on the Mississippi*. It is said to be the first typed draft of a book ever submitted to a publisher.

Sholes, however, lived long enough to see some of the changes his machine had brought about. It spelt the doom of male clerks, hitherto laboriously copying letters in long hand in a copper-plate script at the maximum rate of 15 to 20 words a minute. It opened the doors of business to women, creating a new profession for them. These women were soon typing at the then incredibly fast rate of 40 to 100 words a minute.

Sholes was perfectly right when he declared: 'I feel I have done something for the women who have always had to work so hard.' These early 'lady typewriters', as they were called, needed to be sturdy women. An average woman could hardly be expected to depress keys—what was needed was a blacksmith's touch. Later advances solved this problem as the typewriter reached, by stages, its present ease of operation combined with efficiency of performance.

The jobs provided to 'lady typewriters' were not an unmixed blessing. They were looked upon with suspicion and considered to be dangerous women who went husband-hunting or broke up the homes of respectable city officers. A typing exercise they were often set was 'The Wages of Sin is Death.' The British Government took the initiative in 1888 of employing a couple of ladies in the Inland Revenue

Department. They wore long celluloid cuffs and high stiff collars, and were locked in a room and fed through a hatch.

Today, it is impossible to imagine a typewriter without a shift-key mechanism or a machine typing capital letters only. It was not till 1878, however, that the problem of the two 'faces' was solved without increasing the number of keys by placing two types, a capital and small face of the same letter on each bar, and adding the shift key. At about the same time another typewriter was devised containing twice the number of keys and, incredible as it may seem, it competed with the other model for a number of years. What was it that decided the issue in favour of two faces on each key? The touch system of typing!

The typist today is able to see what he or she is typing. In early machines the bars were arranged in a circular 'basket', located underneath the carriage, which necessitated raising the carriage to see the typed lines. These machines operated on the down-stroke principle, in vogue till 1833. Front-stroke machines came several years later with type-bars placed in a segment in front of the carriage, the type printing on the front of the cylinder.

The immensity of the effort that went into typewriter manufacture can be gauged from the fact that upto 1870 about thirty-three inventions in five countries were recorded. After 1873, America alone accounted for two hundred and twenty-eight makes out of a world-wide total of four hundred and twenty-nine. But the number was reduced to sixty makes by 1900. It rose again in 1914 to a hundred and thirty, till today only five manufacturers remain even in the country where the demand for typewriters is the biggest in the world, estimated at many hundreds of thousands annually.

Typewriter manufacture is comparable for the precision and intricacy required to the manufacture of telephones and watches. Before Naval Godrej's efforts, typewriters had not yet been made in India. After profound and prolonged study of the processes of manufacture, and an assembly of the world's best typewriters, Naval and his team of engineers evolved a machine comparable to any available then. They were able to do so because of their vast, well-equipped factory, and technical know-how coupled with the experience of nearly sixty years in specialized fields, and a skilled labour force of thousands.

Naval knew what he was up against. He knew also that if the precision and intricacies of typewriter manufacture were mastered, India would be the first to produce typewriters in Asia, including Japan. Government sponsorship (most of the early typewriters made by Godrej were purchased by the Central and State Governments to encourage Indian industry) coupled with the motto of self-reliance dinned into him by his father and uncle, egged him on to manufacture the typewriter as a prestige product. He made this decision at the time when foreign firms were not in favour of actually manufacturing typewriters completely in India. Production was inspired further by the belief that, as the country advanced, it had to itself produce what it needed. In striking contrast to firms that were either selling imported machines at profitable prices, or partially assembling some parts in the country, Naval went on to manufacture complete machines.

Since Godrej already had sufficient capacity for their requirements of standard machines, it stood to reason that foreign interests installing any appreciable capacity were likely to supplant this indigenous capacity and keep their plants busy. The extensive and up-to-date plants in the Godrej factories had been producing a variety of quality goods at progressively lower prices. With the installation of the necessary new machines at Vikhroli, involving heavy capital outlay, it became possible to undertake precision jobs like typewriter manufacture. Technicians were specially trained to master this precision job. The Woodstock machine—an American model—was followed. At a later stage a collaboration with Optima of Germany was brought in.

As their basic raw material, Naval used alloys of special ferrous and non-ferrous metals to get the quality required. Of the 1,800 components in a typewriter, only the types, key-tops, rubber platen and one spring—of the value in all of Rs 30—were imported. But these parts would soon be made by Godrej themselves. All the other parts, with all their dies, jigs and fixtures were designed and executed by Indian engineers. Two types were manufactured—the Pica typing ten letters to an inch and the Elite, twelve letters. Plans were already afoot as soon as the necessary keyboards were finalized to bring out typewriters in Hindi and other national languages.

As a group of the Bombay Management Association remarked after a tour of the Godrej factories: 'It was most encouraging to see the vast amount of planning that has gone into its production and to virtually see the whole product being put together from components manufactured in the same concern.' Utmost care was exercised at every stage of manufacture, from the selection of the right materials for the different components, correct heat treatments and rigorous tests with the latest type of electronic equipment and heat-treating furnaces and hardness-testing machines, right down to the final and exquisite finish and electro-plating and enamel painting.

An unsolicited tribute to their capacity and skill was paid by the regional supervisor of the world-famous American Typewriter Company who, on visiting the Godrej works, confessed himself to be amazed at 'the very impressive plants' and opined that 'your organization is important enough to undertake any machinery production.' Another well-known firm of engineering consultants referred to the manufacture of the all-Indian typewriter as 'a great step forward and another proof of the inherent ability that can be developed in India.'

There were sceptics also. When Sohrab mentioned to a well-known Union Minister that Godrej were planning to manufacture typewriters, the disbelieving Minister taunted him saying that if they did so, he would eat every bit of the typewriter! Well, the Minister had to eat his words instead when in due course a Godrej typewriter was indeed presented to him!

If it took Sholes, through Remington, thirteen years to gain entry into the American market in 1881, Godrej too had a tough time, though for different reasons. They had to face stiff competition not only from the established and reputed firm of Remington, but also from another manufacturer, Halda, who too was making headway in the Indian market. But this apart, the first Godrej typewriter, M-9, had a hard touch causing unnecessary fatigue to the typist. In spite of this, with the concerted efforts of typewriter salesmen who went from office to office, 9,000 typewriters were sold between 1955 and 1959. An improved model, M-8, introduced in 1959 showed slightly increased sales of 12,000 till 1961.

But the touch was still hard. Complaints kept pouring in till 1965 when Godrej put its feather-touch M-12 in the market, after which there was no looking back. In 1967 typewriter manufacture was taken up in Plant 3, Vikhroli, with Godrej entering into collaboration with Buro Maschine Werke of East Germany and marketing the VEB Optima Model. This had a scientifically designed full-size keyboard with 46 keys (92 characters), which meant that there were six extra keys with useful functions at no extra cost. The other remarkable feature of this machine was that it had an interchangeable carriage with three different sized carriages, 25 cms., 38 cms. and 47 cms., easily transferable on the same base machine. The M-12 came with a two-year guarantee, unlike the one-year guarantee of Godrej competitors.

In fact the M-12 was precision-made, with the help of German technical skill acquired through sixty years experience in typewriter manufacture. Each one of the 2,220 parts went through rigid tests on 1,733 precision gauges during manufacture and assembly. The machine was designed to please and built to last, and was available in two attractive colours, bright brown and Everest green. The carriage would not jump or wobble. It was dependable, strong and adjusted to stay in alignment even after years of use. The time taken for the type-bar to spring back into place after printing, was minimal to suit the typist's speed. If he typed very fast, the keys wouldn't jam; if he typed at medium speed, the machine would not jump spaces. It had a touch control knob for hard or gentle typing, depending on the number of copies the typist wanted. It had a line-ruling device, made of clear plastic, with four notches to enable the typist to make horizontal and vertical lines, which was indispensable while tabulating.

Small wonder then, that between 1965 and 1970 the production doubled to 24,258 machines. With the collaboration with VEB Optima ending in 1970, another model, named after the founder of the Company, the Godrej AB, was introduced.

This was a remarkable combination of functional design, light weight and superb workmanship. Typing was fast, easy and less tiring on the Godrej AB—thanks to its light responsive touch. All controls were streamlined and conveniently grouped within easy reach of the typist, for greater typing comfort. Its clear characters, even impression and uniformly-spaced print were easy on the eye. Its other features were quick-return type-bars and alert space-bars for faster typing, left- or right- hand margin setting on full width of carriage, instant colour selector at one's fingertips; full-width tabulator with conveniently placed tabulator-bar, tab set and tab clear keys. Like the M-12, it also had an efficient push-button service in the interchangeable carriage, which prevented accidental jamming.

Godrej were familiar with the demands of modern offices. They made it a point to keep redesigning and improving typewriters, model after model, to keep pace with changing requirements. The Godrej AB was also offered with a special English keyboard with mathematical symbols, and government-approved keyboards in Hindi, Marathi, Gujarati, Tamil, Telugu, Kannada and other Indian languages. At that time special keyboards for the Thai and Russian languages were also manufactured. Special typewriters (with right-to-left carriage movement) for Arabic, Urdu, Persian, etc., and keyboards for specific European and other languages, were also offered.

The AB was on the market for nine years, from 1971 till 1979, during which period 1,58,159 AB typewriters were sold, making an average of 17,500 machines per annum. After a stint of nine years, the PB model was introduced. This one was named after the founder's brother, Pirojsha.

The PB Godrej typewriter proved even more popular and its demand far exceeded expectations. It was put on the market for three to four years from 1980 to early 1983, during which over one lakh typewriters were sold, an average of nearly 33,000 typewriters per annum, as compared to the earlier average of 17,500 per annum.

The Godrej PB offered the optimum combination of light touch and speed. The ribbon movement was specially designed for high sensitivity and the key lever mechanism was simple and robust. The typist could get failproof automatic reversals, reduced load, and a light-as-air touch while typing. The ribbon track selector allowed three positions, thus giving 33 per cent more ribbon usage. Intermediate connecting links were provided on the key lever to reduce vibration, eliminate clashing and increase speed. An additional feature was linear ball-bearings, which facilitated smooth and easy carriage movement.

Godrej were going full steam ahead, against Remington and Halda, and a new entrant in the market—Facit.

Finally, in April 1983 the Godrej Prima was introduced. It took pride of place in the market, designed for even greater efficiency, easy, effortless typing, and smooth carriage movement, once again ensured by linear ball-bearings with hardened and ground stainless steel guides. The Prima figures speak for themselves. In thirteen years, from 1983 to 1996, a whopping 6,06,000 Prima typewriters were sold, an average of 46,600 per annum. Whereas, upto 1983, in 28 years, Godrej had sold 3,13,214 typewriters; in less then half the time, in the next thirteen years, they sold almost *double* the quantity.

Godrej have not only made tremendous strides in the manual typewriter market, but today hold a 65 per cent market share. The baby of 1955 had not only come of age, but during a span of forty-two years had given to the Indian and foreign market, six different models (M-9, M-8, M-12, AB, PB, PRIMA) in three different sizes and a variety of vernacular languages, including Hindi, Urdu, Kannada, Tamil, Telugu, Malayalam, Marathi, Gujarati, Bengali, Assamese, Oriya, Gurmukhi, and for export in a few select foreign languages.

Typewriters are recognized the world over as having contributed immeasurably to business efficiency. The Godrej typewriter evolving over a period of time to embody the latest ease and efficiency features contributed to the same end in India, and at about half the cost of imported makes. For this product as for others, Godrej did not ask for any price protection.

This was in accordance with the tradition established by Ardeshir and Pirojsha of keeping the consumer in mind always. Before the advent of Godrej, the Indian user had to pay anything from hundred to three hundred per cent more for typewriters, and that for quality that did not always come up to Godrej standards.

Spurred on by their achievement in this highly specialized field, Godrej took the initiative in organizing National Speed Typing Championships annually in which, on an average, as many as 30,000 competitors participated. The most promising of these competitors was young Abhishek Jain who, at the age of twelve, won the championship first in 1989 and then again in 1991. Such was his promise that Godrej were encouraged to sponsor his participation in an international contest at Brussels in Belgium in 1991. He fulfilled the high hopes his sponsors had of him by winning the Junior World Speed-typing championship.

Abhishek went on to better his own record at the twentieth World Typing Championship at Istanbul in 1993. Fifteen years old, he was the only Indian to cross the 20,000 stroke mark in what is called 'manual typing'. Because of his age he had compulsorily to enter the contest in the junior category. But this did not deter him from surpassing the senior champion Silviya Barancokoya, a Slovakian, to earn the title of world champion in speed-typing.

Small wonder, then, that Abhishek regards the Godrej Prima manual typewriter as 'my prize possession that has enabled me to give of my best.'

Again, in June 1996 Abhishek entered the International Youth Meeting and Typing Competition held at Bonn, Germany and won the World Speed-Typing Championship, clocking the speed of 135 w.p.m. The competition was tough. Competitors were allowed ten minutes to copy as much of a typed copy as they could. The maximum ratio of error allowed was 0.5 per cent. All kinds of typewriters whether mechanical, electrical or electronic were permitted. Even, personal computers were allowed in the competition. This time Abhishek used the Godrej Write On electronic typewriter instead of the Prima manual typewriter.

Godrej also sponsored Dr Rajinder Singh, a dentist by profession, of village Cheog in Solan, Himachal Pradesh, as India's entry to the World Championship of Typewriting in Sofia, Bulgaria, on 14 July 1985, and Italy in 1987. The World Championship Contest in Speed-typing is held by INTERSTENO (International Federation of Shorthand and Typewriting), Germany, every two years to coincide with the INTERSTENO World Congress. Rising to this challenge on both occasions, Dr Rajinder Singh raced past all the others to be the fastest typist in the world on his Godrej Prima.

Both Dr Rajinder Singh and Abhishek are from the Punjab.

There was another interesting achievement that was to find a place in the Guinness Book of Records. In 1986 Shamboo Anubhawane typed on a Godrej Prima for 123 hours completing 8,06,000 strokes—a marathon achievement by any standard,—starting on Monday, 18 August 1986 at 12.00 noon and concluding on Saturday, 23 August at 3.00 p.m.

Some years ago Godrej moved on from manual to electronic typewriters. Manual typewriters were and are still in demand and Godrej manufactures as many as 50,000 of them a year, in different sizes, in all the thirteen Indian languages as well as in some select foreign languages. As for electronic typewriters, their production grew from 7,500 in 1990-91, to 9,500 in 1991-92 and to 10,000 in 1992-93. They are manufactured in several Indian as well as foreign languages like Bangla, Russian, Polish, French, Czech and Arabic (Persian and Maghreb languages).

Anticipating the trend of increased office automation and use of computers in manufacturing operations, Godrej have developed a team of dedicated professionals for designing and manufacturing a wide range of electronic business equipment, including, apart from electronic typewriters, word-processors, dot matrix printers, keyboards, multilingual terminals and engineering workstations.

10

SUPERMAN PUF

If the typewriter has come to be regarded as an indispensable adjunct of the modern office, the household refrigerator unquestionably occupies pride of place in a modern home, particularly in a tropical climate like ours. In this age of gadgetry, this super-gadget has won the hearts of housewives the world over and has definitely come to stay. Having mastered a high-precision job like typewriter manufacture, Naval under Pirojsha's constant encouragement turned his attention to the highly developed science of refrigeration. The opportunity was provided by the availability in the early fifties, at a reasonable price, of general purpose machinery like conveyor belts and ovens needed for making refrigerators from the General Motors refrigeration plant.

Refrigeration is an outstanding case of how science instead of being in conflict with nature has derived inspiration from its well-established law that cold prolongs the life of organic matter by inhibiting growth and decay. When organic substances were deep-frozen, it would seem there was no limit to the time over which they could be preserved, provided they were kept air-tight. The astonishingly well-preserved specimens of pre-historic fauna that have come to light from amidst the ageless snows of Siberia and Alaska, provide a dramatic illustration of this remarkable phenomenon.

Man's first attempts at refrigeration were naturally confined to the use of natural ice. But owing to the short duration and cost of transport of natural ice, ways and means had to be developed to make artificial ice, which ultimately led to the establishment of the refrigeration industry. 'The vastness and importance of this industry today,' avers Chief Engineer S.F. Desai, who was closely associated with the manufacture of the Godrej refrigerator in its initial stages, 'can be gauged from the fact that as far back as in the twenties the manufactured-ice industry of the United States alone comprised an investment of a thousand million dollars.'

Cold storage is, according to Desai, one of the essential uses of refrigeration. 'The season for certain fruits and vegetables, which would normally be a few weeks, is drawn out to as many months or more by its virtue; commodities like eggs which are plenty can be made to hold out much longer, if necessary; in fact, but for refrigeration, modern cities like New York which receive over a thousand car loads of perishables every day, would be hard put to feeding its teeming populace.'

Refrigerators, whether ice or mechanical, operate on the same principle: the absorption of heat from the food compartment by a physical change of the refrigerating medium, ice to water in the one case, the liquid refrigerant to a gas in the other. Owing, however, to the greater convenience, economy and performance of the mechanical or automatic refrigerator, the latter has practically superceded the ice refrigerator.

Mechanical refrigerators, again, may be of the absorption or compressor type, both having a closed system wherein the refrigerant, the medium used for refrigerating, circulates. In the early twenties an absorption type refrigerator was devised that had no moving parts at all and, paradoxically, produced cold through the application of heat. This heat source was either kerosene oil, gas or electricity. The electric compressor refrigerator scored over the absorption refrigerator in that it weighed less and provided more usable space within the same external dimensions. The once noisy compressor of the electric refrigerator was by constant experimentation made so quiet and its reliability and durability so improved that it replaced the gas refrigerator.

The modern compressor refrigerator, as manufactured by Godrej, has been described as an elegant piece of furniture hygienically finished, both inside and out, and lavishly appointed to conduce to the highest degree of utility and convenience of service. It consists of outer and inner bodies between which is packed a high efficiency non-conductor of heat such as glass-wool. As an insulating material for refrigerators, glass-wool has ideal characteristics. Not only is it hygienic, non-hygroscopic, rot-proof, light and permanently durable, but also has about the lowest coefficient of thermal conductivity. The inner body earlier used to be vitreous or porcelain-enameled, whereas the outer body was in white or in coloured enamel finish. Inside fittings vary with different models but generally there is a freezer with ice-trays for producing ice-cubes, fruit and vegetable compartments and miscellaneous shelves and racks.

Naval began, as was his wont, by reading all the relevant literature on refrigerators to make himself fully conversant with the processes of its manufacture, its origins and subsequent developments. Meanwhile, research at Vikhroli was proceeding apace. It became clear to Naval that while the entire refrigerator manufacture could be undertaken, the heart of the refrigerator, its hermetically-sealed unit, comprising the compressor, oil pump, electric motor to drive the compressor, oil to lubricate the moving parts, the liquid refrigerant and the receiver would have to be imported initially. There were also the condenser, the evaporator, expansion valve and the thermostat all suitably interconnected to the sealed unit with copper tubing to form a closed circuit.

Usually, during a cycle of operation, the liquid refrigerant flows from the receiver into the expansion valve where it is throttled as it flows from the high pressure which exists in the receiver to the low pressure existing in the evaporator. In this passage the liquid gets evaporated, the heat required for the evaporation being drawn from the refrigerator and its contents. The vapour is next drawn into the compressor which then delivers it under pressure to the condenser. Here the latent heat of vapourization is drawn out from the compressed vapour by the cooling air around the condenser whereupon the vapour is again converted into liquid and returned to the receiver. From the receiver it once again flows to the expansion valve to start another cycle. The desired temperature is ensured by regulating a thermostat which, once set, will function automatically to maintain that temperature, regardless of the surrounding room temperature.

Naval turned to the General Electric Company of the United Kingdom who had been producing refrigerators from the twenties. Their earlier models were sold for as much as a thousand dollars, twice the cost of an automobile. A market survey conducted by GE (USA) had revealed that while there was a significant market for refrigerators in America, they could be produced at a lower cost with high reliability. Designers throughout the company were requested to submit their ideas. Chris Steenstrip's idea, conceived originally by a French monk Marcel Rudiffren, was selected for development in 1925, earning him the title of 'Father of the Monitor Top Refrigerators'. This became one of GE's most successful products. The original patent on the refrigerating machine was granted in April 1930. Thirty-nine additional patents followed in rapid succession.

A pilot-project was undertaken by Godrej. When tests proved satisfactory, full-scale production started. The first model to come out of the Godrej works was a seven cubic-feet model in gleaming white enamel exterior and porcelain-enameled interior finish; a half, but roomy freezer with ice-trays or, for frozen foods, removable hygienic shelves, automatic temperature control and interior light, extra door compartments including egg-rack and butter chamber and fruit and vegetable drawers.

This model was worked by a high economy sealed-in refrigerating unit supplied by the General Electric Company and with a guarantee for its life and performance. It was a sore point with Naval that just as in typewriter manufacture he had to eventually collaborate with Optima of Germany, in refrigerators he had to begin by using the GEC compressor unit. It would take him four years with the installation of specialized machines for the manufacture of these units to repeat the feat with refrigerators. By 1962 these units were manufactured in India. The ultra-high dimensional accuracy required for some of the components of the sealed unit made it indispensable to employ processes like fine-boring and micro-honing. When two surfaces moved in relation to each other and still had to hold a seal against high-pressure or vacuum, the finish had to be as fine as possible. With micro-finishing, surfaces could be flattened within one light band i.e. about 12 millionths of an inch—less than a hundredth part of a human hair!

India's first refrigerator, made by Godrej in 1958, was sold for the incredibly low price of Rs 1,885 plus sales-tax as applicable. There was no excise duty then for the fortunate few who seized the opportunity to have a refrigerator in the home. In 1968 came a new model with capacity of 255 litres, but with a full-width freezer. In 1970, again, Godrej introduced the 165-litre model with table-top, comprising one aluminum shelf, one glass shelf and a vegetable crisper at the bottom. This model captured the imagination of the public being the right size for the Indian home and was affordable for the average middle-class family.

With the introduction of these smaller models, the total installed capacity of refrigerators almost doubled. Whereas in 1970 the refrigeration industry put 37,000 refrigerators on the Indian market, the very next year, in 1971, the number increased to 86,000. In 1973, Godrej came out with a 165-litre model, but with two aluminium shelves and a glass shelf at the bottom, much to the delight of the Indian housewife who now had more space to place her groceries.

As market trends kept changing from time to time, the need was felt to increase the capacity of the larger model as well. In 1974, the 290-litre model was introduced. This had an automatic defroster. Just by pressing the red button on the thermostat, the defrosting was taken care of. This saved the housewife the trouble of defrosting, emptying, wiping and cleaning.

The glasswool insulation gave way in 1987 to polyurethane foam insulation dramatically personified in the silver-clad, goggled figure of PUF which, because of its superior insulating properties seal in the cold for longer periods, formed a protective wall around the refrigerator, tight-sealed the gap between inner and outer walls, reduced external sweating and did all this at almost the same price as ordinary glasswool insulation. PUF cooled better, saved money and space, made the refrigerator super-strong and extra hygienic and preserved the finish—in the many benefits it conferred, it was a superman in icy realms.

In 1981, however, there was a crisis. Prices crashed following what was described as a price war. Among the many causes were the slack winter season, the increase in bank interest, which the dealer had to pay, and above all the tax policy of both the Central and State Governments. The excise duty, which the customer had to pay, was between 40 per cent on the 165-litre refrigerator and 80 per cent on the larger 290-litre refrigerator, the State sales-tax was between 15 and 20 per cent and the octroi tax at 4 per cent. But the price cuts resulted in bumper sales. The demand particularly for Godrej refrigerators was unparalleled in the history of refrigerator manufacturing in India.

Subsequently, Godrej have started working on an environment-friendly refrigerator. Two models are suggested, the polyurethane foam model with cyclopentane and the cooling system model with hydro carbon. Cyclopentane is considered the more environment-friendly and is also more easily available. There is, however, a slight fire risk, which can be controlled by adopting the right safety measures. Godrej-GE Appliances are therefore working on developing the Cyclopentane model.

Refrigerator manufacture has come a long way since its inception in 1958, with far-reaching results. It has ushered in a whole new life-style among India's large middle-class segment. The Godrej refrigerator continues to be updated practically every year, since 1987, with the introduction of new models of different sizes and different colours, incorporating the very best in technology and utility features. It was as if Naval had redefined the challenge of the pioneer, not in only being the first, but in recognizing a real and long-term need, and working towards its fulfilment with determination and flair.

11
ONLY THE BEST

Godrej's pioneering efforts in the refrigeration line did not elude important transformation in soap manufacture, which was started by Ardeshir. Naval's elder brother Burjor, equipped with a degree in mechanical engineering, Diploma Ingenieur (Dipl-Ing), and the prestigious doctorate in technical chemistry (Dr. Ing) of the Technical University of Berlin, Charlottenberg, was instrumental in bringing about far-reaching changes in this soap manufacturing unit. By installing the very latest equipment and attaching an equally well-equipped research laboratory, it became a unique, well-conceived, large-scale factory at Delisle Road.

Getting the coveted degrees was quite an adventure for

young Burjor who commenced his studies there in 1933. War clouds loomed on the horizon and Nazi Germany was the powder keg. Having acquired the Diploma Ingenieur in general machine-building, Burjor was about to obtain his Master's degree when his studies were interrupted by the outbreak of the War. 'It was terrible', Burjor recalls. 'I was very scared. I was told to leave immediately . . . and luckily I got into the last train from Cologne to Paris.'

After the war Burjor got permission from the Allied Military Command to go back to Germany, but on a condition that seemed impossible to fulfill. He was to complete almost a year's course in just three months. The Examining Officer asked him, 'Will you be able to complete it in such a short time?' 'I must!' Burjor replied. He worked as if his life depended on it, which in a sense it did. He stayed back till the very last day. 'They were good enough to take my examination on a Saturday,' he recalls gratefully.

But there were other little misadventures. An indoctrinated German girl told Burjor, as he was negotiating the price for a second-hand machine to purchase for the metal products company back home, that Germans hated such bargaining. Perhaps she mistook him for a Jew. Then again, the Curator of the Berlin Museum, who took special care of him, didn't look like a typical German and, worse, was of an independent outlook. He was attacked by Goebbels as a Jew, probably a ploy, Burjor thinks, to try and make him a member of the Nazi party. 'That was the Nazi way of doing things.' But the Curator filed a suit against Goebbels and won. The incident made Burjor realize 'the importance of standing up for one's principles.'

Back in Bombay Burjor developed a conscious culture of research and development at the factory, setting aside sizable resources for this activity. In fact, research was a tonic for him. In an interview with this writer he affirmed: 'When I did research my motto was: Only the best is good enough for me. And that brings prosperity if the researcher is capable.'

No truer words were spoken. Over the years this unceasing, relentless, single-minded pursuit of research has resulted in many triumphant successes in the shape of new products, better designs and formulations and, most important, import substitution. Indeed, in a company which lays great store by continuity, research is the crucible where today's dreams are melted down and shaped into tomorrow's realities.

The first of these successes was the deglycerination of soap-making oils to recover glycerine. The process is known as Hydrolysis. Under this a mixture of Oil and Water is split into glycerin and fatty acids using high pressure autoclaves at a temperature of 235-240°C. The steam pressure is attained in 28-30 (ATM-Atmosphere). The normal air pressure the whole world lives and breathes is 1 (ATM). When glycerine began to fetch a high price in the export market from 1962 onwards, soap-makers in India who had let glycerine go waste in their factories became particularly interested in plants for its recovery. But as the potential amount of glycerine products from each maker was small, such plants were not feasible. Besides, their operation entailed high levels of technical skill. Burjor realized that instead of a central recovery glycerine plant to cover a number of small soap-making units, a central fat-splitting plant was the efficient solution, making it possible to recover a bigger amount of glycerol. In 1953, less than two decades after high-pressure splitting was adopted in the USA and Europe, he installed the sophisticated Wurster and Sanger high-pressure fat-splitting plant, which was the first plant of its kind in India.

Saving of glycerine through high-pressure fat-splitting has had worldwide repercussions. During World War II glycerine which is used for the manufacture, among numerous things, of nitro-glycerine, was conserved in most countries compelling those who wasted it to use fatty acids. Use of fatty acids confers several advantages: better recovery of an important and costly by-product i.e. Glycerol; the saponification (reaction of caustic soda with fatty acids) time is brought down considerably, hence soap-making is faster; and soap-making from fatty acids eliminates the danger of incomplete saponification. The danger lies in pockets of caustic soda remaining as such in the end product and this would be harmful to the skin causing itching, burning and irritation. These acids being the right raw material for the small-scale laundry soap industry, it was in the national interest to utilize the entire existing capacity for their production. Besides, as the surplus glycerine from all over the world was then finding its way to the United States, valuable foreign exchange could be earned.

In India itself Godrej supplied glycerine, manufactured to BP, USP and other specifications, to textile mills, pharmacies, confectioners, industries like paint and varnish, ink, cosmetics and cigarettes. The other vital raw material, fatty acids including stearic acid was supplied to textile, rubber, aluminium and leather industries and to grease manufacturers.

Burjor did not relax after the success of his fat-splitting plant, but led the field in making soaps from fatty acids. By the use of fatty acids dangers connected with incomplete saponification were avoided, because the saponification or, rather, neutralization in the early stage was easy and quick. After the soap was made free from fatty acids, it could be finished in the kettle, as the soap-boiling pan is known— right after saponification, since no salting out is required. Besides, no nigre is produced. It is well-known that much of the usual loss in the process occurs in the nigre and that its disposal is always a problem. By using fatty acids, soap production can be standardized to a degree not possible with the conventional process. Moreover, caustic potash or any organic alkali may replace part of the caustic soda. Thus glycerine can be recovered from semi-boiled and cold-made soaps as well as soft (potash) soaps. In the case of shaving soap, for example, it is well-known that excess of glycerine causes diminution of lather. Therefore, by using fatty acids, the glycerine content can be controlled at will.

Adopting a bold approach to technology, (Burjor was never averse to flouting tradition), and having inherited a pioneering spirit, he almost single-handedly revolutionized the manufacture of soaps and later of detergents. While other soap-makers, not only in India, were using the arcane technique of 'fitting', he refused to do so as he could see no merit in it. 'Fitting is an . . . art!' he remarked. 'With science you can be very sure. I converted the art of soap-making into the science of soap-making.' He added that unless the person who does the fitting is experienced in the art, the quality suffers. 'Thus, there is dependence on such workers who may demand a fantastic price for their services, and behave like prima donnas.'

By way of explanation of the 'fitting' process, the traditional method of soap making was based on saponification of oil. During this process, glycerine is released as a by-product. This glycerine recovery required the fitting process wherein common salt was added under intermittent heating conditions. Here human skill (and hence art) was involved in adjusting the temperature of the kettle and the addition of the right quantity of salt. If these parameters were not observed properly, there was the danger of the whole mass of soap changing 'phase' and thereby going waste. In the modern process of making soap directly by saponification of fatty acid, this danger was totally eliminated. Hence it became a science.

Ever since scientists have known that germs can breed prolifically in the human skin, they have searched for an effective germicidal soap. These germs are of two kinds, the transient and the resident. The transient variety is connected with the normal contact of the skin with the environment. But resident bacteria thrive on the skin for an indefinite period. Ordinary soap readily removes the transient bacterial flora, but the resident bacteria far more slowly. Resting in the deeper layers of the skin, the resident bacteria become difficult to reach and slow to be destroyed.

The efforts of scientists have been more often than not frustrated by the fact that germ-killing ingredients which proved highly effective in other antiseptic products, were found unsuited for use in soaps. The so-called germicidal soaps often irritated the skin without harming the germs. But the discovery of a whitish powder, hexachlorophene, better known by its trade name, G-11, changed all that. In fact, G-11 was acknowledged world-wide as the outstanding contribution of chemistry to the soap industry.

G-11 was a result of exhaustive research by the versatile German-born chemist Dr Wilhelm S. Gump, assisted by the noted bacteriologist Arthur R. Cade, in the laboratory of the Givaudan Company, suppliers of aromatic materials to the cosmetic, perfume and soap industries. Wilhelm Gump synthesized several substances and numbered them consecutively in what has come to be known as the G series. Of the materials so numbered, two were found to have promising possibilities, G-4 (dichlorophene) and G-11 (hexachlorophene), the former being a powerful fungicide. The latter, after the most exacting tests by numberless physicians, medical schools, hospitals and dermatologists, proved to be the most effective in destroying skin bacteria when used in soap.

A summary of the results of these tests showed that the regular and exclusive application of soap containing 2 per cent G-11 over a period of five days reduced bacterial flora of the skin to 5 per cent of the normal. A remarkable characteristic of G-11 soap was that a certain portion of G-11 was retained on the skin after the lather was rinsed off. This residual G-11 prevented the very few germs still on the skin from multiplying, and killed new germs deposited on the skin between washings.

Surgeons went on to give the most convincing proof of G-11's efficacy by employing it in the surgical wash. Tests revealed that a six minute wash—not scrub—with G-11 soap reduced far more bacteria than the traditional ten minute scrub. Moreover, the alcoholic rinse was found to be not only unnecessary but undesirable, as it dissolved the residual G-11. Checks made on the hands of the surgeons who had worn surgical gloves for an hour revealed that, when ordinary soap was used, the bacteria count doubled, but when soap containing G-11 was used, there were only half as many bacteria.

Because of this, hospitals in America and Europe changed from the ten-minute scrub to a three-minute wash with the new soap containing 2 per cent of G-11. Before this was put into force, however, surgeons were required to use G-11 soaps regularly and exclusively in all their personal washings both at home and in the hospital.

It became obvious to Burjor that such a soap would be ideal for India's tropical heat which gives rise to a number of irritating and acutely uncomfortable skin diseases, many of them communicable, especially in overcrowded cities, dwellings and public conveyances.

Perspiration was by itself odourless. But once stale, bacteria formed, smelt offensive. G-11 soaps were therefore successful as deodorants because of their bacteria-destroying quality. Another of its important functions was to preserve clothes. Body odour was easily transferred to clothes, which required not only frequent changing of clothes, but more vigorous washing, which shortened their life.

Burjor was further impressed by the early promise of G-11 'as a factor in protecting public health, aiding individual comfort and sanitation and preventing certain types of diseases.' The popular *Reader's Digest* in its issue of September 1950 had predicted: 'G-11 will find jobs wherever skin bacteria are a problem.' This was followed by *Fortune* devoting considerable space to the fabulous success story of the development of a soap with G-11 by one of America's largest firms. When corroborative evidence from various irrefutable sources of G-11's unprecedented performances started piling up, Burjor lost no time in obtaining a license for the exclusive use of G-11 in India for manufacturing soaps and other toilet preparations in which G-11 was effective.

It was in these circumstances that India got Cinthol, the only proved germicidal soap, followed by Cinthol Toilet Powder. Launched on Independence Day, 1952, enriched with Fougere perfume, the reception Cinthol received from Indian users was truly phenomenal. Not only did the soap give the user that clean and refreshing feeling all day, so welcome in a hot, dusty country, but it also made him or her acceptable and agreeable in company.

Godrej Soaps were now in a position of strength. But soap-makers throughout the country, particularly those in the small-scale cottage industry sector, had to struggle for survival against the assault by the multinational. They would have perished but for the formation in 1934 of the Indian Soaps and Toiletries Makers Association (ISTMA) with its Head Office in Calcutta, later shifted to Bombay. The Association was therefore like a sheet anchor to them, giving them a voice and making it possible for that voice to be heard. The fact that Sohrab Godrej and Naval Tata of TOMCO stood together against the threat of the multinational, gave strength to the Association enabling it to look after the interests of these threatened soap-makers. The Association's primary aim was to ensure their survival. Among its lesser aims, apart from the obvious one of protecting the interests of its members, were to educate the public against the use of adulterated products, to promote scientific research calculated to advance the trade and, perhaps too ambitiously in the dog-eat-dog soap business, to 'promote a feeling of fraternity and co-operation among its members.'

A common problem agitating all toiletries manufacturers was the penal excise duty of 120.75 per cent levied in the early thirties on their products. This was perhaps the highest duty for any item of mass consumption. The ISTMA pleaded with the Ministry of Finance that this was retarding the growth of the industry and encouraging the manufacture of spurious products, which are serious health hazards, besides helping the import of smuggled goods. Its plea to bring the duty in line with other consumer products of mass consumption, that is at the earlier level of 25 per cent, fell on deaf ears.

Among other problems taken up by the Association were the criteria of eco-labelling of toilet soaps and synthetic detergents; the Motor Vehicles Act restricting loading to 9 tonnes instead of 13, which would lead to sharp increase in transportation costs; the threshold level of assessable value for attracting excise duty; the end consumer price, inclusive of all taxes; and the alleged practice of unjust enrichment by collecting excess duty from consumers and then claiming refund from government; and so on.

The Godrej contribution to ISTMA has been a significant one. In fact, Godrej and ISTMA have been likened to Damon and Pythias—inseparable. Originally known as the All India Soap Manufacturers Association and based in Calcutta, the organization acquired a legal entity when it was incorporated under certificate No. 1392 on 11 September,

1937. Rechristened as ISTMA, Godrej provided it with accommodation in Bombay at the Vikhroli complex for 26 months from 8 August 1973 until it acquired its own offices at Dalamal Chambers, Bombay. A grateful executive body recorded its appreciation as per the minutes dated 29 July 1975.

Adi Godrej was its President from 1985-86 to 1987-88, giving the body time, a sense of direction and considerable expertise.

ISTMA's motto was 'Be clean, use soap, be sure, buy Swadeshi.' It is interesting to record that ISTMA, in its interaction with the public and the government, had originally locked horns with the Lever triumvirate—Lever Brothers, Hindustan Vanaspati Manufacturers and United Traders Limited. In 1956, however, Hindustan Lever, formed by the merger of these three bodies, became a Limited Company, seeking to acquire a national character with its name Hindustan Lever Ltd. Incidentally, the proposal to admit Hindustan Lever Ltd. as member was seconded by Godrej in a singularly gracious gesture. With HLL's inclusion, the ISTMA, already a vocal body, gained considerable strength with the active help from HLL's data base, organizational infrastructure and lobbying ability. Its Executive Committee became fully representative of all the zones with adequate weightage given to regional members. This representation, however, was limited to the interests of large-scale manufacturing units numbering about forty-four.

Other achievements to Burjorji's credit were to come later. Outstanding among these was his realization that alpha olefins were ideal raw material for the detergent industry because of their hard water resistance, high foam characteristics, synergy with soap and other surfactants, excellent biodegradability and mildness on the skin. He invented a process to make alpha olefins from natural fatty acids, a technique that was patented in many countries.

Apart from overcoming all the shortcomings of earlier detergents, this process also prevented wastage of laundry soap. In his characteristic way Burjor acknowledged his indebtedness to a scientist from Lurgi, the famous German chemical plant manufacturers, who first drew his attention to the acceptability of alpha olefin sulphonates. Godrej's old rival, Hindustan Lever Ltd., who had been lobbying for several years to set up a Linear Alkyl Benzene plant did not, however, agree with this hypothesis. This will be discussed in its proper place in the second volume of the Godrej story.

Burjor was singularly fortunate that along with his life's calling he found his life-partner. Early one sunny morning as he was driving down to the Godrej factory at Lalbaug, he chanced upon 'a very pretty girl with rosy cheeks.' Enquiries revealed that she was Jai, daughter of the medical practitioner H.P. Dastur, who happened also to be his father's relative and friend. Luckily for Burjor, Jai too found him 'an interesting person with a good sense of humour.'

Burjor and Jai were married after a six-month courtship. She gave him the understanding and encouragement he needed in his solitary, trying and demanding research work. Often, he would get completely lost in it. She would be called upon to remonstrate, in her own gentle way, that he give more time to his home. 'It was for his own good,' she modestly claims, 'for his health.' Even so at the height of his career Burjor reserved Saturday evenings to go to the movies with his wife. A teacher by profession, singularly gifted, Jai had the rare knack of establishing a one-to-one relationship with her students, winning their confidence and endearing herself to them.

Apart from research, Burjor was interested in comparative philology particularly of the Indo-European languages. In his usual methodical and meticulous style he mastered the German language and spoke it correctly and fluently besides having a deep affection for it. For several years he was the Honorary Consul-General of Austria. He was also very active in the Indo-German Chamber of Commerce and was its President at one time.

Always ready to make time for academic institutions and professional societies, he was Chairman of the Prof. J.G. Kane Memorial Trust which bestowed many benefits on the Department of Chemical Technology, University of Bombay.

Like his father and brothers, Burjor too considered poor economic growth 'the bane of India' and its poverty 'a disgrace'. He advocated a two-point programme under the circumstances. First, to keep down the population growth by humane birth-control methods and, second, to stimulate economic growth as much as possible, mainly by removing the 'road-blocks'. One road-block was the degeneration of trade-unionism in the country. Trials of strength between employers and employees made no sense in today's world, as some countries had practically eliminated strikes and lock-outs. Only continued negotiation made sense. Another road-block was the attitude of the government which, 'to say the least, is irresponsible'. Recalling an assurance made at the time the so-called public sector was started, that government would not interfere in the internal affairs of the private sector, he deplored its constant interference, as for example, in the matter of payment of honoraria to working directors. India, according to him, was at present a rich country inhabited by poor people. Compared to other countries we had several material resources. In order to develop this vast country, it was necessary to devise 'a scheme whereby those on the lowest rungs of the ladder get the highest incentive, whereas those on the highest rungs should also have at least some incentive to improve matters. In short, it is necessary to mobilise all our resources.'

Burjor practiced the art of living he so passionately propagated. Like Ardeshir and Pirojsha he was not discerning in family matters. At the same time he was the most clear-headed man this writer has known. Exuding an air of quiet confidence, his deep knowledge and research put him on sure ground, enabling him to stand four-square to all the winds that were blowing. And these winds, in the dog-eat-dog soap business could, as we shall see, be quite harsh. Just as uncle Ardeshir stood up to the renowned British safe-maker Chubb and even humbled him, so Burjor stood up to the giant multinational, Hindustan Lever, and, if not humbling it, at least refused ever to be cowed down by it: 'I was never awe-inspired by HLL. Their far greater volume was of great advantage to them. Once, when oil prices rose, their then chairman, Cecil Petit, cut soap prices to kill competition. I had come to know at that time that Petit was to be replaced by Mr A.J.C. Hoskyns-Abrahall. I spoke to the latter by telephone, and after a few minutes he restored the *status quo ante* and asked me whether I was satisfied. Needless to say, I thanked him.'

Burjor's personal traits set him apart from most Indians. More than any other quality, he valued thoroughness. A customer complained once that because of some particles in the Godrej shaving soap, he got blemishes on his skin after use. Burjor ordered each and every shaving soap in the factory to be X-rayed to determine what was wrong. Always very punctual, he expected others to be the same. Extremely health-conscious, he didn't want flowers to be kept on his desk as they attracted flies. Before taking a sip from the glass of water on his table, he would hold it up against the light to check for any dirt. Workers would leave finger stains when pushing open the glass door of his room—he had a plastic sheet stuck on the door with the request PLEASE

USE THIS SHEET. Always precise and courteous, but a man of few words, Burjor gave the impression of a man removed, absorbed in his own thoughts, whose being was on a higher plane than most others. Yet, he had a wry sense of humour that sparkled most unexpectedly. He impressed this writer in the many years he had known him as a somewhat paradoxical person, seemingly restless in his pursuit of research and yet at the same time totally at peace with himself.

For three years in succession, Burjor was included in the First Five Hundred International Award of the International Biographical Centre, Cambridge, England. The other award he greatly prized was the International Cultural Diploma of Honour of the American Biographical Institute awarded in 1991. Some time ago he was the recepient of the International Man of The Year (1991-92), again from the Biographical Centre of Cambridge, 'for his services to the entire and perfect prevention of pollution of groundwater and surface-water caused by detergents.'

Never forgetting that he himself hadn't been blessed with the most communicative of fathers, Burjor made it a point always to be close to his family, particularly to his two sons Adi and Nadir. They would often go to the beach together. Their conversation would revolve around serious subjects like chemistry, geography or the world situation. Burjor would always have lots of anecdotes to recount.

The moment he realized that the time was right, he delegated responsibility to his sons so that he would be free to conduct his research. He confessed being proud of his sons, and happily acknowledged their considerable contribution to the Godrej enterprise. Half-seriously he added: 'They are both autonomous. But, unfortunately, they are not free from the cussedness of human nature. There was a song in Germany in the twenties, the purport of which was: Every person is cussed. It was so, it is so and it will remain so.'

His sons would be responsible for expansion with new products and collaborations, develop the company's marketing techniques, and further modernize the firm introducing the latest scientific management system like the Japanese Kaizen system. They would ensure an uninterrupted profitability record with a turnover at the time of writing of over a thousand crores and proudly coin the slogan 'The name is the promise.'

12

A Way To Sell

To get the full measure of Godrej's achievements as industrialists, account has to be taken not only of their skills in engineering and manufacturing, which were quite extraordinary, but also of their responsiveness to the concept of marketing as distinct from and prior to selling, and to professional management.

The Godrej sales approach has reflected the image of a growing company, changing with the times. In the early fifties the selling of Godrej products was hardly a problem. Because of the shortage of steel whatever was manufactured was sold and demand was always in excess of supply. Bombay city had three showrooms, one in a Kalbadevi

A Way to Sell

by-lane, another more prestigious one on Veer Nariman Road in the Fort area and a third in Godrej Bhavan. The rest of India too was covered by branches set up at Calcutta (1928), Delhi (1930), Madras (1931), Hyderabad (1939), and finally Kanpur (1939). Having a showroom at each branch was essential for the obvious necessity of displaying heavy items like Storwels, safes, steel office-tables and chairs.

In the seventies, after forty years of development, the need to go in for branch expansion was felt. Godrej found it necessary to have their own branch and sales offices, particularly in each State capital and, if the need arose, even to have two or three branches in one State. This exercise was begun in 1977 with the opening of the Lucknow branch followed by branches at Ahmedabad and then Chandigarh. Expansion was slow but steady and came to constitute a network of twenty-eight branch, sales and area offices. In practically every State there was Godrej representation which correspondingly boosted sales. Each branch was supported by an experienced sales force and backed by an efficient service network. Trained salesmen and mechanics were largely responsible for the good image of Godrej.

P.D. Muncherji who worked for thirty-seven years in Godrej and retired as General Manager (Locks Division) in 1994, recalls: 'We at Godrej resorted to a strategy or sales approach when doing our selling. We would first find out what the customer wanted to buy. If we did not know, we would make it a point to ask him. We would go a step further, and find out what the customer's or his company's problems were, and then show them how we could work together with them and solve the problem. The problem could be of limited budget; the problem could be of space; shorter delivery, etc.

'It was so much easier to sell someone what they wanted to purchase than it was to convince them to purchase what you were selling. It was essential for us to find out who did the purchasing, for every company had its own system, procedures and head of purchase. This strategy we adopted in Godrej helped us to a very great extent in doing our selling. We were not always successful, accepted refusals with a smile, and always took it as a part of the game of selling.'

The greatest possible attention was given to pricing, which became a function of manufacturing costs. So many factors had to be taken into account—raw material costs, potential demand, target-groups, promotional expenses, distribution arrangements, and the prices of competitive products. Above all, what was important were the values that Godrej cherished and wanted to stress upon houses, offices, banks, and to promote their standards of excellence, positioning themselves above their competitors.

Then there were dealers throughout the country. The association of Godrej with their dealers has always been a close and warm one, lasting in some cases over several generations of a family. In the words of S.N. Vyas of N.P. Vyas & Co., wholesale dealer for Asansol: 'It is a strange mixture of emotions for us (on the occasion of the Godrej centenary); it makes us feel proud. Pride for having had the enviable privilege of a glorious association with the house of Godrej since 1946.' This relationship is defined in greater detail in the second volume of the Godrej story.

But soon growth was to exact its price. Controlling over two dozen branches from Bombay itself proved to be an insurmountable task. To ease the load, the solution was to divide the country into four regions, North, South, East and West and to appoint four Regional Managers at Delhi, Madras, Calcutta and Bombay. Regionalization, introduced in late 1988, meant that the Managing Director and General Manager (Marketing) who had till then to keep in touch with several branches all over the country, now had to deal with only four Regional Managers. Meetings were held every month between Head Office (Marketing) and each of the Regional Managers, and at the end of each marketing year, reviews were made of each branch's performance during the year.

Called marketing, this was essentially a selling process—finding customers for products already being made. Marketing, on the other hand, was the process of helping industries to decide *what* products to make in the first instance. As C. Northcote Parkinson, M.K. Rustomji and Walter E. Vieira have pointed out in *Marketing—Key To Business Success Today*, business firms pass from the stage of being production-oriented to become finance-oriented and then with increasing competition to become sales-oriented. 'However, they have also found that with rapid economic and technological changes, they have had to become market-oriented, since sales-orientation alone could not ensure success. At this stage, the marketing concept replaces the sales concept.'

Three major lines illustrate the development of this concept through Naval's initiative in Godrej, lines that fulfilled existing needs and anticipated the needs of the future—machine tools, typewriters and refrigerators. Machine tools were developed out of necessity for Godrej's own use during the War years when they could not be imported. Typewriters posed a formidable challenge—Godrej would be the first in Asia to manufacture them, beating even Japan in the process. As for the manufacture of refrigerators, opportunity came on a platter, as it were, with the availability of the necessary equipment at a reasonable price. Opportunities come to every man, but it takes a great man to seize them and to manufacture a product, considered to be a luxury in the home, but which soon would become a necessity. In just forty years the demand for refrigerators zoomed beyond expectations, with Godrej taking the lead in sales.

Like several other companies in India in those days, Godrej too relied for decades on the organization-chart with its structures of responsibilities and of authority, and its associated set of position descriptions. This had helped the sales department to function smoothly. But times were changing. The new buzzwords were professional and scientific management, which had already found acceptance in leading companies in the USA, UK, Germany, France and others in Europe. Great progress was made in developing managing skills, and the speedy growth brought about prosperity in these countries and a higher standard of life for their people.

Harvard Business School, Massachusetts Institute of Technology (MIT), Yale, Stanford, Cornell, among others, were turning out professional managers who were expected by dint of their training to be able to tackle everyday business problems. A need for them was felt even in India. 'If you have a problem, hire an MBA,' became the accepted slogan. As companies grew and came across gray areas of business in which they had less confidence or expertise, the belief spread that the MBAs were the best qualified to tackle these areas of business.

Like several leading industrialists, Naval too was looking for newer and better ways to sell. He realized that professional management had come to stay and that the need for professional managers would inevitably grow. It would be necessary for these managers 'to look into the faces of the people we manage. And to realise that *they* are our most important resources,' as Kenneth Blanchard and Spencer Johnson remark in the introduction to their *The One Minute Manager*. Naval, like his father, not only looked into the faces of his workers, but knew most of them by name and was conscious above all else that they were the company's most important resource. How people managed people made all the difference.

Godrej had been particularly fascinated by the managerial practices followed by the managing agency system, after the East India Company stopped its commercial operations around 1840. The managing agency's assets were skill in management, integrity and an experienced set of partners. They had such versatile skills that they could manage a conglomeration of businesses including anything from a tea plantation or colliery to an engineering factory. However, the nineteenth century managing agency firms became anachronisms in the twentieth century because they did not keep up with the times. They essentially remained traders, did not industrialize and refused to take risks. During the inter-war years, companies like ICI, Levers, Dunlop, etc. set up manufacturing activities in India as opposed to the managing agency firms. Interestingly, Indian managing agency houses also made attempts at setting up industries. Some of them set up the first Indian textile mills.

The arrival of the multinationals in 1930 was the last landmark in the evolution of professional management in India. With World War II, the demand for Indian managers increased considerably because most foreigners were called back home to be enlisted in the war effort. Thus it was that the heritage of the Indian professional manager became a curious one—an amalgam of the skill and adventure of his trader forbearers in the distant past, the managerial styles introduced by the colonial powers and later on the multinationals. In the fifties, the so-called Indian professional manager was typically the one who was educated at prestigious universities abroad and had more or less adopted a foreign culture and values to such an extent that he could be termed as more international in character than Indian.

A defect Sohrab was quick to point out in the current management courses was that the books being written and published in foreign countries discussed cases relating to decisions involving millions of dollars and pounds. Managers when they came to work in Indian organizations, found that what they studied could not be applied in practice. Foreign texts did not fit into the Indian context, it was 'like importing foreign medicines for local diseases.' There was the example of a company that tried to implement McGragor's Theory of Motivation in toto, but realized, within two years, how foolish it was to practice the theory as all the pre-requisites were not present. The company concerned was brought to the brink of ruin. Sohrab's plea was that the concept of professional management should be interpreted not in view of degrees and diplomas, but in terms of application, attitudes and approaches.

Accordingly, the first batch of management trainees were recruited by Godrej from the Indian Institute of Management, IIM, Ahmedabad in 1968. The interview board included the directors and senior managers of Godrej & Boyce. The trainees had to undergo a two-year training (which later was reduced to one year) at various manufacturing plants and had to do an in-depth study of all the products manufactured by the Company. Besides, they were by turn assigned to the departments of sales, accounts, delivery, showrooms, field sales, etc. in order to familiarize them with their working. The selection of a batch of management trainees for both the metal products and soap companies became an annual affair.

Several younger family members, Adi (Burjor's son), Jamshyd (Naval's son), Nadir (Adi's younger brother) also went abroad to acquire training in management. Adi took a BS and MS in Engineering and Industrial Management from MIT. Jamshyd graduated in mechanical engineering and did a post-graduate degree in business administration from the Illinois Institute of Technology. Nadir completed a BS in chemical engineering from MIT, an MS in chemical engineering from Stanford University and an MBA from the Harvard Business School. Tanya (Adi's daughter), did her BA in economics and political science from Brown University.

With a network of professional managers in employ, the next step was to decentralize the sales department and introduce what was called Product Management. For each product, namely, refrigerators, typewriters, Storwel, steel office furniture, locks, machine tools, forklift trucks, industrial systems, steel foundry, a Product Manager was appointed to promote the sales of the product he was looking after.

The Product Manager, in consultation with the General

Manager (Marketing), had to co-ordinate his efforts with the manufacturing plant and central delivery, on the one hand, and with the branches and wholesale dealers, on the other. Products had not only to reach the various markets, but distribution had also to be looked after. The Product Manager had to ensure that stocks were not allowed to pile up at the manufacturing level or in the branch warehouses, particularly during the off-season, so that capital would not be blocked in any way.

A continuous tab had to be kept at every point, manufacturing plants would have to be advised by marketing about what and how much to produce in a particular month as per the market demand. But then, there were other factors, too, which had always to be considered, and chief of them were the availability of steel, raw materials and components, the availability of transport to different sectors, the formation of truckloads.

Better interaction between branches and the manufacturing plants had to be developed, as also an efficient order processing system so that timely deliveries could be effected. Delivery schedules were slow in coming, and delivery dates continued to pose a problem. Godrej products were being sold, but the need was felt for more aggressive marketing strategies for the different product lines. There was also the need for better teamwork between marketing, the branches, production and other support services in order to overcome competition by ensuring consumer satisfaction.

In Godrej Soaps too these changes generated an improvement-oriented culture. Adi Godrej joined the company in 1963. Realizing that commissioning production facilities was just not enough, over thirty depots were established all over the country to ensure proper servicing of markets and reduce time between order placement and execution. Later, these depots took over the function of clearing agents. By 1993 the sales force was expanded from 45 to 400 salesmen. Already there were nearly 2,000 distributors; the retail dealer network comprised seven lakh dealers in the urban and fifteen lakh dealers in the rural markets.

Similarly, the Foods Operation had nearly 2.5 lakh outlets. Correspondingly, the total outlay in publicity rose from Rs 2.3 lakhs in 1963 to Rs 24.5 crores in 1993.

This material growth would not have been possible without the commitment and dedication of staff members and workers. The evolution of the Godrej Kaizen System, which helps bring about total employee involvement by encouraging and empowering all employees to make continuous improvements at the worksite was a major step in this direction. In concrete terms the Kaizen System led to seventy per cent reduction in changeover time on the shop floor, reduced inventories by forty per cent and spares and repairs cost by fifty per cent, besides leading to low energy consumption by rendering one of the two high-pressure boilers redundant.

Thus, it was that the instinctive or intuitive management practised by the doughty old managers in Pirojsha's days gave way to modern scientific management. But the basic principles and values are equally applicable to the ancient systems of management as they do to the 'one-minute managers' of today. These are enshrined for all practical purposes in what is known as the SWOT formula, described as 'a good management tool for the managers, like a thermometer and stethoscope for a doctor'—'S' to concentrate strengths, 'W' to recognize weaknesses, 'O' to evaluate opportunities and 'T' to counter threats. The values remain the same, only the application has been made scientific, enabling Godrej to sow better seeds over a wider field and gather richer harvests.

13
GLOBAL PRESENCE

An important concern of Sohrab, who has travelled to about 160 countries, including Antarctica, was that Godrej should acquire a global presence. The market of the future was a global one. The burning problems of the present like population control and environmental degradation were global. Often, in his writings and speeches, Sohrab referred to population, environment and development as the Holy Trinity.

Appointed Chairman of both the companies Godrej & Boyce and Godrej Soaps in January 1973, Sohrab took special care in acquainting himself with as many business activities and disciplines as possible. 'I sometimes thought,' he chuckles, 'the stork brought me to the wrong family.' His interests as a young man lay elsewhere—in journalism, choreography, mountaineering, tourism with its many beneficial effects. 'My father was single-minded,' he says. 'The karkhana was his whole world. He tended to be autocratic with us. He insisted, for example, on my sitting for the B.Sc. degree. My interest was in the arts. I told him I would take degrees in both science and arts, but he refused. I felt terrible, then, though eventually I got reconciled to it. The trouble was, he had little time for us. Though all his energies were spent on being successful as an industrialist, he never properly initiated us into industry. Left everything to us, as it were.'

But the discipline enforced by Pirojsha made him realize, at a callow age and against his natural inclinations, that he would have to adapt himself to his destiny, ordained by birth. The discipline could sometimes be exasperating and took a lot to get used to.

Fortunately for Sohrab, he came across the *Uplift of India* by Sir Visvesvaraya in which he argued that only through industry could the country become prosperous. 'Prosperity through industry'—the slogan was like a revelation to him. His outlook changed totally.

Against the rigidity of his father, Sohrab found comfort as a child in the warmth and gentle understanding of his mother Soonabai—'A mother is a mother still, the holiest thing alive.' Like any other fairly well-to-do boy of his age and time, he was sent first to Queen Mary's and later to St Xavier's High School, then to St Xavier's College from which he graduated in Science. The family in the meantime shifted from Grant Road to Cumballa Hill (with weekends spent in Versova), and finally to their property at Ridge Road where they reside to this day.

Sohrab has happy memories of these places, particularly

Versova. Their neighbours then were the very old Dadabhai Naoroji and young Rustom Masani who was to become Dadabhai's biographer. To Sohrab they all seemed very nice and friendly; the ladies in particular would catch hold of the six or seven year old Sohrab to ask him all sorts of questions. They were always curious to know what was going on in each household, what they had to eat for lunch or dinner, who visited them and so on. The little fellow would answer all their questions with the utmost seriousness, getting named as a 'reporter' in the process. *'Ai reporter aiyo!'* the Parsi ladies would make fun of him. Maybe they were right, for Sohrab was always interested in the press, and had a special regard for war correspondents. Among his friends as a young man were some representatives of the famous French news agency, AFP.

Soonabai was really the soul of the family, a radiant personality, looking after Pirojsha, his family and his and the neighbours' children. She had always been active and when in 1920—Sohrab was eight years old then—she passed away, life came to a halt for him. He just couldn't reconcile himself to the loss. His ayah would try to console him that she wasn't really dead, but had only gone to reside in the clouds, but he saw through her: 'They shouldn't have done all that because I never stabilized.' Neighbours and friends too were puzzled and concerned. What is happening to the boy, they wondered. Other peoples' mothers die, but they don't behave like this. Why is he taking it so much to heart? His was a suffering of the spirit which they could not comprehend and he couldn't convey to them. 'For a long time afterwards,' Sohrab recalls, 'I wore mother's locket. But greater than my own sense of loss was my sadness for my two younger brothers and sister who would never know a mother's love. Naval was only three and a half then. Such a lovely child! Burjor, too. Later in life, once, when Burjor was in a great difficulty and felt lost, my conscience pricked me that I hadn't done enough for them as the eldest.'

With the passage of time after Soonabai's demise, Sohrab became reconciled to the finality and inevitability of death. But for this early encounter with tragedy, the loss of Pirojsha and, later, under tragic circumstances, of his younger brother Naval to whom he was particularly close, might have been unbearable.

Sohrab made up his mind that if he was to remain in industry, he might as well be as good an industrialist as involvement, example and study could make him. Over the years, Pirojsha had impressed upon him that given the nature of the Indian economy their efforts should have a three-fold purpose. Firstly, they should see that customers were always satisfied so that they would buy more and more goods. This in turn would lead to more goods being produced and the government would get more money by way of taxation. Secondly, they should work in such a way that they made profits to be able to pay taxes, among other things, and thirdly, the people who worked for them should get adequate wages along with various benefits. He believed that the fundamental reason for their organization's existence was the satisfaction of consumer needs. In the process of fulfilling consumer needs, the organization would make profits which are a logical outcome of customer satisfaction. Profits could not, however, be independent of product quality and consumer satisfaction. Customer service, as a corporate philosophy, was therefore ingrained in Sohrab at a very young age.

The Godrej association with steel as a basic raw material being such a long one, a great disappointment of Sohrab was that even so many years after Independence, they were forced to import steel, besides other materials, and that too at a time when foreign exchange reserves were dwindling. One of the shortcomings of the mixed economy was that not only steel, but aluminium, cement and power were not in the hands of the private sector, so that if the public sector was not properly run, the country's economy suffered. In 1979-80, for example, additional production worth at least three to four thousand crore rupees could have been achieved, if there were no bottlenecks of coal, power and transport. Lack of proper infrastructure was a further impediment to progress.

In the Indian economy, fissiparous tendencies resulted in groups of people being played against one another. There was no attempt by industry at cooperation or co-ordination. Sohrab, like other enlightened industrialists, was not against the public sector provided it was run well and co-ordinated with the private sector. The private sector actually was publicly financed to a large extent, and the so-called public sector was actually a State sector. The terms 'public' and 'private' were therefore not quite appropriate. 'There is nothing so private about the private sector,' Sohrab argued, 'It is for the benefit of the community, and the so-called public sector which is supposed to benefit the public, is actually controlled by the State and does not benefit the public to the extent it is expected to.' He laid particular stress on the publicly financed sector because eighty per cent of the revenue realized by the government was derived from this sector. 'Why should we keep quiet about this?' he asked.

The concept of a mixed economy laid down by Jawaharlal Nehru was not, according to several industrialists, impartially implemented. They were not making a case for the private sector being better. Rather they were only pointing out that it had in practice shown that it could deliver the goods because some sort of personal incentive and a keener spirit of competition were involved. Indian industrialists were called upon to place before them the example of Japan;

particularly the aspect of cooperation where the whole country worked, as a famous writer remarked, 'as Japan Incorporated.' The Japanese were under a totalitarian regime but, strangely, they took the democratic path and experienced phenomenal growth. As an overpopulated country, India could best be compared with China. But China had a system of government that automatically eliminated a lot of political problems.

Sohrab constantly liaised with people in various ministries, interpreting his uncle's and father's beliefs to them. He would recall a prayer in Sanskrit which, translated, means, 'May we prosper together and enjoy our prosperity in common; let our exploits be joint endeavours.' Brought up on the Gandhian philosophy, he along with other industrialists felt that Gandhi who was critical of industry would have changed his mind if he had known that modern industry had created an elite class of workers who had improved their social status, with good working conditions plus good housing. In the past, it is true, workers were made to work in unhygienic, unventilated factories for long hours; they had hardly any time for their families, had no benefits and enjoyed no holidays. But conditions were changing.

The trouble was that, like trade, from 1947 industrial policy in India was highly restrictive. Domestic industry was subject to a wide array of detailed and discretionary government controls. Such controls took various forms such as barriers to entry and expansion of capacity through industrial licenses, reservation of large numbers of industrial products for the public as well as the small-scale sector, highly time-consuming procedures for exit of firms and prices and distribution controls on various products. A young entrepreneur found it very difficult to function easily, and therefore he resorted to anti-social methods, and what is called a parallel economy began to function. 'Wage goods' was a word commonly used, but enough was not done to give basic amenities to the people, to people who could manufacture things on a large scale and tap its benefits, and which would in turn also benefit others.

There was discrimination against industry in favour of agriculture. Because of political reasons, and because the agricultural sector had its own lobbies, it was not taxed, whereas some parts of the industrial sector were over-taxed, even up to 100 per cent and more. This was a golden opportunity to make sure that the rural sector did develop and that it generated its own income to contribute to the country's prosperity. The Government had a good scheme to help industrialists who wanted to do something to better the lot of the people in the countryside.

Industrialists did deplore the fact that many people, particularly politicians, had not taken the trouble to understand how businesses were run, what profits meant, and that profits were to be allocated for several purposes; that maintenance and future security of a company required conservation of profits. In spite of everything, however, the national saving rate was quite good. In this context, Sohrab was, however, critical of sections of the very privileged who made a vulgar display of their wealth, which set a bad precedent, got talked about and vitiated the industrial atmosphere.

Economics could not be dissociated from social problems. Respect for work had to be instilled. The trouble in India was that workers were not made to feel as if they were part of a benevolent system and that they were working for the general good, as a result of which, if they worked better, they would get better rewards.

The other important hurdle to India's success was discipline. Here again, the examples of Japan and Korea were relevant. The Koreans had a tightly controlled economy, but they had also been made to feel that working together in a united manner could bring about great changes in the country. Growth had to be achieved through consolidation. In the private sector this was done as a matter of course because of the imperative of footing the bill. But a number of projects started by the government did not run consistently. The infrastructure, which was mainly within the government's purview and on which a large part of industry depended, had to be well-maintained. There was a great need for cooperation in industry. 'We should be wary not to fall into the traps that the politicians lay for us', Sohrab warned, 'and make sure that we do cooperate. Otherwise the fate of our country is very dim.'

Indian industry was trying hard to acquire expertise in capital markets and ensure for itself a global presence. As part of trade delegations to various countries, Sohrab made it his mission to project products of Indian industry as a whole including Godrej products, naturally, and to try and promote mutual trade-relations at an international level. With freedom won, trade between Britain and India was on an even keel. India was poised for a quantum jump in its growth. It had all the elements necessary for this—large technical manpower, a developing industrial infrastructure, an active capital market, a large and growing domestic market for consumer goods. The aim of these various missions was to bring together businessmen of India and the other countries and to reduce the information-gap existing between them. The missions covered a fairly wide spectrum of industry, including chemicals, engineering goods and consumer goods. The members sought, among other things, technology transfer, joint ventures in countries like Malaysia, Singapore and Latin America and collaborations with buy-back arrangements.

An important event in this direction was the establishment in 1982 of the Council of European Economic Community Chambers of Commerce in India. It was intended to promote, foster and extend commercial and industrial relations between India and members of the European Economic Community, and to develop commercial exchange between industry, trade and business in their respective countries.

The main snag in further strengthening these economic relations was the adverse trade balances that India had with the European Economic Community. The trade deficit was as much as 50 per cent of India's global deficit! Although it was primarily the responsibility of India to increase its exports to the Community, some encouragement from the EEC countries was necessary to augment exports from developing countries like India. Some European countries like France, West Germany and Netherlands had already established agencies for this purpose. Sohrab wondered whether the EEC itself could establish an agency to coordinate and strengthen such efforts. Of course, the generalized system of trade preferences introduced by EEC had benefited developing countries like India. However, the quotas fixed in the early sixties needed to be revised on the basis of available resources and recent developments in each country. Sohrab cited the example of India which should have a higher quota than most countries since the textile industries in India depended upon the cotton grown in India itself. India could not be compared with a unit like, say, Hong Kong which had to import its cotton or yarn requirements.

An International Chamber of Commerce Congress with trade delegations from various countries was held in Delhi in February 1987. Sohrab followed this up in 1988 by undertaking a whirlwind tour as part of the Indian trade delegation to Spain, Portugal, Belgium and France. Apart from import and export, the question of further transfer of technology and joint ventures in diverse fields were taken up. There was vast scope for strengthening and increasing trade-relations with each of these countries. Temperamentally and culturally Sohrab felt closer to Europe than to other countries. He had enjoyed much interaction with France: as President for nearly three decades of the Indo-French Technical Association and a Vice-President and, later, President of the Indo-French Chamber of Commerce and Industry, among others. France realized the market potential in India way back in 1958. The French Government founded the ASTEF (Association pour l'Organisation des Stages en France, which later came to be known as Agence pour la Co-operation Technique, Industrielle et Economique: ACTIM) to train Indian scientists and engineers and to acquaint them with French industries, French production methods and technologies. Another objective was to keep the trainees in contact with their French counterparts so that they could keep abreast of the developments. From 1958 to 85, 2,500 Indian scientists, technologists and engineers were provided with technical training or obtained higher education in France practically in all fields of science and technology.

Sohrab had a long and profitable association with the Indo-French Technical Association (IFTA). He took over as President in 1970 from Dr Homi Sethna. At a symposium held in Bangalore in 1985, he pleaded for closer co-operation between the two countries in various matters. The French machine-tool industry was about three and a half times bigger than its Indian counterpart. French industry had earned fame for continuously evolving technology in the field of special purpose equipment for nuclear energy, aircraft and automobile industries and railways. As for the status of the industry in India, in 1984 it registered a production of 200 million dollars worth of metal-cutting and metal-forming machine tools. In spite, however, of its high standing in world markets, France ranked as low as seventh in import of machine tools by India. What was therefore needed was a proper nurturing of the Indian market.

Global Presence

At the Bangalore seminar, Sohrab recalled the Prime Minister's words that India's emphasis was now on higher technology, better management and quality excellence. He stressed that language barriers could easily be surmounted and that it was up to French trading agencies to ensure a proper evaluation in India of French products and technology. What was needed was a positive approach and a strategy of co-operation. To the French participants in the seminar he appealed: 'India is on the move and if you will give her your hand at this moment it will be most appreciated and you will earn a lot of goodwill for your industry. Educational and useful information about new developments in the French machine-tool industry is something I would like to stress to enable the users of your products to understand and profitably produce parts, components, at attractive prices in our country. During your present visit special effort should be made to find partners and collaborators with a view to produce in India some of your machine tools under licence.'

True, France was 10 years too late. Still a start could be made to take advantage of the sincerity and goodwill of IFTA members towards France. During 1984 the Indian Government approved of 752 products for foreign collaboration, followed in the first half of 1985 by 440 more products. Out of these, 258 products involved participation by foreign companies. His recommendation was that French machine-tool manufacturers should work out some kind of a joint arrangement in the area of research and development in machine tools. This was quite a practical proposition and could prove to be of mutual benefit if a part of the programme was devoted to designing in India and the rest was done in France.

The climate in India was inviting. The royalty rates and down-payment currently offered by Indian industry were fairly attractive. French collaborations were looked forward to, particularly as France had stressed the importance of culture through the ages and had evolved a unique way of life which included interest in different cultures.

Selling Godrej products abroad was a far cry from making Godrej internationally known. Exports were, for a number of years, handled by the sales department under Rustom Sanjana. It was only after a separate export department was established, and brother-in-law, K.N. Naoroji (who was till then working in Imperial Chemical Industries), took charge in 1967, that the export drive gathered a certain momentum. No doubt greater attention to exports and devaluation of the rupee also helped. Almost all Godrej products, particularly steel furniture, security equipment and machine tools became globe-trotters, earning valuable foreign exchange from Russia, East Africa, the Middle East and the Gulf countries. Even so they made a poor showing. Naoroji believes that with quality considerably improved and prices made more competitive, the performance would improve in the years to come.

It was necessary for Godrej to establish a global presence. They began with Indonesia and struggled for ten years, but had to leave given the unfavourable industrial climate. They were, however, successful in Malaysia. When the Malaysian Industries Minister visited Pirojshanagar, he was most impressed. Thanks largely to the kind intervention of Malcolm Macdonald, the High Commissioner for UK in India, who wrote to some British firms in Malaysia, Sohrab received a most cordial reception when he visited the country. Godrej launched their factory in Johore Bahru in 1967 under the name of Godrej (Malaysia) SDN. BHD. With time, another factory was put up in Singapore under the name Godrej (Singapore) Pte. Ltd.

Godrej began with the manufacture of steel office equipment. The range of office-tables, unlike in India,

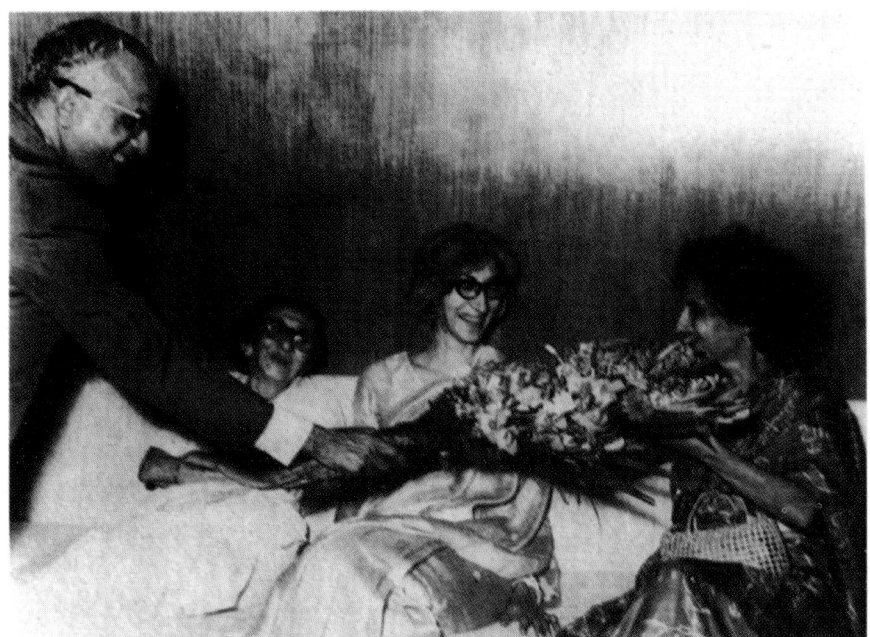

K.R. Gokulam offering a bouquet to Jaiben Godrej. On her right is Soonuben Godrej. Next to her is the renowned educationist, Cooverbai Vakil, who was the creative spirit behind the Godrej Udayachal Schools at Pirojshanagar

A section of the Mangrove Nursery at Pirojshanagar, Vikhroli

The very first housing quarters built by Pirojsha in 1952 for his workers

Hillside housing for the Godrej staff

Exhibits at the 'Web of Life' exhibition organized by the Udayachal School students from 14 to 19 December 1995

At the Annual Sports Day at Vikhroli (left to right): Burjorji P. Godrej, Adi, Jamshyd, Smita, the late Pirojsha B. Godrej, the late Naoroji P. Godrej and Sohrabji P. Godrej

The Udayachal High School building at Pirojshanagar

Vijaya Dhamankar, a Hindi literacy teacher at Pragati Kendra, conducting Hindi literacy classes

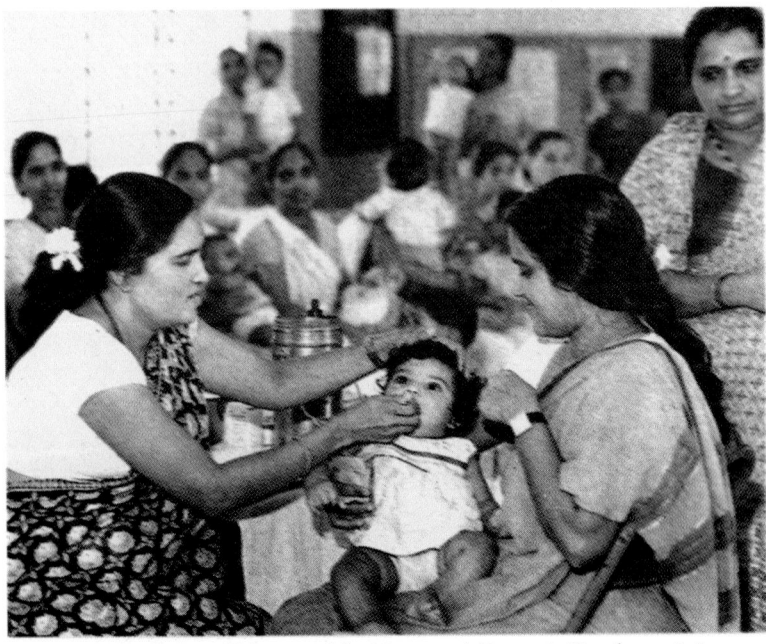

Sudha Ambedkar, Public Health Nurse of Pragati Kendra, giving an oral polio vaccine to a child during the immunization camps in 1973-74, one of the best programmes conducted by Godrej in Maharashtra if not in India

At the Sheriff's public meeting in Bombay on 9 January 1973, to mourn the death of Pirojsha B. Godrej (left to right): N.H. Tata, Mayor R.K. Ganatra, Governor Ali Yavar Jung, Sheriff J.G. Bodhe, Smt Sumati Morarjee, N.D. Sahukar. Mayor Ganatra addresses the meeting which is presided over by the Governor of Maharashtra, Ali Yavar Jung

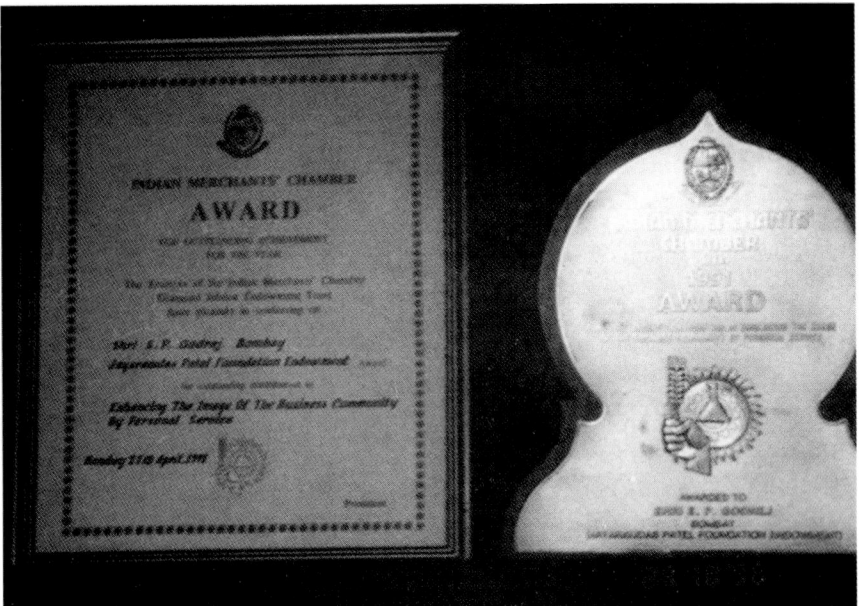

The Indian Merchants' Chamber honours Sohrabji P. Godrej for 'outstanding contribution in enhancing the image of the business community by personal service'

The American Biographical Institute Research Association honours Burjorji P. Godrej with the post of Lifetime Deputy Governor

The American Biographical Institute honours Burjorji with the International Cultural Diploma of Honour

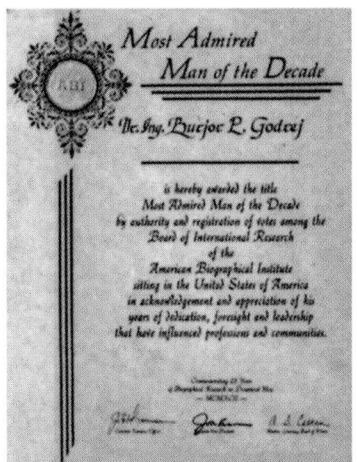

Other select awards and honours conferred on Burjorji P. Godrej

Padma Bhushan awarded in 1976 to Naoroji P. Godrej in recognition of his contribution to Indian industry and society as a whole

The late Naoroji P. Godrej at a felicitation function on being awarded the Padma Bhushan, organized by the Godrej Central Works Committee on 8 February 1976 at Pirojshanagar. On his right is his elder brother, Burjorji P. Godrej

Presentation of a Godrej typewriter to Prime Minister Indira Gandhi. N.P. Paul, a Senior Liaison Manager of Godrej, is seen at the extreme right

Sohrabji P. Godrej at a TV conference in Delhi on 17 April 1970 organized by the Indian Society of Advertisers. (Left to right): Naoroji Godrej, Keshab Mahindra, Prime Minister Indira Gandhi and Y.A. Fazalbhoy

At the inauguration of the state-of-the-art Godrej - GE Appliances Mohali Works, Chandigarh on 28 February 1996. (From left to right): B.J. Wadia, Vijay Crishna, Chief Minister of Punjab, Sardar Harcharan Singh Brar, and S.P. Godrej

Sohrabji P. Godrej with Lord Attlee at the Birla Hall on 27 February 1961

The Sheriff's condolence meeting. (From left to right, 1st row): Smita Vijay Crishna, Sohrabji P. Godrej, K.N. Naoroji, Mrs N. Palkhivala, the late J.R.D. Tata Jehangir Nicholson, the late Burjorji Godrej, M. Doshi and Mrs Katy Dastur

Sohrabji P. Godrej with Madame E. Cresson, French Minister of Industries, and J.R.D. Tata at the Indo-French Chamber of Commerce Annual Meeting held at Taj Hotel, Bombay, on 8 December 1985

Dr V.K.R.V. Rao addressing a Rotary weekly meeting on 14 July 1964 on 'Perspectives of Indian Economic Development over the Next Ten Years'. S.P. Godrej, President of the Club (left) and R.G. Saraiya (right) are present

Sohrabji P. Godrej with Prince Philip, the Duke of Edinburgh. On the left is Mr Gavin W.H. Relly, Chairman, WWF–South Africa

Adi with Malcolm Forbes Jr in 1995

Lilian Carter acknowledges greetings of the Godrej employees during her visit to Godrej industrial garden township, Vikhroli, on 15 February 1977. Also present are (left to right): Senator Percy, Lilian Carter, Jamshyd N. Godrej, Sohrabji P. Godrej and Chip Carter

Adi Godrej with former Finance Minister, Dr Manmohan Singh, Harsh Goenka and Ajit Gulabchand in 1995

Adi Godrej with Nani Palkhivala, Verghese Kurien and others, on the occasion of award of the Dadabhai Naoroji Prize to Verghese Kurien in 1995. Adi is President of the Dadabhai Naoroji Foundation

Jamshyd N. Godrej, President of the CII, with Jyoti Basu, Chief Minister, West Bengal, on the occasion of the CII Conference at Calcutta on 6 April 1994

included single-pedestal and double-pedestal desks made in an attractive combination of rosewood or teakwood tops and steel body structure. They have also manufactured filing cabinets, compactors, steel cupboards, security lockers and chairs.

Steel for their manufacture had been imported from Taiwan, Japan, Korea and Indonesia. All the workers are very co-operative and most of them are Chinese, with women making up 30 per cent of them. In Singapore which is duty-free, the wages are almost double of what is paid in Malaysia because of the very high standard of living. The infrastructure in both countries is very good, with excellent natural resources. Godrej faces competition from ten other manufacturers, all of whom, including Godrej, are involved in considerable export.

Sohrab keeps himself abreast of what is happening in the companies. Weekly top-level meetings enable him to be in touch with the latest developments and to keep in touch with the companies' policies. If ever there is a serious complaint about a product or a service, in the spirit instilled into him by his father Pirojsha, he gives immediate personal attention to it.

When, sometimes, his company was by-passed, Sohrab reacted quickly. In 1982, the Jammu & Kashmir government had purchased 250 typewriters from Godrej. In spite of their giving excellent service, at highly competitive prices, the following year the government purchased 500 typewriters from another company. Immediately, Sohrab wrote a letter to Dr Farooq Abdullah, Chief Minister of Jammu & Kashmir, reiterating that the quality of the Godrej typewriters was 'equal to, if not better than, other makes' and that 'most attractive price terms for bulk supply' were being offered.

It's another matter that Godrej still did not get the order.

When in 1973 the Drugs Controller, contrary to world experience with hexachlorophene, prohibited the manufacture of cosmetics containing this compound, Burjor Godrej wrote a strong letter of protest to the Prime Minister, Indira Gandhi. He said, 'If the European Common Market, Sweden, Switzerland, Finland, Austria, etc. are allowing and will allow in future also, the use of HCP in cosmetics, is there any reason why it should be banned in India? To say the least, the Drugs Controller, India, is acting as if India were an appendage of USA, and even going a step further.' Sohrab followed with another letter pointing out that hexachlorophene was 'irreplaceable as a chemical of its kind' and, far from being risky, 'there is great risk in *not* using it.' He added: 'We feel strongly that decisions regarding scientific products should be taken on rational lines; otherwise in our scientifically developed country one could not take responsible initiatives.'

The Drugs Controller was, however, adamant. Godrej filed and won a suit in the Bombay High Court for using hexachlorophene in toilet powder. But it was a pyrrhic victory. Because of the prohibitive price of hexachlorophene brought about by the unfair action of the US Food and Drug Administration, it could not be used in toilet powder. Dr Eric Jungernan, a highly respected consultant, summed up the entire controversy with a damning indictment: 'The toxicity of hexachlorophene was political.'

On one occasion in Calcutta, Sohrab was present at a function addressed by the then Governor, Dharam Vira. Referring to the unsettled conditions existing in the city then, the Governor remarked in passing that things had got so bad that even Godrej cupboards were being broken open. He was referring to an incident in the patriot C.R. Das's house. Disturbed by this Sohrab rang up and spoke to his daughter.

Laughingly she told him not to get so ruffled, as it was only a wooden cupboard that had been broken open by some miscreants!

But Sohrab has never been content to be an industrialist and nothing more. Like uncle Ardeshir, he is of a restless nature and, like his brothers Burjor and Naval, he has varied interests. International affairs, the 'population holocaust', environmental pollution and degradation, the preservation of wildlife and of our heritage, natural and man-made, are matters of the deepest concern to him. From an industrialist he has grown to be a concerned citizen. He tries to balance his companies' affairs and his world interests in an intricate minuet, without missing a step. The problem isn't the balancing, but the time needed for it. If Sohrab were granted one wish above all others, he would cry: 'Let my day last longer than 24 hours!' His life is a race that began the day he entered the Lalbaug factory, a marathon race against time to make up for the many lost years.

14
MR ENVIRONMENTALIST

Sohrab stayed with his father on the third floor of their 40-D, Ridge Road house, 'The Trees'. At dinner they would often discuss the karkhana that, as we have seen, was an obsession with Pirojsha. But as the karkhana became established, Pirojsha's interests widened. Inspired perhaps by Gandhi's writings, he would often remark that just because they made money didn't entitle them to use it as they wished. What profits they made had to be ploughed back into the business, and what remained had to be held in trust for those less fortunate than themselves. Pirojsha was always modest about Godrej's achievements. They were small as compared to what the developed countries had achieved; in

Mr Environmentalist

India they had a long way to go still.

The two problems of gravest concern to Pirojsha were the fast rate of population growth and, as a result, the multiplying slums with the degradation to which they lead. Believing as he did in Darwin's theory of evolution and observing the conditions in which people lived, he once told Sohrab that at this rate of population growth a time would come when Indians would have to learn to sleep standing to occupy the minimum space!

He was convinced that population control was the first necessity to prevent the erosion of economic gains and the consequent human frustration and unrest. So far as his own workers were concerned, he could provide them with comfortable and hygienic housing at heavily subsidized rents at Vikhroli and, through the Pragati Kendra, to disseminate information regarding family-planning. But that wasn't nearly enough. Sohrab recalls how every time they passed Worli and saw the ugly tenements built by the British with only slits for windows, Pirojsha would be considerably agitated that workers who lived there were deprived of fresh air and had to be in darkness even in the daytime. He believed that real progress could only be achieved in a milieu of general advancement all around. He therefore urged his son, whose connections made various fora available to him, to drive home the population-environment nexus at every available opportunity. Sohrab did this with an almost religious fervour. He didn't seem to be conscious of the irony of a bachelor propagating family-planning, and in the process of stressing the nexus he earned the sobriquets 'Mr Environmentalist' and 'F.P. Godrej'.

The statistics were damning; thirty per cent of the population having an inadequate income, 48 per cent still illiterate, 70 per cent having no access to pure drinking water, 30 per cent villages having no electricity and 70 per cent yet to be connected by road. The dreaded prospect, by

2025, of overtaking China, which has a much bigger area, as the most populous country of the world. In a nutshell: India compressed 14 per cent of the world's population on 2.4 per cent of the world's land and sustained it on 1.5 per cent of the world's income. The problem was difficult and complex and quite daunting because it had to cover over 860 million people, from diverse linguistic and cultural backgrounds, spread over 5 lakh villages and thousands of cities and townships, of a wide and varied topography.

In his campaigning Sohrab received considerable inspiration from Russell W. Peterson, President of the world-renowned National Audubon Society whom he often quoted and with whom he corresponded. 'Aside from the threat of nuclear war,' declared Peterson in an address to the Institute for World Affairs, University of Wisconsin, on 11 December 1984, 'population growth is the most pressing environmental issue of our times. Almost every environmental problem, and almost every social and political problem as well, either stems from or is exacerbated by the growth of human population.' As a result 'a culture of poverty is being transmitted down the generations, sacrificing human resources and impeding social progress.'

Peterson went on to quote from Pranay Gupte's book *The Crowded Earth* based on field research in several Third World countries which stated that the world responds readily to what he calls 'loud emergencies' like famines, earthquakes, etc. But the world is not so responsive to the 'silent emergencies in which more than 45,000 children perish every day from preventable causes. This tragedy, and the related tragedy of 400 million children who go to bed hungry each night, go relatively unnoticed.'

In his speeches and writings Sohrab pointed out that the worst consequence of over-population—the population holocaust, as he calls it—is that the community and its environment cannot function as an ecological unit in Nature.

Land cover, which is already inadequate, is being further denuded. About fifty years ago 45 per cent of India was covered by forest and it had, next to Brazil, the largest varieties of trees and plants. Today the forest area had been reduced to a mere 12 per cent. Our lifeline rivers, the fabulous gigantic Himalayan ranges, vast life-giving forest areas had been polluted or devastated. We were misusing precious land resources by allowing sick, useless cattle to graze upon it.

In a city like Bombay over-reclamation had weakened the shoreline and was destroying its sustaining wetlands. Wetlands, in fact, were a neglected source of wealth. Gandhi's words about the importance of village uplift had been forgotten with the vast majority living in squalor. Our wildlife was threatened along with its habitat. The tiger, for example, required vast and extensive territory of its own type for survival, which in turn could preserve the habitat, mainly forests.

Of utmost concern to environmentalists was that the accumulation of all these factors had brought about a crisis of character in our people in their fight for a better quality of life—even survival, coupled with greed and materialism in some sections of society. The population holocaust had not only numbed the physical fibre of our people, but the constant deprivation had also damaged their mental faculties. 'Because of many centuries of suffering and exploitation,' says Sohrab, 'even equality of opportunity is not enough for our masses. They often need spoon-feeding, as it were, to get the skills into their hands and minds. Because they lack even basic skills, they cannot get jobs, except as labourers.'

Recalling Gandhi's words that in our country there was enough for everyone's need but not for everyone's greed,

Sohrab pointed out that when Gandhi said this, the population was within manageable limits (342 million), which it is no longer! Today the basic needs of our people like adequate housing, sufficient food and drinking water, could not be fulfilled. Again, a grave shortage existed of primary health-care centres. People could not even benefit from medical care because of their unhealthy and congested living conditions. Diseases like TB and malaria, eradicated at great cost and with the help of international agencies, were resurfacing with a vengeance. Or take leprosy. India had more leprosy patients than a more heavily populated country like China. The point is that because of abominable congestion in our country and our propensity for patchwork solutions, there was all-round degradation.

A basic shortage was that of food. The 'Grow More Food' campaign became quite successful—for a fairly long, but limited period—with the evolution of new strains and the planting of more and better seeds, all on highly scientific lines, thanks to the initiative of Dr M.S. Swaminathan, an agricultural scientist of world renown, and others. We even had a surplus, which, alas, was notional since a large majority of the people had low purchasing power. But, after adopting artificial methods of cultivation, the soil had become impoverished. The use of insecticides also did considerable damage. But then, no scheme, however laudable, could serve the needs—especially of an impossibly vast population for indefinite periods. Hence, the necessity of all-out help to continually evolve new scientific methods as a way of life and to serve our masses.

The pity was that our four-decade-long multi-pronged Family-Planning programme, costing nearly Rs 5,500 crores, had not made a dent in our population growth. Considering that India was the first country to adopt family-planning as a state policy, the first to establish a birth-control clinic in Mysore in 1930 and that the International Planned Parenthood

Federation was founded here, it had continued to lag behind the other countries which started their programmes much later. Apart from the Population Foundation of India, of which J.R.D. Tata was the Chairman, the Family Planning Association of India with Smt Avabai Wadia as its President, there is the International Institute for Population Sciences, was located at Bombay (one of the few such institutes in the world) where considerable research on demography was in progress and which should help to provide a scientific basis to population control.

Godrej set an example of what the corporate sector could do in this regard. The failure of family-planning policies in the country as a whole made Godrej realize that population control could not be brought about without improving the quality of life of employees through providing houses with clean and green surroundings and education for their children, preventive and curative medical facilities and a welfare centre to look after the psychological and emotional problems of workers and their families. From the very inception of the Vikhroli project, an integrated and holistic approach was therefore taken. Two dispensaries were commissioned for factory employees at the workplace and at 'Upchargraha' in the residential colony. Almost all children residing in the colony were immunized against diseases like measles, mumps and diphtheria. All pregnant women were looked after in the ante-natal clinic right from the confirmation of pregnancy to the delivery. Follow-up was also done after delivery at the post-natal clinic. A condom dispenser was installed. In fact, the Godrej family-planning clinic became a government-recognized centre.

To propagate the message of family-planning, surveys were undertaken in the colony to enlist eligible couples for the purpose and also to convey information about various family-planning methods. Group discussions to develop a positive social attitude towards family-planning were organized, along with film shows, skits, dramas, exhibitions, poster contests, and so on. Information was also imparted through the monthly bulletin *Darpan* and on salary slips.

In the early fifties employees and their children were found to be suffering from under-nutrition. The management started supplying lunch and snacks in factory canteens at highly subsidized rates. About 1,500 calories were provided per *thali* lunch. Children were given free milk in the pre-primary school and snacks at highly subsidized rates in the primary and high schools. All children were medically examined regularly. As a result, nutrition level in children considerably improved, from 40 per cent under-nutrition and malnutrition in 1966 to 1 per cent in 1994.

Recently, a Health Clinic for creating health consciousness among women was opened. It provides a health package programme with about 10-12 lectures on nutrition, yoga, physical health, the spiritual aspect of health, child psychology and inter-personal relationships. A Youth Clinic has also been started to prepare girls for adjustment to college life.

India has lagged behind in spite of being one of the highly industrialized countries, having made significant strides even in advanced technology and in scientific management. The need is to develop the right mental attitudes and implement the right priorities. More and more Indians should be made to feel strongly about the burning need to plan their families in their own interest. This approach should acquire the force and momentum of a people's movement and come to be considered as a mark of patriotism.

A change of attitudes is therefore called for in India. Basic to this change is sound education. Take the example of France where, with cent per cent literacy, traditionally the most important minister after the Prime Minister is the

Education Minister. In India, on the other hand, education is tagged on to human resources development, a laudable exercise which nevertheless has not singled out education as an indispensable single force. Again, enlightened countries generally budget more for education than defence, whereas in India, our budget for education stands nearly at the bottom of the scale in importance, a niggardly 2 per cent. Particular attention needs to be given to female literacy, for there is a very close correlation between fertility and female literacy. In Kerala, for example, because of universal literacy, particularly female literacy, the birth rate is much lower than in other states.

Trade unions, as voluntary bodies in whom workers repose their faith, are in an advantageous position and should be made to feel that it is their obligation as a national duty to help in imparting family-welfare education, disseminate information, arrange counselling and distribute non-clinical contraceptives through union outlets. The committed media too could help greatly in creating public awareness as a national duty and privilege. Scientists also have a crucial role to play in regard to over-population by intervening in the social process, codifying and assisting in the process of sustainable and just development. Finally, enlightened and sincere politicians should take the initiative to bring this about instead of just exploiting the existing vote-banks composed of ill-informed voters.

Industries like Godrej owe their success, among other things, to scientifically evolved marketing of their products. 'Unfortunately—I should say, tragically,' comments Sohrab, 'we do not give to issues of vital national importance even one-tenth of the importance we give to selling merchandise on profit. But make no mistake about it. Runaway population growth is a threat, which biologists, ecologists and demographers recognize to be at least as serious as that of nuclear war.'

Closely linked to the carrying capacity of ecosystems is the concept of sustainable development. Accordingly, the underlying correlation between population, poverty and pollution has to be analyzed against the background of the ecosystem's capacity to provide support for development and for maintenance of an acceptable quality of environment.

As a result of the Godrej endeavours for family-planning and environmental protection, Sohrab was invited by Prince Bernhard of the Netherlands, the then President of World Wildlife Fund-International, which is closely linked with the International Union for Conservation of Nature and Natural Resources (TUCN), to be a founder-trustee of World Wildlife Fund-India (now World Wide Fund for Nature-India) of which he later became President. He also became, with his father's encouragement, a member of the exclusive '1001-A Nature Trust', Chairman of the WWF-India National Steering Committee on Population and Environment, and Vice-Chairman of the People's Commission on Environment and Development (PCED).

Pirojshanagar, the Godrej industrial garden township, epitomises a blending of Man, Machine and Nature. The uniqueness of this area is its well-maintained natural environment, which has not only been protected but greatly enhanced! The survival rate of trees is high, largely because everyone here—including the children of the Godrej-run Udayachal Schools—is conscious of the importance of trees. For the past many years a well-stocked tree bank is maintained here and saplings are generously distributed, free of cost, to voluntary organizations engaged in afforestation work. The Godrej and, particularly, Sohrab's reverence for trees brings to mind a telling comment made by Ralph Waldo Emerson, more than a hundred years ago. In Paris during the Revolution of 1848, Emerson noted that the trees on the boulevards had been cut down for barricades. 'At the end of a year,' he observed drily, 'we shall take account and see if the Revolution was worth the trees.'

The Godrejs are particularly proud that a large expanse of mangrove forest, perhaps the best on the west coast, adjoins this township. This valuable and endangered mangrove expanse, which is a haven for water-birds, is vital for the protection of the hinterland and as a spawning ground for fish. At great financial expenditure, the mangrove is being maintained and protected from poachers by the Soonabai Godrej Trust. It received high praise recently from M.F. Ahmed, Inspector-General of Forests, who described this mangrove patch as 'acting as lungs in the industrial area of Mumbai.'

It is said that the only causes worth fighting for are lost causes. For Sohrab the population-environment nexus is not entirely a lost cause. He does despair of the delay and lethargy, and feels like personally shaking up people to an awareness of the impending dangers. But he hasn't lost hope. In the final analysis, he believes, it is individual values that fuel social changes. Progress towards a sustainable development depends on the awareness, motivation and the sense of responsibility of each one of us to Mother Earth and to future generations.

Sohrab's dedication to the cause has subsequently led to many honours being bestowed on him, and a National Conservation Centre being established, in memory of his late father. Meanwhile, another activity has been close to his heart, that of a Rotarian, provided the 4-Way Test is seriously followed.

15

SOCIAL CONCERNS

The spirit of Rotary is native to the Indian way of thought and life. From time immemorial India has been advocating the ideal of 'service above self' as the best means of reaching the kingdom of God. The Vedas speak of this ideal in ennobling terms, asserting it to be the only means for a 'Karma yogi' to realize the ultimate reality. By heritage, training and temperament, India is eminently suited for the growth and development of an organization like Rotary.

To an Indian, the symbol of Rotary—the rotating cogwheel—is a reminder of the Ashoka Chakra, the national symbol. The wheel also reminds him of Lord Vishnu, the Protector of the Universe and his famous weapon,

Chakrayudha. According to Hindu mythology, the Vishnu Chakra is associated with the power of protection from evil, ignorance, misunderstanding and confusion. Similarly, Rotary's Four Way Test—Is it the truth? Is it fair to all concerned? Will it build goodwill and better friendship? Will it be beneficial to all concerned?—and the Rotary philosophy with its emphasis on karma, dharma and world brotherhood enables a man to do his best for himself and his fellowmen, acting as a balm in a troubled world.

A developing country like India provides ample scope for service. The population explosion and the consequent environmental degradation, made critical by the traditional evils of casteism and communalism, are eating into its vitals and stunting its growth. Here is a field where Rotary, believing as it does in fellowship and world brotherhood, can render yeoman service. Rotary can also play an important role in combating illiteracy. Widespread corruption and, worse, the practice of protecting and even deifying the corrupt, inefficiency and ill-health are some of the other problems facing India which call for concerted efforts of the whole country to remove them: Rotary can play an important role in initiating such efforts through revitalisation.

Sohrab became a member of the Rotary Club of Bombay in November 1952. He assumed the responsibility of Joint Secretary in 1957-58, became Director in 1959-61, In-charge, International Service, then Vice-President in 1963-64 and President in 1964-65. The same year the Rotary International President, Charles W. Pettengill issued a challenge to fellow Rotarians the world over to 'Live Rotary.' Among the guidelines he suggested for this purpose, were to apply Rotary principles to all business relationships; exercise community leadership by attacking a significant community problem and participate in the matched district and club programme and accept an opportunity for community service.

As in all that he did, Sohrab took his duties as Rotarian seriously, maintaining a hundred per cent attendance and sometimes even more, attending when abroad the Rotary meetings of those countries, exchanging flags and trying to build bridges of friendship between India and other countries. Even when attending international conferences held by organizations like the International Chamber of Commerce, the International Planned Parenthood Federation and others, he tried to put the accent, whenever relevant, on India and Rotary.

The fact that the four basic principles of Rotary coincided with the motivating force of the Godrej enterprise was to an extent responsible for Sohrab's keenness as a Rotarian. 'I would say that the Rotary philosophy with its emphasis on karma, dharma and world brotherhood enables a man to do his best for himself and his fellowmen. Rotary is an excellent organization to do good things in life, which may be difficult for an individual to do by himself. For the same reason I agreed to become Sheriff of Bombay in 1982.'

Akin to the spirit of Rotary was the growing consciousness of the social responsibility of business. Leaders in industry all over the world had for the past few years been acquiring a new philosophy under which they felt that business is a part of society and had an obligation to the community in terms of social problems, even if to some extent it took a toll of their profits. Some of them went so far as to say that 'the first responsibility of business is to operate for the well-being of society'. The new move reflected a certain amount of genuine altruism, but it was also to some extent a consequence of continued attacks on business. Company chiefs had been shaken by the protests, for example, of the consumer crusaders of America. The crusaders insisted on knowing what the companies were doing for the community and the nation. To quote Henry Ford, 'Businessmen will have to put as much emphasis on immediate social progress as they do on productivity and profits.'

In the same vein, the British Management Review commented: 'In economic affairs the primary purpose of an enterprise, and so of management's responsibility, is the provision of goods and services in accordance with the requirements of the consumer.' A celebrated authority on management, E.F.L. Brech amplified this by saying that 'whatever its particular form in terms of ownership or control, an enterprise cannot escape basic responsibility to the community in which it is located. Thus it is well recognized that the community looks to an enterprise to fulfill certain standards of social performance in whatever it produces or sells regardless of its size, form of proprietorship, whether corporate, co-operative or some form of partnership.'

Godrej were one of the earliest firms in India to realize this. In fact, as mentioned earlier, several measures they introduced for their workers anticipated labour legislation in the country. Both Ardeshir and Pirojsha were conscious of their total responsibility, both to their business and to the community. If Japan today is a great nation economically, Sohrab has never tired of pointing out, much of the credit goes to the ingenuity of its businessmen and their willingness and determination to serve the nation in their passion for profit, which in turn takes care of the welfare of the people. Since business life in India was inextricably linked with the people in terms of millions of consumers, their ultimate welfare and happiness was, in a way, a guarantee for the growth and continuance of the business. It was therefore imperative that in addition to making a fair and adequate return on capital, the industry or trade had to think in terms of obligations to the community, beyond its natural and legitimate concern for profit, for its own enlightened survival. In the complex economic and business life of the country, every enterprise had a manifold responsibility—to itself, to its customers, workers, shareholders and the community. It was the task of management to reconcile these separate and sometimes conflicting interests in fulfillment of its responsibilities.

The overall success in fulfilling such responsibilities was of course dependent on the economic policies pursued by the government. India was passing through a stage of transition where, on the one hand, there was a revolution of rising expectations and, on the other, there were constant hurdles which made fulfillment of these expectations difficult. The businessman was unhappy because he was not able to completely fulfill his role as supplier of goods and services to the community. The community was unhappy because it did not get the optimum satisfaction it was entitled to in the goods and services it bought. To fulfill its responsibilities in protection of the consumer, the government stepped in, not just as a watchdog, but as an active participant in vitally important economic decision-making. This had far-reaching consequences on the relationship between trade, industry and commerce. The result was economic controls which restricted the freedom of trade and industry to produce and to distribute what they wanted to and consequently put limits on the freedom of the consumer to buy what he wanted. These restrictions gave rise to a class of unscrupulous and spurious businessmen who exploited the market scarcities for their own personal gratification, causing heart-burning among businessmen and industrialists who became the helpless victims of the situation. The business community as a whole became the target of criticism, as caring only for profit and not for the fulfillment of social objectives.

A dire need therefore arose for a change of outlook, so

that politicians and others would not fritter away their energy and time attacking the private sector's irresponsibility, when it actually contributed nearly 80 per cent of the revenue realized by the government, to which had to be added the amounts paid by individuals in industry. Considering all the constraints of a tightly controlled economy, before the recent liberalization policy, the fact that industry had been functioning somehow in India and thereby yielding socio-economic benefits to the country was something to be thankful for. 'Atheists have remarked jokingly,' Sohrab wryly comments, 'that in India one has to believe in God to justify India's viability.'

The main responsibility was to ensure that the source from which all these benefits accrued should remain sound, that is, the efficient running of the business in the interest of all those connected with it; shareholders, through safeguarding their interests; consumers, through the supply of quality goods at the right prices, and through provision of reliable after-sales service; workers, through a combination of wages and amenities like housing, medical care, education, mainly, and, above all, through the construction and proper maintenance of up-to-date airy factories with exemplary working conditions; and government's through the payment of taxes. Housing particularly, for which there was a crying need, was another example of social responsibility which business could assume. However, it had become very difficult to implement it because of various impediments, particularly the Land Ceiling Act.

Pirojsha and Naval believed that the singlemost important objective of taxation, to raise the required revenue, without stifling growth, was being frustrated in India by inequities in the taxation policies. Many taxes existed that raised very little revenue and impeded growth. The wealth tax was a very good example of this. It raised less than 100 crores, which is less than 0.2 per cent of Central Government receipts. Such taxes discouraged saving and efficient investment which are necessary for growth. Then again, excise duties on so-called luxury products were pegged at very high levels, often beyond the point at which maximum revenue can be raised. The 100 per cent excise duties applicable on everyday toiletries were a case in point. The move, in 1983, to reduce excise duties on several items including electrical appliances, was a welcome though belated recognition by the government that it was counter-productive to peg excise duties at too high a level.

The tax system, according to Sohrab, could and should be simplified: 'It is a shocking fact that in spite of having a fairly high savings rate in the world, we have had a very low growth rate. This is entirely due to the fact that savings are invested very inefficiently, particularly in the public sector where rates of return are very low. The first step is to get a firm grip on government-spending. Administrative expenses should be reduced by eliminating unwanted bureaucracies, and government investment should be curtailed by opening up more sectors to private enterprise and foreign investment. Once the government spending is reduced, the tax system can be rationalized. In a country such as India with low per capita incomes, an income-tax can never raise much revenue. The major emphasis has to be on indirect taxes. The best system is to peg taxes on all products at a uniform rate. A value-added tax is necessary to avoid the high level of multiple taxation that is prevalent in India today.'

Direct taxes in a country like India not only did not raise much revenue by impeding growth, but led to a waste of energy in legally avoiding and, what is much worse, in a massive and blatant evasion of taxes. Although not a tax expert, Sohrab ventured the opinion that other than entirely abolishing all direct taxes, perhaps the simplest system was to have a flat rate tax with very few or no special deductions. For instance, in India one could have a simple system whereby all incomes below Rs 50,000 per annum were exempt and all incomes above that bracket were taxed at a rate of 30 per cent.

Black money in India was largely due to our taxation system: 'There is no black money in Hong Kong which has a free economy and low levels of taxation. Black money in the Indian economy is of two kinds: black money raised by a violation of price controls and black money created to evade direct taxes. The solution to the first is the elimination of price controls and the solution to the second is elimination of high rates of direct taxation.'

With a view to lend teeth to the legitimate needs of consumers and the enlightened pursuits of business, a Fair Trade Practices Association (FTPA) was established in October 1966 with the dual objective of promoting fair trade practices in industry and trade in the interests of the consumer, and to create greater public goodwill towards the business community. As its President from 1972-74, Sohrab issued a clarion call: 'The Indian consumer has to realise that to set things right he has to become a positivist and an activist instead of being hesitant and negative. He has to understand that nothing comes free and consequently if he is interested in getting good quality products at the right price, place and time, he has to work for it. Others are there to aid him, but they are helpless if the consumer's own attitude is one of apathy.'

Consumers needed to be informed and educated regarding their rights and the courses of action available to them to protect their interests. Publicity could be given through the radio, television, documentaries, advertisements in dailies and so on, and Consumer Protection Weeks could be held to create increased awareness. Two erroneous impressions had to be dissipated. First, that the FTPA was a political gimmick designed to benefit only a few top industrialists and, second, that the very existence of an organization like the FTPA would be a tacit admission of the prevalence of unfair trade practices. The business community was in no position to totally deny the charges of malpractices, although many of them had their origin in government's misconceived policies. Rather than lose by default, business should protect its true image by serious and sincere efforts. There was no need to feel apologetic about this for, though the reputation of business had been getting worse, its performance by reasonable economic or social standards was satisfactory: Sohrab, however, pointed out, 'But at the same time, we in the business community have to realise that what is important is not how business conceives its role and performance, but how the intelligent section of the public view it.'

J.R.D. Tata, a Patron of the Fair Trade Practices Association, stressed the need for the formation of a trade and industry organization confined to businessmen with a proven record of straight dealings. The constitution of such an association, he insisted, should ruthlessly make it obligatory to expel any member guilty of malpractices. Tata who had recently received the Madras Management Association's business leadership award, suggested as a measure of retrieving the soiled image of industry and trade, that private enterprise should set up some mechanism of a social and management audit to which, periodically, business units should submit themselves.

Analyzing the reasons for the poor public image of business and industry, which was preventing the private sector in particular from playing its full part in the economic revival of the country, Tata deplored the fact that their image was far from being commensurate with the massive contribution of the private sector during the last half century. As a result many sound projects of importance to the country put forward by honest, competent and resourceful companies were being frustrated to the detriment of the country's economic development: 'The vast majority of India's entrepreneurs, large and small, are patriotic and socially conscious men, who do not ask for special favours or large profits, nor seek monopoly or concentration of wealth and power. All they want are the opportunities, to exercise their initiative and skills to apply their resources for the country's benefit as well as that of their shareholders, labour and customers and to be left alone to get on with the job.'

Sohrab liked Bombay (Mumbai) and, as a conscious citizen, deplored its degradation. At one time Bombay was one of the most beautiful cities in the world, clean and well-maintained, with an efficient transport system, well-maintained public services, and, even its rampant poverty alleviated to some extent by a basic human dignity. The only solution, of course, was decongestion, giving incentives to people to move into other places and disincentives against their moving into the city. But this wasn't enough. The problems that agitated the city were the same as those affecting the rest of the country; galloping population growth, 'the population holocaust.'

Cities like Tokyo and New York suffered from the same problem. But these cities had amusement parks, swimming-pools and other amenities which provide relief for their population. Bombay by contrast had its abundant *zopadpattis*.

In a seminar on urban development in May 1985, several suggestions were made. Divert future growth to other areas:

'Immediate sizable investment in New Bombay is a must.' Develop new growth centres, shift activities further to the north. Divert offices and industries' locations away from the city.

A detailed study of the carrying capacity of Bombay city in terms of water supply, sewage disposal, electricity transmission, transport and so on was needed. 'Why do we carry on as if there is unlimited potential to expand these services? The first water supply scheme for Bombay cost 100 crores, the second scheme cost 500 crores, the proposed third scheme will cost 800 crores. Where will we find the funds?' Sohrab asked.

Another problem facing the city was the growing encroachment on footpaths, public areas, etc. Considering that the municipality was spending over Rs 500 crores on the sewerage project, he failed to understand how a few lakh rupees couldn't be spent to enforce the removal of encroachments. Side by side with removing what was unauthorised, he was deeply concerned as an active member of the Indian Heritage Society, about protecting and preserving what was of value; buildings, structures, precincts of historical, architectural or cultural value, sea scapes.

What lent weight to his views wasn't only that they were the result of deep-rooted convictions, but the fact that he was so closely lined with the Godrej companies which were setting an example in fair trade practices, workers' welfare, family-planning, environmental protection and mangrove preservation. Sohrab's achievements in these areas are, by their very nature, intangible and very often, by the same token, they remain unrealized. But they are not any the less significant. Sohrab, like his father and his brothers, was concerned by the population explosion and consequent environmental degradation which have today reached the extreme of endangering our very survival. He believes passionately that preserving our heritage of historical buildings and monuments in this first city is a duty enjoined on us by the past. Aggrieved by the crimes wrought in the name of religion, he propagates nature worship as the ideal, being common to all religions. It is said that travels make the man. Having travelled to almost all countries, finding in their stages of development, their cultures and ways of life. a basis of comparison to his own country and his own people, he is conscious of how much, in spite of our tremendous scientific advances, there is still left to do. He tries in his own way to do the best he can. To quote Robert Browning:

The little man, with a little thing to do,
Sees it and does it.
The great man, with a great thing to pursue,
Dies ere he knows it.

Sohrab is a fast thinker so that most of those who work with him find it difficult to keep pace with him. He is, besides, an obsessive perfectionist. A marketing expert makes the point that there is a distinction between striving for excellence and striving for perfection in that while the former contributes to the task and also imparts a sense of satisfaction to the performer, the latter carried to excess leads to unnecessary delays and confused priorities. Sohrab wouldn't agree. And, as if to make the point, he, the seniormost among Godrej workers, works the longest hours of all.

16

THE LARGER CITIZENRY

Necessity doesn't always mother invention. True, when during the War Godrej couldn't import machine tools for their own use, they decided to manufacture these tools themselves. But even if there had been no War and the necessity to import them hadn't arisen, Naval would in due course have gone ahead with the manufacture of machine tools out of his deep conviction that these would test the mettle of Indian industry and shape and chart its future course, and more basically, that the right tools were needed for the right jobs. Because of the lack of sophisticated research in these fields, Indians had to make do with antiquated, inadequate implements in a vast range of activities from farming right down to clothes-washing. While this might be all right in other fields of endeavour, it would never do in industry. The manufacture of machine tools was even more significant in the long term than that of typewriters and refrigerators and its fruition would entitle Naval to be named as a Titan of industry.

The first mechanical presses and press-brakes were made in 1942 for use in almost every plant at Godrej. Over time these presses and press-brakes along with shearing machines were manufactured in a wide range of models and capacities from 2-tonnes force to 1000-tonnes force. Very much later many of these models became available with modern computer digital controls. Some of these machine tools were manufactured with established world leaders and over the years equipped the press shops of many discerning customers in transport, defence, power-generation and metal-fabrication industries in India and advanced countries abroad.

In the late seventies diversification took on an exciting new turn when, prompted by success in the sheet and plate metal working industry, Godrej, under Naval's leadership, commenced manufacturing process equipment. This involved the use of newer, more challenging and exotic materials, and resulted in due course in sizable import substitution. Manufactured under the stringent specifications of national and international inspection agencies, Godrej came to supply a range of custom-made sophisticated equipment for the chemicals, petrochemicals and fertiliser industries, aerospace and nuclear applications.

Godrej have placed from 1961 till date over four thousand machine tools in Indian and international markets and are forging ahead with a range of technologically superior machine tools, which are more versatile, speedier, more dependable now than earlier, and trouble-free and user-friendly.

Holding a wide comprehensive portfolio of sheet metal working machinery, the Godrej product range includes mechanical presses, mechanical press-brakes and guillotine shears, hydraulic press-brakes and guillotine shears with optional CNC controls, special presses for specific applications, state-of-the-art high-precision and coil-processing lines.

India's largest indigenously built mechanical shears were manufactured by Godrej for Chittaranjan Locomotive Works in West Bengal in 1985-86. A fully automated 250-tonne cold extrusion press system was made for MICO in Nasik. India's first high-technology, high-precision, lamination press lines capable of speeds up to five hundred strokes per minute were also manufactured, followed by plastic-injection moulding machines. In fact, Godrej are in a position to offer the entire machinery for sheet metal processing shops, either manufactured indigenously or supplied under agency agreement from foreign manufacturers like LVD of Belgium and L. Schuler of Germany.

Godrej have, over the decades, developed and maintained the best in machine-tools building and quality control facilities. The future looks even more promising with new products being developed.

The Godrej toolroom, one of the best equipped in the country, supplies intricate precision tools, jigs and fixtures to a select list of demanding customers. The reason for this extremely high standard of excellence obtained in the toolroom goes beyond the highly sophisticated jig-borers to the rare skill and attitude of the workers whose talents have been sharpened over many years of training and experience.

Realizing the tremendous role machine tools would play in the future, Naval guided the Indian Machine Tools Association through its formative years and was its President from 1971 to 1973. He established the pioneering international exhibition known as IMTEX, the showcase of the machine-tools industry. IMTEX was hosted seven times on the sprawling, landscaped grounds of Pirojshanagar. The first exhibition in 1965 had about ten exhibitors. The seventh, and last in his lifetime, had 400 participants! Organizing this wasn't an easy task. All the facilities available in running factories were required to demonstrate machine tools, especially the large ones. Besides, it was an expensive proposition with a covered area of 50,000 sq. metres, with a connected electrical load of 12,000 KW for both power and lighting. Six restaurants were installed to cater to different tastes. All the necessary facilities were made available for conducting business satisfactorily. Machinery and equipment worth over Rs 75 crores was displayed, the majority indigenously made and the rest from several advanced countries.

Naval soon became the authoritative voice to speak on the trials and tribulations of the machine-tool industry in India, its slow growth and heavy dependence on imports, and how these could be remedied. The basic fact to be borne in mind was that this industry was one of low profits, high capital investment and long gestation periods. The advance in technology was now very fast, and the introduction of computers and electronic systems had projected the industry into the age of mechatronics. Speaking on the occasion of the Sixth IMTEX Exhibition on 6 February 1986, when N.D. Tiwari, Union Minister of Industry, presided, Naval listed the factors why the machine-tool industry had lagged behind in India in recent years:

- This industry was under severe constraints of licensing policy and MRTP/FERA restrictions until recently.
- Upgrading of technology was not demanded by users until the recent revolution in the automobile sector.
- The Government of India had been following a policy

of protection from imports till very recently. As a result, a certain level of complacency had crept into this industry.
- The fiscal controls were stacked against industry, making it uncompetitive vis-a-vis foreign manufacturers.
- The import duty on specified machine tools on Open General Licence was 35 per cent. The import duty for machine tools imported under approved projects was 45 per cent. However, the import duty on components was 85 per cent. The import duty on raw materials could be as high as 150 per cent.
- There had been no new entrant of significance in this industry for more than 20 years due to the very low level of profits in this industry. Historically, the international machine-tool industry had been confined to entrepreneurs who have been essentially technicians, engineers and innovators.

Naval pointed out that in the last ten years the lowest share of imports in the total consumption of machine tools was 34 per cent in 1977. In 1985, however, the share of imported machine tools in the total consumption had risen to 60 per cent. He believed that the industry had to face the challenge and plan to reduce machine tools in the total share of consumption to 40 per cent in the terminal year of the Seventh Plan (1990).

The machine-tool industry had already taken certain steps to stem the tide of imports which went up from 44 crores in 1975 to 200 crores in 1984, but the government too had to cooperate to balance the trade in machine tools. The steps already being taken by the industry were technology upgradation and technology imports. More than 23 foreign collaborations were signed in the previous two years, for NC/CNC machine tools alone, and also for non-CNC machine tools. Further, inhouse research and development generally, and particularly at the Central Machine Tool Institute at Bangalore, had been stepped up considerably. So also investment by existing manufacturers had also considerably increased, and every major manufacturer had undertaken modernization office facilities.

Government too could cooperate by reducing the import duty on raw materials and components which should not in any case exceed 50 per cent of the duty of the complete machine imported into India. It was recommended, firstly, that customs duty on raw materials and components should not exceed 25 per cent *ad valorem*. Secondly, excise duty on finished machines when manufactured in India, which then was 12 per cent, should be reduced to 5 per cent. Proforma credit should also be allowed on all inputs of raw materials and components which could be set off against Central excise duty on finished goods. Thirdly, the cost of plant and machinery should be allowed to be written off on a Straight Line Basis in 3 years. Term loans should be available at no more than 10 per cent interest with repayment schedule over 10 years. Credit authorization should be given up to 6 months of production. The import of second-hand machine tools should be totally banned. Expenditure on research and development which was about 2 per cent of the value of production should be increased to approximately 5 per cent so as to reduce India's dependence on imported technology.

No country in the world was totally self-sufficient in the production of machine tools. The countries that came closest to self-sufficiency were Japan and West Germany. India should aim, according to Naval, to meet at least two-thirds of its requirements in this connection. He expressed his confidence that, given an environment that placed the Indian producer on the same fiscal level as his foreign counterpart, the Indian machine-tool industry would be able to meet the challenge. He pointed out that there was a considerable time-lag between the policy announcement of the government and its implementation by the industry. This industry by its very nature needs long gestation periods to implement changes.

S. Moolgaonkar of TELCO had made the same point in his speech as Chief Guest at the IMTEX Exhibition in 1982. He said that the Indian machine-tool industry had to develop the competence to meet the changing demands of the market without having to resort to continuous import of technology. The popularly exhorted concept of technology assimilation was more relevant then than at any time in the past. What was even more important was that this should be done in the most cost-effective manner. In his Presidential Address, at the 1986 IMTEX exhibition, Union Minister N.D. Tiwari made the interesting suggestion that while TELCO, HMT, Kirloskar and other big units had their own Research and Development units, what was needed was 'a collective type of research' through a high-level centralized Research Co-ordination Council. If collective research was undertaken, the six crore rupees currently being spent by the industry on Research and Development could multiply fourfold.

The thrust Naval gave to the machine-tool industry at home and, to some extent, through the IMTEX Exhibitions in the international sphere as well, marked the climax of his industrial career. Of the many reasons for his spectacular success, the close rapport he enjoyed with his workers and engineers was a conspicuous one. The rapport the workers had with his father was born of authority and respect. A somewhat aloof figure, Pirojsha had always kept his distance. But Naval was different, he mixed freely with them. They were in a real sense his 'buddies' who had helped him to set up his industry. In the early stages when numbers were

The Larger Citizenry

limited he knew most of them by their first names. Like them, he too had begun at the bottom sharing their sweat and toil. Very early in his career, working as an apprentice in blue overalls in the toolroom at the Lalbaug plant, he noticed that the plant manager and the fitter could not between them lift up the heavy motor to hold against the press side, align it and bolt it. They dared not ask him to lend a helping hand; after all, he was the proprietor's son. To their astonishment, without a word, Naval rolled up his shirtsleeves, went up to the manager to help lift the motor so that the fitter was free to align and bolt it. It was this readiness of his to work shoulder to shoulder with his workers that established a bond between them and assured him of their unswerving loyalty. Each and every product the company made he knew thoroughly. Every machine that was bought he'd inspect, see it unpacked and installed in his presence. He knew the strengths and deficiencies of his workers. A stern and unforgiving disciplinarian, if he ever found a worker shirking or leaving his plant in a hurry before the bell rang, he would dismiss him on the spot. At the same time he was forgiving of genuine mistakes.

As a hot-blooded young man, Naval had quite a temper, but, as he matured in years, he learnt how to control it. Soonuben recalls an incident that took place in his salad days. Along with an English gentleman, a tenant of Godrej's, Naval went to receive a foreign guest on a P & O liner berthing in Bombay. The Englishman was allowed to go up, but Naval was stopped at the gangway by a policeman on duty. A hot argument followed during which Naval snatched the baton the policeman was wielding threateningly. Naval was taken to the police station and made to appear before a magistrate at Esplanade Court the next morning. Fortunately, for him, the Magistrate was both wise and witty, and saw the humour in the situation—a citizen indignant that while his tenant was allowed to go up he was not, and a policeman outraged that the very symbol of his authority had been snatched from him. Naval was let off with a warning, that such a thing shouldn't be allowed to happen again.

An evangelist of productivity, Naval believed that productivity was the key to success in every sector of the industry from plants to service points and dealer outlets. He wanted productivity to go beyond operational systems to the workers themselves. Productivity to him was an attitude of mind which would enable the workers to achieve better results for their efforts, lower costs, reduce time and derive the satisfaction and sense of fulfilment that comes with doing a job well. He tried his best to instil this attitude of mind in his workers. It would change their outlook, make them concentrate on the contribution they were making rather than on the rewards they would be getting and inspire them to devise better and more effective methods of doing the job. It would give each worker a competitive edge within the organization for his own growth along with the company's. The rewards would always follow.

Naval appreciated the other man's point of view even if it was contrary to his own. Rustom Sanjana, who was quite outspoken by nature, recalls many differences of opinion he had with Naval. When on retiring, Sanjana went to bid Naval goodbye, he apologized for having unwittingly given him offence at any time, emphasizing that whatever he had done was in the best interests of the company. Warmly, shaking his hand, Naval assured him, 'Sanjana, we need people like you. What is the point of having only Yes-men?'

Stories doing the rounds at Vikhroli make Naval out to be a larger-than-life figure, which indeed he was in his genuine care and concern for the workers. We have seen how the entire layout, landscaping of the Vikhroli township was planned in great style by him. Even for designing the

The Larger Citizenry

workers' flats he would personally sit with the architects, which experience proved to be later helpful in planning Godrej Baug.

Once a senior supervisor suddenly died leaving behind a young widow with two minor children. Payment of her husband's Provident Fund amount would, in the normal course, have taken considerable time. Neighbours and colleagues had somehow managed to pay for the funeral expenses, but the poor woman had nothing to feed her children with. The Vice-President (Corporate Services) approached Naval, explained the woman's plight and suggested that, as a special case, 20 per cent of the Provident Fund should be paid to her. Naval listened in pained silence. 'Give her the entire amount,' he said. 'If there's any problem later, we shall see.' He even permitted her to continue living in the company's quarters and to keep sending her children to the Vikhroli school.

Naval wished to do something to help children of school-going age. It was this concern of his that led his wife, Soonuben, to undertake to look after the workers' children. She recalls the time they started teaching with just seven or eight children in an old grain warehouse in the early fifties. She had to go from house to house using all her persuasive charm to recruit children for this school. The white sari-clad lady, tall and slender, with the winning smile, became a familiar and friendly figure moving about among the workers' wives. Unfortunately, schooling was something that meant little to them in the early years. Discipline was foreign to their nature. The children would absent themselves every now and then, giving the excuse that they had gone to their native place. Soonu never taught in the school, but her perseverance won, and, by the time the regular school was built, the workers began to show increasing interest.

A visit to the school is an experience to cherish. Here, on

a sunny morning, groups of little children are engrossed in making rangoli patterns. There, in a corner, another batch is busy making *gajras*, and a third group is working on a *toran*, threading marigolds interspersed with mango leaves. When the task is finished there is much rejoicing with a song in praise of flowers. Learning by observing is encouraged. To learn about insects the children are sent out in the garden to watch an anthill or to a corridor corner to observe a spider spinning its web. Groups of children are digging in the garden to grow vegetables or are taken for study-trips to the post-office, the market, the railway station or on a bus ride, so as to be motivated by first-hand experience. 'A young child learns best from what it sees and experiences itself— not from what he is taught in a classroom', observes Ms S.D. Choksey, the Principal of the primary and pre-primary sections. 'So we see to it that the child has the right learning environment.'

The classroom rigidity of desks and benches is deliberately broken, as often as not, classes are held under the trees in the abounding gardens. Mathematics becomes a game, grammar a puzzle to be solved. Drama, puppetry, picture composition become effective means for developing communication skills. Waste becomes precious raw material, with empty cartons, used typewriter ribbons, discarded packages, toothpaste tubes, softdrink bottle-caps, etc. utilized to make animals, puppets, toy vehicles, furniture, etc. The re-cycling of waste is transformed from theory into practice. Waste computer paper is used for drawing, spraying, sticking, tearing or cutting and a variety of pre-writing activities.

The children are also made to interact with visiting schoolchildren from Australia and England. They are encouraged to participate in various international competitions in essay-writing, painting, etc. Says Ms D.B.J. Jahina, Principal, Udayachal High School (now retired, and replaced by Mrs K.H. Billimoria), 'All these activities enhance a child's self-esteem. They also get many options when it comes to choosing a career.'

Involvement of parents as the child's best allies is encouraged. Parents are invited to help in the classroom or to accompany children on picnics. They run a parents' library and are currently engaged in an ambitious literacy programme, teaching small groups of illiterate parents.

How far are these innovative methods successful? The results speak for themselves. For the past several years consecutively, the SSC results have been above 95 per cent. Today, Udayachal boasts of almost 4,000 students with 162 teachers, which works out to a teacher for every 24 students, which must establish some sort of record in Bombay's teaching institutions. Apart from Soonuben, other members of the Godrej family take keen interest in the running of the school. Jaiben Burjorji's wife, used to teach English as a first language and mathematics, and also English as a second language to Gujarati-medium children. In each case she would teach a class from the fifth to the SSC. Pheroza Godrej, wife of Managing Director Jamshyd, organizes and participates in teacher-development programmes.

Both the school's principals are highly qualified. The staff and teachers are probably among the best-trained of any school anywhere. The school building is spacious, with airy classrooms and wide verandah. Equal facilities and opportunities are given to the students irrespective of whether they are rich or poor. The school has among the best school libraries in the city with more than 54,000 books, some of them dating back to the early years of the century. The teachers are allowed to give tuitions only after school hours and only in the school and free of charge. Giving tuitions at home is prohibited. Extra-curricular activities are encouraged, like pottery, clay-modelling and other crafts, singing and sports for primary students, painting and crafts for the pre-primary and needlework, metalcraft and carpentry, commerce and computers for secondary students. There are two types of camps, with tests in trekking, first-aid and so on.

A unique feature of the education imparted at Udayachal has been the annual exhibition organized by the students themselves under the watchful eye of their teachers. Last year (1995), for instance, the exhibition organized was rather intriguingly entitled, 'The Web of Life'. Life as seen through the eyes of children, was captured here in all its shades and aspects. Right from the origin of life on earth to the birth of mankind and its evolution to the complexities of living; from the interdependence of living creatures to the maintenance of ecological balance; from the progress of science and technology to family-planning to the loss of life through wars and natural phenomena. The subject was looked at from various viewpoints such as language, science, art and craft and social science, thus bringing out the inter-connection of subjects in the curriculum. Besides highlighting certain scientific, historical and geographical facts, the exhibition was linked to the environment, to social problems and philosophical issues like the quest for happiness.

According to Naval's son Jamshyd who successfully took his father's place, running the school cost the company two crore rupees a year. There was no screening but, to drive home the necessity of family-planning, only the first three children of each family (now reduced to two) were accommodated.

Naval, like other family members, followed the footsteps of his father in his philanthropy. He gave of his wealth to a wide variety of charities. A follower of the Zoroastrian precept of good thoughts, good words and good deeds, he was a sincere practitioner of philanthropy which Zoroastrianism enjoins as the greatest of virtues. A self-taught man, he poured vast sums into education and other grants: hospitals, clinics in Bombay and elsewhere. Brought up in an atmosphere of the social contract, this was his abiding contribution to the larger citizenry of India. 'To give away money is an easy matter, and in any man's power,' declared Aristotle. 'But to decide to whom to give it, and how large, and when, is neither in every man's power nor an easy matter. Hence it is that such excellence is rare, praiseworthy and noble.'

In the first instance Naval contributed expertise, energy and funds towards housing for his employees and eventually through Godrej Baug for Parsis. One of his few unfulfilled goals was the model township he had planned for the less privileged, named after his mother, to be constructed by the Soonabai Pirojsha Godrej Foundation.

The Godrej companies give as much as 32 per cent of their profits to a wide variety of philanthropic causes. The Godrej Foundation, founded in 1972, is a charitable trust open to the public at large and to all communities. It renders educational aid to students going abroad and studying locally, and gives medical relief to the poor and those needing various treatments. It also aids and promotes culture, fine arts and allied institutions, and extends help in case of natural calamities. It also extends help to the homeless, which has given birth to the prestigious Godrej Baug complex. The P. Godrej Memorial Wing at Breach Candy Hospital and the Spastics Society of India are other examples of the same benevolence. Blood banks, libraries, schools, orphanages and many allied institutions have been supported and aided.

Similarly, the Soonabai Pirojsha Godrej Foundation, owns land at Pirojshanagar, which has been extensively used in preserving and maintaining the mangroves at Vikhroli.

Believing strongly in the ripple effect of a healthy nation, Naval has initiated, through the Pirojsha Godrej Foundation, the Foundation for Research in Community Health (FRCH). Despite our rich tradition in the field of health, the majority of people in India who live in the villages and slums still do not receive any meaningful form of health care. Drawing upon expertise from various disciplines such as medicine, social science, management, documentation and economics, the FRCH determines the reasons for this failure and to attempts to evolve cost-effective alternative strategies which could be utilized on a countrywide scale. Studies undertaken by the Foundation have revealed the importance of socio-economic, cultural, environmental, political and human factors which have hitherto not been given due recognition and without which the knowledge and technology available would not succeed in achieving health goals.

One of the FRCH's bold and original schemes in the process of conducting its field-studies was the training of semi-literate village women in the Mandwa Project. An article entitled, 'Helsman Extraordinary' in *Parsiana* (January 1991) described how the project started. Invited to the Godrej bungalow in Mandwa, the noted plastic surgeon, Dr Noshir Antia, who was the driving force behind the Foundation, couldn't understand how people coped and survived in their dismal surroundings. Recognizing the rural folks' competence, Antia wondered whether they could be taught to help themselves. Assured of Naval's financial support, Antia launched the project with a young doctor from the J.J. Hospital and a young graduate from the Tata Institute of Social Sciences—which eventually was to have repercussions on the government's health policy. Seeking to establish links with the rural community which would serve as a channel for transferring knowledge at the grassroots and enable them to maintain better health in their own surroundings, the project ultimately trained a woman from each of the twenty to thirty villages sunk in poverty.

Education was imparted by trained nurses in the local dialect and eventually these women were able to give injections and vaccinations, to diagnose the diseases that needed modern drugs and to ensure that the medicines were administered to the patients in their villages. Training was given once a week under the shade of the surrounding trees; and Naval would on occasion come and sit quietly on the ground like the rest of them, recalls Antia.

The Mandwa project even acquired a centre designed by Jal Gobhai. Eventually, however, the project had to be disbanded in just ten years for various reasons. A major reason was excessive interest at the grassroots level without the local and zilla parishad leadership being given the importance they felt they deserved. There was also a failure to provide the expected higher level of services like X-rays. The refusal to permit the project's vehicles to be used during elections also created unnecessary ill-will. Again, the village bigwigs, chauvinists to the core, resented the importance that the women got. They started making all sorts of absurd demands on Naval. When these were rejected, there was violence and finally a shutdown. 'Naval and I were adamant,' recalls Antia, 'but he was very disappointed. He was interested in people, looking after them. We worked for ten years, spent nearly 20 lakh rupees, but no one knew about it—that's the difference.' Naval's wife Soonu recalls the occasion when a woman needed a ceasarian operation, but there was not enough light above the table. Naval immediately interjected: 'Why didn't you call me, I would have held up the light for you.'

The project was wound up in 1983. But the lessons learnt endured. Those trained in modern hospital-based clinical medicine got the unique opportunity to understand and appreciate entirely different problems of health and illness and the socio-economic and political factors underlying them. It was seen how the commonest and even the major killer and maiming diseases could be controlled at remarkably low cost at the village and community levels by workers supported by a very modest referral service. The greatest achievement of the Mandwa experiment, according to Dr Antia, was in the field of health education, where a village woman, once convinced, could transmit the knowledge and technology to the rest of the community in a manner which no external media could ever hope to achieve. It demonstrated the importance of the cultural factor in communication.

Brought up in a Gandhian and nationalist atmosphere like uncle Ardeshir and father Pirojsha before him, Naval and Sohrab went on to try and fulfill another national imperative with the establishment, along with his friend Vasant Sheth of Great Eastern Shipping, of the Foundation for Medical Research, in which about thirty specialists worked dedicatedly towards finding a cure for leprosy. The country had about 3.2 million leprosy patients out of the total estimated world figure of 11 million. The Government of India and many national and international organizations were active in this field, but in spite of over two decades of the National Leprosy Control Programme, there was as yet no marked decrease in the incidence of the disease.

The basic concern of the donor-trustees of the Foundation was whether man was at the crossroads in achieving a breakthrough in the discovery of a treatment for leprosy. Vasant Sheth recalled how on several occasions when he would lose his patience at the slow progress, Naval would intercede to tell him that basic research always took time. Naval was not only deeply interested in periodic scientific audits being carried out but, whether it was a working day or a holiday, whether in Bombay or Mandwa, in meeting these scientists, both foreign and Indian, to learn from them at first hand whether the search for a cure was continuing on sound lines. 'Amongst Naval's greatest achievements,' says Sheth, 'his love for real or fundamental research with a pragmatic objective may be recorded as an extraordinary part of his character. Pure research takes years and requires large funds. He came to realize that without this research there cannot be any real development. In this matter he was very different from common business people who think only of immediate profits and not long-term real developments.'

It was Naval's interest in housing that led to his association with the Parsi Punchayet which, for a man of his integrity and outspokenness, was less than a happy one. A.J. Davar recounts in his study, 'Non-Zoroastrians in Zoroastrian Precepts and Practices,' how under the influence of the priestly class, Parsi leaders persuaded the British in the late 1700s to establish the first Punchayet (a council exclusively elected by eligible Parsis) in Bombay to settle religious and social disputes. 'But the law courts consistently refused,' notes Davar, 'to give it law-making or law-enforcing powers in these areas.'

Naval's motive in joining it was, as he stated in the Manifesto dated 3 December 1984 announcing his candidature, 'to do whatever is possible for the good of the community. My father was at great pains to instill in his sons a sense of duty for the upliftment of the community and the people at large. The fact that my family name is known for its indelible mark on Indian industry and Parsi philanthropy is not enough for me, I would personally like to do whatever I can for my community, and I feel that the Parsi Punchayet could be revitalized to meet the aspirations of the members of the community.'

Admitting that the Punchayet could not be expected to perform miracles, given the constraint on its resources, Naval went on to state: 'the revamping of its management and administration would go a long way in raising the Punchayet to its apex status, which this great and ancient institution is destined for.'

The following goals were stated: 'The twin facets of housing—new construction and repairs—would be engaging my urgent attention because I feel that this is the most pressing problem which the community is facing at present.'

Naval had other goals too. Davar pointed out how, denied executive powers, the Punchayet ended up by wielding only vast financial power as the custodian of Parsi trusts and properties rather than holding a position of pre-eminence on socio-religious practices or religious doctrine. Naval's goals included the setting up of houses for the priestly class and a central fund for their education and amelioration. He also wished to provide more employment opportunities for the unemployed in the community, to educate young boys and girls to enable them to acquire the required skills to be self-sufficient and to initiate schemes to provide technical education by reviving certain technical institutes that the community already possessed.

The vast Godrej Baug, developed on Punchayet land, was intended to eventually house about 5,000 families. Naval wanted to computerize the Punchayet's accounts, to introduce an open house policy whereby all seven trustees as well as the main administrative officers would be available on certain days of the month to face and answer whatever charges or requests the community chose to make. He desired also to institute a regular system of overhauling the Punchayet's residential properties to obviate ad hoc repairs, to appoint a truly good administrator and give him enough rein to do his job.

None of this came to pass, largely, perhaps, because he resigned over the issue of collecting about Rs 40,000 in donations from those whom he recommended for allotment of flats from the 50 per cent donor quota in buildings constructed by Godrej in the Baug. As Naval told *Parsiana* in the interview after the event, if recipients of Bombay Parsi Punchayet's scholarships worth Rs 5,000 could be asked to contribute to its building fund, why not beneficiaries of flats worth Rs 3.5 lakhs. 'Where can you get such a place for Rs 40,000?' he had queried. He was careful to add, 'I have done this openly. Whatever money comes in is given back to the Bombay Parsi Punchayet for further construction.'

The Board of Trustees of the Parsi Punchayet were of course shocked by 'the sudden and unexpected resignation of their valued colleague Seth Naoroji Pirojsha Godrej as a Trustee of the Parsi Punchayet.' They passed a resolution recording his valuable services, on 14 October 1986, in these words:

'Mr Naoroji Godrej was uncontestedly elected as a Trustee and joined this Board on 25-2-1985. During his short period of trusteeship of the Punchayet, he gave a much needed boost to its building programme and for the welfare of the Parsi Community in general. Being one of the heads of the Godrej Industrial Complex, his vast experience of public and industrial life and his mature advice were extremely helpful to his colleagues in arriving at important decisions on various matters.

'Mr Naoroji Godrej was associated with the Parsi Punchayet Trustees along with his late father Mr Pirojsha as a member of the Godrej Foundation Advisory Committee during the years 1941 and 1943 and gave useful guidance in the conduct of the farms.

'Mr Godrej is as capable, industrious and versatile as the eminent founders of the Godrej Industrial Complex, his uncle Ardeshir and his father Pirojsha.

'These eminent predecessors had the welfare of the labourers at heart, which Seth Naoroji Godrej has inherited.

Even the Punchayet Staff have also tasted the benefits of his liberality.'

The amount of time he spent on the housing project was incredible, recalls Jamshyd. From the time of ground-breaking he was known to go every Saturday to review the progress. Right through his long illness, on his way to hospitalisation and on discharge, he desired to drive through Godrej Baug to see things for himself. 'He was hurt that his co-trustees didn't back him up.' He resigned because he found he was unable to function. 'He joined to help the community,' says Soonu. 'When he realized he couldn't do much, he withdrew. He was never interested in holding on to a chair.'

Naval's backing of the controversial Athravan Educational Trust is another example of his sturdy independence. The controversy arose out of the fact that the Trust had originally been set up for the amelioration of Parsi priests, but when the Constitution was drawn up it was found that a whole lot of other objectives were outlined. This created some bad blood in the community. But Naval decided to find out for himself. Ignoring all that was said against it, he not only accepted trusteeship of the body, but provided space for its functioning in Godrej Bhavan. His ability to assess a situation for himself regardless of what people said was also evident in his decision regarding the Bombay Parsi Punchayet's membership of the Federation of Parsi Zoroastrian Anjumans in India. It was feared that Bombay which had more Zoroastrians than the rest of India put together might be forced to accept the viewpoints of other Anjumans whose total voting power at the Federation's Executive Committee was greater, even though the number of Zoroastrians was less than the Bombay Parsi Punchayet's. To overcome this problem, Naval suggested that the Federation's unwritten code, ensuring the autonomy of member Anjumans, be embodied in its constitution together with a proviso that the body would make no representation to the government without the approval of the Bombay Parsi Punchayet. The Federation willingly accepted Naval's condition and the issue was settled amicably.

What might Naval not have achieved had he lived even a few years longer! But time which heals can also wound. Over and above his social and charitable concerns, one of Naval's pet beliefs was that in a highly industrialized city like Bombay, it was imperative to have a permanent exhibition centre particularly for machine tools. Ninety acres of ideal land suitable for this purpose were available at Vikhroli which he offered to the State Government at a very reasonable rent in the hope that, if accepted, all the interested associations and government agencies could join hands to bring the project to fruition.

But before the negotiations could be completed, an event occurred that shocked and outraged Naval's immediate family members, the larger family of his workers and the country's business and industrial circles—an event that was eventually to cruelly cut short Naval's career, not in its prime, but at its pinnacle.

17

THE TRAGIC FLAW

It was 8.10 p.m. on 8 January 1979. Naval with his son Jamshyd had just returned from Vikhroli to their 40-D, Ridge Road residence when the door bell rang. Naval opened the door to be confronted by a dishevelled, excited stranger wielding a deadly Rampuri knife. Before Naval could recover from the shock, the stranger stepped forward and stabbed him twice in the abdomen. As he fell and lay bleeding on the floor, his daughter-in-law Pheroza rushed to help him and, alarmed by the commotion, his mother-in-law Gulbai came running to the door. The stranger wildly attacked the pregnant Pheroza, stabbing her also in the abdomen and thigh and then plunged his knife into Gulbai's stomach. Before Jamshyd, who was in the kitchen fetching a glass of water, could rush to his family's help, the assailant fled.

The assault threw business circles generally into a state of panic and highlighted the grim reality of deteriorating labour-management relations. It came in the wake of a spate of violent incidents involving rival trade-unions and managements. Three workers were killed in the Siemens' plant at Kalwa, after clashes over Dutta Samant's efforts to form a rival union. On 13 November 1977, the Personnel Manager of Britannia Biscuits was stabbed in the back and seriously injured. Two prominent labour leaders and four others were arrested. In a similar manner the management representatives of Forbes Chemicals, Cooper Engineering, Star Chemicals, Subhash Textile Mills, Shivaji Flour Mills and Zenith Steel Works had been assaulted. The continuing lock-out at Premier Automobiles was also brought about by interunion rivalry between Dutta Samant's and R.J. Mehta's unions.

Frantic telegrams were sent to the Central Government by, among others, the Indian Merchants' Chamber, the Maharashtra Chamber of Commerce, the All India Manufacturers Association and the Association of All India Engineering Industries. The messages correctly claimed that the assault was incited by a militant trade-union leader and was more a reflection of trade-union rivalry than of management-worker conflict.

In the meantime, a frantic Jamshyd rushed his father, his wife and grandmother to the Breach Candy Hospital. Because there was only a single operation theatre available, Pheroza who was pregnant was operated on first, while Naval lay in agony. Pheroza had a miscarriage, and Naval was hospitalized for almost two months, with noted doctors Farokh Udwadia, Fardoon Soonawalla and Kersi Dastur fighting for his life.

The immediate reason for the attack on Naval was never

clearly established. It was said that it was because he was handling the negotiations, taking a fair and firm stand, never giving in. Even the Union Minister for Labour told Sohrab that it was a political matter and had nothing to do with employer-employee relationships.

The Crime Branch of the Bombay Police arrested the militant trade-union leader Dr Dutta Samant and three others, all members of the INTUC, in connection with the assault. They were remanded to police custody for a week. The case against Samant was that the assault was a desperate gambit provoked by the realization that he had all but lost hold over the workers at Godrej, one of the largest engineering units in the western region.

Such was the outrage felt in trade circles generally in Bombay that a mammoth public meeting was held on Friday, 12 January, which expressed indignation and concern 'about the gangsterism in industry and trade obviously instigated by just a few so-called union leaders. The dastardly assault on a leading industrialist and his family members at his residence on 8 January 1979 has shocked and filled with indignation not only all the representatives of trade and industry, but also the public at large.'

The resolution continued: 'What is even more serious is that this assault is a part of a chain of such assaults which have come in quick succession over the past year or so. Even if the wheels of law and order might have been moving in these cases of assault, the distressing feature is that neither the people instigating such assaults appear to be deterred in their utter lust for such actions nor the people have so far seen any signs which could relieve the reign of terror.'

The meeting decided to meet the Chief Minister of Maharashtra to put on record its strong protest and to make a few suggestions for industrial peace in the city. It stressed that only certain union leaders had been indulging in cruel and cowardly assaults for forcing their demand, either upon the management or upon the rival unions. In view of the numerous representations made to government, it should come out in a forthright manner and name the culprit—be he the employer or the union—without sitting on formalities or permitting political considerations to stand in the way. The apathy with which things had been allowed to deteriorate was deplored and it was made clear to all concerned that employers would no longer allow themselves to be taken for granted and that they would themselves resort to effective measures so as not to expose themselves and the employees any more to such dangers.

Later, the entire congregation of small, medium and large businessmen called upon the Chief Minister and voiced their feelings, urging upon him to take immediate and strong action to restore the confidence of the citizens of Maharashtra. The Chief Minister took due note of their feelings and gave a categorical assurance to take several corrective measures.

Naval recovered, but only partially. His health was badly affected and he was not the same man again. As he lamented once: 'This has taken ten years from my life!' Twelve pain-racked years were still vouchsafed him. But the discipline of a lifetime took over. He returned to work as if nothing had happened, with redoubled energy as if aware of Time's winged chariot drawing near. With singular reticence he didn't blame his workers or even refer to the incident.

In the meantime the Commissioner of Police, J.F. Ribiero, filed a case (Sessions Case No. 305 of 1979) against the accused, among whom were Dr Dutta Samant, who was alleged to be the instigator and the actual assailant Shankar V. Savardekar. P.R. Vakil was engaged as the Special Public Prosecutor. The case against Dutta Samant could not be proved, but Savardekar was convicted and awarded various sentences, some of which were directed to run concurrently.

It was believed that pressure was brought to bear by the Government on the Prosecutor not to pursue the matter beyond the actual assailant to the alleged instigators. Savardekar went in appeal against the conviction. The High Court admitted the appeal, but upheld his conviction with a few minor alterations. The outcome was not entirely satisfactory, but, as has been said, scales are too often in the eyes of the goddess Justice rather than in her hands. And Naval and his family didn't pursue the matter. The only happy outcome was that when the Breach Candy Hospital needed to have a Charity Wing, Godrej gave 20 lakh rupees to found the Pirojsha Godrej Memorial Wing and an annual contribution towards its upkeep.

Naval's stabbing and death twelve years later had in them the elements of Greek tragedy. The perfidy in the motives of those who were responsible. The irony that this should have happened to one who cared and did more for his workers than most other industrialists and who won their respect and admiration, and their love.

The 'tragic flaw' in his character that made him believe that, having no enemies, he had nothing to fear. The twist of Fate that made him do, that dreaded night, what he almost never did—open the door himself soon after coming home. The shock and pain borne stoically for twelve years from the partial recovery to the inevitable, untimely end.

The end came early in the morning of 8 August 1990. The body was taken to Vikhroli the same morning and laid in state, flower-bedecked, in Plant 15. Grief-stricken family members stood behind, heads bowed. Relatives, friends, co-workers in their thousands, their families too, the children he had loved so well, filed past paying their last respects, a sad, unending column.

It was a day of heartbreak. Few could restrain their tears.

But there is a continuity in human affairs that survives even death. Naval bequeathed an example to be followed, like his uncle Ardeshir and father Pirojsha before him. Whenever friends or family members visited him in hospital, concern writ large on their faces, he would say: '*Soo thayoo? Jara haso ni!* (What's wrong? Smile a little!)' Just before his death, with all his family members around him, he told them 'to hold together' whatever happened, so that what they had built together would last and grow.

His achievements were truly remarkable. He carried on, and enhanced the tradition established by Ardeshir and Pirojsha. He pursued their commitment which was two-fold—to the highest industrial standards and to basic human values. Writing in *Meditations on Freedom*, Leonard Read quotes Cervantes's words that the road is always better than the inn. He goes on to comment, 'Those who settle on fame or fortune as the inn, and having arrived, call it quits, miss the whole point of life. Realistically, there is no inn, no ultimate point of arrival. It is the road now and forever—finite man probing infinity, finding his way, endlessly. All that matters are the lessons learned along the way.' So did Naval carry on in the belief that India can do it. Any doubt expressed about the country's ability to be self-reliant irked him. On one occasion, he along with Jamshyd had called on the Industries Secretary, Maharashtra State, with a proposal to manufacture computers and peripherals by upgrading their typewriter division. The Secretary inquired which technology they were importing. Quick came Naval's retort, softened with a laugh: 'We do not believe in importing technology, we develop it.'

Mention needs to be made in this connection of an

individual who was a formative influence in Naval's life, for whom he had a great regard which was amply reciprocated—the outstanding Indian scientist, the late Dr Homi Bhabha. They were such good friends that Naval would often visit the BARC. The cladding for its picturesque dome was done by Godrej. Homi Bhabha would on occasions approach Naval for the manufacture of certain highly specialized equipment. Knowing his exacting standards, Naval would sometimes tell him: 'Why don't you import it? You have the means.' Bhabha would retort: 'Of course I have the means. But I want you to make it. I know you can.'

Naval was a man of ideas, which B.C. Forbes calls the raw material of progress. But an idea by itself is worth nothing, as Forbes goes on to say. 'An idea, like a machine, must have power applied to it before it can accomplish anything. The men who have won fame and fortune through having an idea are those who devoted every ounce of their strength and every dollar they could muster to putting it into operation.' Naval's ideas took shape and bore fruit because he had also mastered the three M's of success—making, managing and motivating people.

Two books that greatly influenced Naval were *In Search of Excellence* by Thomas J. Peters and Robert H. Waterman Jr., and *The Art of Corporate Success* by Ken Auletta. No doubt these books inspired him in the day-to-day conduct of the company's affairs. No doubt also, he discovered in the companies they held forward as examples of excellence, (Procter & Gamble, Texas Instruments, Blue Bell, IBM, among others) traits that were responsible for the growth and development of Godrej since the time Ardeshir began with lock manufacture—that the individual human being counts in that it is attention to employees rather than work conditions *per se* that has the dominant impact on productivity, that innovative companies are especially adroit at continually responding to change of any sort in their environment, that

The Tragic Flaw

every worker is 'seen as a source of ideas, not just acting as a pair of hands,' that workers enjoy a personal identification with the company's success, that service is more important than the sale, 'overpowering service, after-sales service.' As Ken Auletta puts it, 'The world's great companies may share at least some common qualities, beyond a quality product. They tend to be entrepreneurial rather than managerial; they have faith in a future vision, and stick to it; they resolve the tension between authority and participation in such a way that employees feel as if it is their company, and yet feel a part of something larger than themselves; they feel secure that they are the best, yet insecure because they are not perfect.'

If there is one thing *In Search of Excellence* illustrates more than any other, it is that success is not to be had for the asking. Thomas Watson, Jr., of the IBM is quoted as saying of his father who launched the organisation: 'T.J. Watson didn't move in and shake up the organisation. Instead, he set out to buff and polish the people who were already there and to make a success of what he had. That decision in 1914 led to the IBM policy on job security, which has meant a great deal to our employees. Almost every kind of fanfare was tried to create enthusiasm . . . Our early emphasis on human relations was not motivated by altruism but by the simple belief that if we respected our people and helped them to respect themselves, the company would make the most profit.' Similarly, Red Pope's description of Walt Disney's methods is recalled: 'How Disney looks upon people, internally and externally, handles them, communicates with them, rewards them, is in my view the basic foundation upon which its five decades of success stand . . . I have come to observe closely and with reverence the theory and practice of selling satisfaction and serving millions of people on a daily basis successfully. It is what Disney does best.' The authors describe how leading companies in America have filled the void created by the breakdown of traditional structures like schools and churches as social centres for the family: 'They have become sort of mother institutions, but have maintained their spirit of entrepreneurship at the same time.'

The 'excellent' companies according to them have a deeply ingrained philosophy that says, in effect, 'respect the individual,' 'make people winners,' 'let them stand out,' 'treat people as adults.' A preponderance of at least some of these basic values like a belief in being the best, in superior quality and service and the importance of people as individuals are noticeable in the Godrej enterprise. But times change and it is in the nature of change for some of these values to be diluted or to be lost sight of. Rustom Sanjana who spent a lifetime serving Godrej, notes the paradox that while in the highly incompatible surroundings at Lalbaug, Godrej acquired a name for excellence, on shifting to Vikhroli which is the country's showpiece, this quality was diluted with unionism replacing the spirit of paternalism. Moreover, the emphasis on quality provoked by severe and even ruthless competition from well-known British makers got weakened in a sheltered market. How great this reputation for quality was, Sanjana recalls by citing two examples. On one occasion, a Deputy Rationing Officer complained that cash from a particular box was frequently missing. He wrote a nasty letter to the company suggesting that their cash-boxes were not unpickable. Godrej challenged him to a test case where they left it to him to select whichever he liked from several cash-boxes and bring an expert of his choice to try and break it open. The cash-box selected was sealed in his presence, the key given to the officer and its duplicate retained by the manager. The only condition laid down by Godrej was that their representative along with the Rationing Officer should be present during the breaking operation.

On the day of the test the Godrej representative enquired

of the Rationing Officer how much time the expert would need to break open the lock. Not more than half an hour, he was told. The expert fiddled with the lock for almost the entire day without success. Towards the evening, instead of admitting defeat, the Rationing Officer made the excuse that the real expert who would have done the job had not been available on that day, so they had brought a substitute. Godrej retorted that they could come on any other day when the 'real' expert was available. A day was fixed for the second time, but a strange thing happened. The expert on seeing the safes exclaimed, 'But I didn't know I would be called upon to break open a Godrej safe. I can't do that.'

A similar case occurred in Hongkong at the branch office of a firm called Pavri Sons. It appears that Mrs Pavri, while crossing in a ferry, dropped her purse carrying the keys into the water. The duplicate keys were also in the same purse. The service department of Godrej were immediately contacted. They wanted a declaration to be signed by the owners of the safe after which the needful was done. But the relevant point is that several expert Chinese mechanics, who claimed they could break open any safe in the world, were dumbfounded in the case of this particular Godrej safe.

Two occurrences, according to Sanjana, affected the Godrej reputation for quality. One was the manufacture of typewriters which was quite an achievement in itself. But till Optima came in collaboration, the quality of Godrej typewriters roused frequent complaints. The second, according to Sanjana, was the manufacture of tumbler padlocks. Because of the limited security they offered, they confused people who believed implicitly that 'Godrej' stood for security. When Ardeshir began manufacturing locks, he made it a point to stress that all locks below 6-lever locks lacked security. But the confusion persisted. A piquant situation arose with the manufacturer issuing a warning to buyers against his own products! An example Sanjana recalls is of Mrs C.D. Deshmukh, wife of the former Union Minister. She once went shopping after locking her house with a tumbler padlock. On return she found that the house had been broken open and burgled. Tumbler lock manufacture was later discontinued.

There is a third factor common to all industries that were once growth industries. Theodore Levitt of Harvard, writing under the title 'Marketing Myopia' in the *Harvard Business Review*, points out how in every industry, 'perversely, a vicious cycle sets in. After experiencing continued growth for a while, managers in the industry come to believe that continuing growth is assured. They persuade themselves that there is no competitive substitute for their product, and develop too much faith in the benefits of mass production and the inevitable steady cost reduction that results as output rises. Managements become preoccupied with products that lend themselves to carefully controlled improvement and the benefits of manufacturing cost reduction. All of these forces combine to produce an inevitable stagnation or decline.' Inevitably, Godrej too are caught in the cycle. But the remarkable thing is that the third generation in the family, while frankly admitting this decline, is vigorously set, with new ideas and the latest efficiency techniques, to arrest it and recover for the name they bear its old glory.

Those who came into contact with Naval found him to be a very decisive person with a sharp, incisive mind. He was quick to lose his temper, but as quickly a smile would light up his face. One thinks of him as always in action, in terms of speed—a quick mind, a quick tongue, quick judgements. Always on the move—the next step, a new project, another milestone to self-reliance.

The Tragic Flaw

Even while in hospital his thoughts were of the future. A month before he died, he was taking a walk on the hospital verandah with his cousins Kerse Naoroji and 'Bobby' Kooka on either side of him. He expressed the need right then to start planning for the Godrej centenary in 1997. One of his ideas was to build a fountain at Marine Drive on the lines of Jet D'eau in Geneva. When he became aware that the end was near, he called his brothers and family members to declare that his last wish was that they should hold together in the future.

Simplicity was the keynote to his character. He was always dressed in white khaddar trousers and bush shirt. He couldn't stand ostentation in any form. His children's and grandchildren's *navjotes* were performed without fuss at home. When the Bombay Parsi Punchayet sought to honour outstanding members of the community, Naval refused to accept the accolade, noting that his brother Sohrab should be given it. The eminent jurist Nani Palkhivala recalls the occasion when Naval and he met at Godrej Baug to discuss the construction of a new building. Naval had, as usual, driven himself there in his small car, attired as always in simple clothes. Palkhivala comments: 'I was proud to be in the presence of a man who had created such enormous wealth for the nation and spent so little of it on himself. The ideal of plain living and high thinking did not have a more dedicated exponent.'

In appreciation of his services the government bestowed the Padma Bhushan on him. But it was like him never to flaunt this honour, so that few people were even aware till they read about it in the obituary notices. S.D. Sulakhe, Secretary, IMTMA, recounts an amusing anecdote in this connection. Hearing the announcement about Naval being awarded the Padma Bhushan, he rang up to congratulate him but was told that he was away at Mandwa. Sulakhe found this typical of Naval's unassuming and self-effacing self that the Award made no difference to the pace of his work or his schedules. What surprised Sulakhe even more was, the next morning, when Naval's secretary rang him up to ask if he had a photograph of his to give to the media, as his family could not locate any! He had not kept any picture of his ready for occasions such as these because he never believed in self-promotion. Eventually Sulakhe found a group picture, which had to be suitably cropped and enlarged.

Naval never knew a mother's love. Soonabai had died when he was only three and a half. The Soonabai Godrej Dance Academy Theatre at the NCPA was gifted by Godrej in her memory. Naval grew up to be robust and healthy, but had an acute skin problem that necessitated his being put on a vegetarian diet. Like Pirojsha and Ardeshir, Naval remained a vegetarian all his life and became a devotee of vegetarianism.

A true Zoroastrian, he didn't believe in the accoutrements of the religion. 'He didn't believe in rituals,' recalls Soonu. In fact, rituals like the segregation of menstruating women were to him a way devised by men of keeping them down. He believed in the upliftment of women and wanted them to have the same rights as men.

Jamshyd recalls how in most conversations with him the important thing that came through was his concern for others: 'He had this great love for doing things for others, even to the extent of being put to personal discomfort. Even on long drives he would insist on driving half the time. There were innumerable instances when he would leave the nicer thing for somebody else. He always gave the credit to somebody else even if he himself had done it.'

High society meant nothing to him. He probably found its make-believe distasteful. He was an achiever. What time he could spare from his work, he would spend relaxing with his family, his brothers, his children and grandchildren. Fond

The Tragic Flaw

of animals, especially dogs, a Labrador named Tuka was a member of the household for as long as he lived. He knew and practiced the secret of relaxation. Apart from this, his great hobby was sailing. Kerse Naoroji, a great sailor himself, accompanied Naval on his sailing expeditions. In the early days he was interested in yacht-racing, in its technical aspects. His yawl *Tir* was built according to his own plan at the Alcock Ashdown Yard. *Tir* had two predecessors, the *Wyvern* and the *Sagitta*. It was in *Wyvern* that Naval and Kerse, accompanied by their wives, sailed to Goa in 1952 without any tindals or paid hands on board. *Tir* was designed and built when the *Sagitta* struck a sandbank near Cochin in the course of a cruise to Colombo. In 1967 Naval and Kerse, accompanied by Mr Cama, sailed to Karachi and back in *Tir*. For this feat Naval and Kerse had their names inscribed on the prestigious 'Scovell Challenge Shield'.

His major love to the end of his days was the sea, as was his father's. Its vastness and timelessness, its hidden wealth, its changing moods, its occasional turbulence and its abiding calm seemed to evoke an emotional response in him. It was as if, fond of sailing, he were pitting himself against the sea, sailing as far as Karachi and the Lakshadweep Islands, even against tide and wind.

The picture one fancies is of Naval riding the waves to eternity, and it was so that his nephew Nadir, Burjor's younger son, envisioned him in a touching tribute, fittingly entitled 'The Captain', written in his memory:

No one quite knows where he can be
I have a vision—a quiet beach
He stands and gazes at the reach,
He boards a yacht, he's out at sea,
He navigates an endless ocean,
And I am lulled by this strange notion.

AFTERWORD

Godrej is a continuing story, 'from generation to generation, and world to world'. The first generation, aided by the second, built a rock-firm reputation, in steel products and soap, for quality production, professional management, consumer satisfaction and marketing capability.

Heading the second generation, Sohrab, the companies' Chairman, widened their horizons to national and international concerns, building the Godrej image and winning world recognition and awards in the process. Younger brother Burjor, senior Managing Director of Godrej Soaps, continued with his life's passion, treading the 'holy ground of research', till the day he died (9 August 1994). He was recently recipient of yet another unique honour 'International Man of the Year', conferred by the International Biographical Centre

Afterword

of Cambridge, England.

Now the third generation takes on the challenges. Jamshyd, Managing Director of Godrej & Boyce, trained by father Naval, is carrying on the steel business in a manner that would have made Naval happy and proud. To get Godrej more in tune with international production practices and quality, Jamshyd has led the company into a bold tie-up, on a basis of equality, with General Electric. Vijay Crishna, married to Naval's daughter Smita, is in-charge.

In like manner, Burjor's elder son, Adi, has with characteristic drive and outstanding marketing skills, expanded Godrej Soaps (of which he is Managing Director) into diverse, highly profitable lines. His younger brother Nadir, also designated Managing Director, has been involved in another group company, Gujarat Godrej Innovative Chemicals, which later became part of Godrej Soaps. The brothers have led Godrej into a strategic alliance with Procter and Gamble for continued prosperity in the country's fast-changing business environment. They have also sought, for the first time on such a scale, some public shareholding, making history in the process.

The frontiers keep expanding. New challenges bring in their wake new opportunities. The story continues, of daring and perseverance, of delightful surprises and quiet achievements.

Certainly a story that needs telling.

APPENDICES

APPENDICES

Appendix A

GODREJ & BOYCE MANUFACTURING COMPANY LIMITED

Corporate Profile
(Date compiled: 23 September 1996)

Registered Head Office & Manufacturing Plants:
Pirojshanagar, Vikhroli, Mumbai (Bombay) 400 079, India
Phone: (022) 5171166/5171177 Fax: (022) 5170900/5171301
Cable: GODREJVIKH

Bombay Branch:
Godrej Bhavan, 4A Home Street, Fort,
Mumbai (Bombay) 400 001, India
Phone: (022) 2078371 Fax: (022) 2072238 Cable: GODREJSAFE

Holding Company of the Godrej Group:
The Company is one of the largest privately-held corporations in India; it is the Holding Company of the GODREJ GROUP, which is one of the largest industrial houses in India with group revenue of Rs 28,000 million (US $ 800 million).

Incorporation:
Established in 1897, the company was incorporated with limited liability on 3rd March, 1932, under the Indian Companies Act, 1913.

Board of Directors:
S.P. Godrej (Chairman), K.N. Naoroji, A.B. Godrej, J.N. Godrej (Managing Director), N.D. Sidhva, N.K. Dhabhar, K.N. Petigara, N.B. Godrej and V.M. Crishna.

Shareholders:
Since its inception, the Company is controlled by the GODREJ family based in Mumbai, India. Its shares are not listed on any Stock Exchange. About 32% of the Company's share capital is held by Pirojsha Godrej Foundation, a public charitable trust.

Godrej: A Hundred Years

Product Range:
The Company has the following eight business divisions, which manufacture and market a wide range of consumer durables and industrial products:

1. **Office Equipment Division:**
   Home Storwels & Furniture, Office Furniture, Storwels & Sliding Door Units, Instafile, Drawingfile Cabinets & Recording Systems, Movable Partition Systems, Book Stacks & Cases, Fire Resisting Record and Filing Cabinets, Cash Boxes and Coffers, Security Equipment-Safes, Strongroom Doors and Safe Deposit Lockers, Mutiflex & Heavy Duty Storage Systems, Workshop Equipment (Tool Storage Cabinets)
2. **Locks Division:**
   Locks & Latches
3. **Manual Typewriter Division:**
   PRIMA Manual Typewriters (available in over twenty different languages)
4. **Office Automation Division:**
   Electronic Typewriters and Word Processors, Dot Matrix Printers
5. **Machine Tools Division:**
   Sheet Metal Working Machines (Presses/Shears)
   Plastic Injection Moulding Machines
6. **Tool Room Division:**
   Precision Toolings (Press Tools/Injection Moulding Dies)
7. **Precision Equipment Division:**
   Precision Fabrications-Chemical, Aerospace, Refinery Petrochemical and Nuclear Applications
8. **Material Handling Equipment Division:**
   Forklift Trucks (Diesel and Electric)

Branches (Sales & Service) in India:
Ahmedabad, Bangalore, Bhopal, Bhubaneshwar, Mumbai, Calcutta, Chandigarh, Cochin, Coimbatore, Faridabad, Ghaziabad, Guwahati, Hyderabad, Indore, Jabalpur, Jaipur, Jamshedpur, Kanpur, Lucknow, Madras, New Delhi, Patna, Pune, Rajkot, Surat, Trivandrum and Visakhapatnam.

Number of Company-owned Showrooms	: 33
Number of Wholesale Dealers	: Over 1,000
Number of Retail Outlets	: Over 5,000
Number of Employees	: 10,700 (including) 1,500 in sales and service)

Bankers:
Central Bank of India,
Mumbai 400 023
Union Bank of India,
Mumbai 400 021
Banque Nationale De Paris,
Mumbai 400 001

ANZ Grindlays Bank plc,
Mumbai 400 001
Citibank N.A.,
Mumbai 400 001

Statutory Auditors:
S.R. Batliboi & Company, Chartered Accounts,
302, Regent Chambers, Nariman Point, Mumbai 400 021

Sales (including Excise Duty) April 1995-March 1996: Rs 6,130 million (US $ 173 million)

Appendices

Major Subsidiaries and Affiliates

Major Subsidiaries (Unconsolidated)	Product Range	Sales (incl. Excise Duty) (April 1995-March 1996)		
			Amounts in millions	US$ in millions
Godrej Soaps Ltd. (67%) (Note 1)	Soaps, Toiletries, Detergents, Fatty Acids and Glycerine	Rs	7,043	198.0
Godrej-GE Appliances Ltd (60%)	Refrigerators and Washing Machines	Rs	6,613	187.0
Godrej Pacific Technology Ltd.(51%)	Office Automation Products	Rs	1,943	55.0
Godrej Telecom Ltd. (73%)	Corded & Cordless Telephones	Rs	62	1.8
Mercury Mfg. Co. Ltd. (52%)	Steel Furniture and Equipment	Rs	59	1.7
Godrej (Malaysia) Sdn. Bhd., Malaysia (83%) (Note 2)	Steel Furniture and Equipment	RM	10	4.0
Godrej (Singapore) Pte. Ltd., Singapore (52%) (Note 2)	Steel Furniture and Equipment	S$	8	5.6
Godrej International Ltd., Isle of Man (Note 3)	International Trading	£	4	6.2
Godrej Properties & Investments Ltd. (Note 3)	Real Estate Development	Rs	282	8.0
Godrej Agrovet Ltd. (Note 3)	Animal Feeds and Agro Products	Rs	1,642	46.0
Godrej HI Care Ltd. (Note 3)	Agro Products Household Insecticides	Rs	1,335	38.0
Major Affiliates:				
Lawkim Ltd. (100%)	Electric Motors (Hermetic)	Rs	1,014	29.0
Godrej Foods Ltd. (65%) (Note 1)	Food Processing and Edible Oils	Rs	1,849	52.0
Godrej & KIS Ltd. (50%)	Photographic Equipment	Rs	58	1.6
Geometric Software Services Ltd. (26%)	CAD/CAM Software Development	Rs	62	1.7

Notes: (1) Shares listed on the Bombay Stock Exchange
(2) Financial Year: January-December 1995
(3) Subsidiaries of Godrej Soaps Ltd.
(4) Rate of Exchange: US$ 1 = Rs 35.5

For further information, contact:
1. Dr K.A. Palia
   Executive Director
   (Finance)

2. Mr P.D. Lam
   Executive Director & President
   (Office Equipment Division)

GODREJ SOAPS LIMITED—A PROFILE
(Date compiled: August 1995)

* Established in 1918
* Household brand name renowned for quality and integrity
* A leading business house in India in consumer products
* Significant presence in diverse industries such as
  — consumer non-durables, office equipment
  — security equipment, electronics
  — consumer products, vegetable oils, foods
  — vanaspati, household insecticides
  — industrial chemicals, animal feeds, agro products
  — real estate and property development
* Strategic alliances with world leaders such as P & G, GE

CORPORATE ENTITIES

Engineering	Chemicals
Flagship—Godrej & Boyce	Flagship—Godrej Soaps
Other Companies	Other Companies
Godrej GE Appliances	Procter & Gamble Godrej
Lawkim	Transelektra Domestic Products
Godrej Trading & Services Co.	Godrej Agrovet
Mercury Manufacturing Co.	Godrej Foods
Godrej Malaysia SDN BHD	Godrej Properties & Investments
Godrej Singapore PT	Godrej International
Godrej Investments	Godrej & KIS
	Godrej Plant Biotech
	Bahar Agrochem & Feeds
	Swadeshi Detergents
	Sahyadri Aerosols
	Wadala Investments
	Ensemble Holdings & Finance
	Vora Soaps
	Godrej Oil Palm Konkan
	Tahir Properties

| Rs 12,676 million | **Annual Turnover** | Rs 13,882 million |
| US$ 403 million | | US$ 441 million |

Total for the Group
Rs 26,558 million
US$ 844 million

Appendices

Gross Revenue—1994-95
Godrej & Boyce Affiliates

Name of the Company	Line of Business	Rs million	US$ million
Godrej & Boyce	Consumer Durables & Industrial Products Godrej Trading & Services Office Equipment	6,200	197
Godrej GE Appliances	Refrigerators & Other Domestic Appliances	5,400	171
Lawkim	Electric Motors	800	25
Godrej (Singapore)	Steel Furniture & Equipment	116	4
Godrej (Malaysia)	Steel Furniture & Equipment	110	4
Godrej Investments	Investments	30	1
Mercury Manufacturing	Office Furniture & Equipment	20	1
	Total	12,676	403

Notes: (1) Gross Revenue comprises sales turnover inclusive of excise and income from other business operations
(2) Exchance Rate has been assumed at US$ 1 = Rs 31.50

Gross Revenue—1994-95
Godrej Soaps & Affiliates

Name of the Company	Line of Business	Rs million	US $ million
Godrej Soaps	Consumer Products, industrial chemicals	6,111	194
Procter & Gamble Godrej	Consumer Products	3,250	103
Godrej Agrovet	Animal Feeds & Agri-products	1,520	48
Godrej Foods	Vanaspati, Oils, Food products	1,480	47
Transelektra Domestic Products	Household insecticides	882	28
Godrej Properties & Investments	Real Estate and Property Development	300	10
Godrej International	International Trade	114	4
Godrej & KIS	Photoprocessing Equipment	50	2
Sahyadri Aerosols	Aerosols Packing	35	1
Wadala Investments	Investments & Finance	23	1
Swadeshi Detergents	Detergents	20	1
Ensemble Holdings	Investments & Finance	17	1
Bahar Agrochem & Feeds	Plant Growth Promoters	15	1

Godrej Plant Biotech	Tissue Culture	5	0
Vora Soaps	Soaps	0	0
Godrej Oil Palm	Konkan Oil Palm	0	0
Tahir Properties	Real Estate	0	0
	Total	13,882	441

Notes: (1) Gross Revenue comprises sales turnover inclusive of excise and income from other business operations.
(2) Exchange Rate has been assumed at US$ 1 = Rs 31.50

Appendix B

Chronological List of Godrej Products

(A) Godrej & Boyce Mfg. Co. Ltd.

Locks	1897
Security Equipment (Safes)	1902
Soaps and Toiletries	1918
Storwels, Filing Cabinets, Steel/Office Furniture and Office Systems	1923
Safe Deposit Vaults	1935
Tool Room, Hospital Equipment and Library Stacks	1935
Machine Tools	1942
Manual Typewriters (First All-India Typewriter)	1955
Steel doors and windows, ERW Tubes and Multiflex Storage Systems	1956
Refrigerators	1958
Forklift Trucks	1961
Steel Foundry	1965
Process Equipment	1976
Electronic Typewriters	1985
Dot Matrix Printers and CAD/CAM Systems	1989
FAX Machines	1992
Washing Machines	
Cooking Ranges	
Window Airconditioners	
Dehumidifiers	

(B) Godrej Soaps Ltd.

Chavi Bar	1918
No. 2	1919

Godrej: A Hundred Years

No. 1	1922
Turkish Bath	1926
Shaving Stick	1932
Shaving Round	1938
Vatni	
Cinthol	1952 (August)
Liquid Soap	1953
DIP Washing Powder	1958
Cinthol Talcum Powder	1960
Shaving Cream (R) Rich	1968
Shaving Cream (M) Menthal	1969
BIZ Sc. Scrubb Powder	1970
Liquid Hair Dye	1974 (May)
KEY Detergent Powder	1977 (January)
Trilo	1977 (July)
Hair Dye—20 ml.	1979 (June)
KEY Bar	1980 (February)
Hair Remover	1981 (November)
Powder Hair Dye	1981 (November)
DEEP Washing Soap	1981 (October)
EZEE Liquid Detergent	1983 (November)
Lime Fresh Shaving Cream	1984
Crowning Glory	1985 (February)
Besto Detergent Powder	1985 (April)
Cinthol (New)	1985 (October)
Marvel	1986 (February)
Fresca	1986 (October)
Vigil	1986 (December)
Mega	1987 (January)
Great Shake	1987 (March)
Fay	1987 (July)
Fresca—150	1987 (October)
DIP Detergent Powder	1987 (November)
Vigil (New)	1987 (November)
Velvette Shampoo	1988 (August)

Appendices

Shikakai	1988 (October)
Cinthol-Lime	1989 (August)
Liquid Cleaner	1989
Velvette Talc	1990 (February)
Marvel	1990 (April)
Tomato Puree	1990 (May)
DEEP (New)	1990 (June)
Limelight	1990 (August)
Nivaran	1990 (August)
Anoop	1990 (August)
Fresca Cream/Cool	1991 (January)
Powder Hair Dye Brown (BR/POL)	1991 (August)
EZEE—200 gms.	1991 (November)
Marvel Lilac/Gold	1991 (November)
Cinthol Cologne	1991 (December)
Vigil—Pink	1991 (December)
Jumping Fruit Juices	1991
Verve Hair Dye	1992 (March)
Cinthol-Sandal	1992 (April)
Evita	1992 (June)
Saxon-Range	1992 (August)
Ganga Toilet Soap	1992 (August)
Cinthol Talc—Satin	1994 (May)
Camay—Classic/Natural	
Powder Hair Dye Sachet	1995 (November)

Appendix C

Testimonials
Regarding Godrej Locks and Safes

From the Bombay Gazette of 24th November 1904: 'Messrs Godrej & Boyce, safe-makers of Bombay, gave yesterday afternoon a public test of the fire-proof quality of safes of their make before a number of persons at their factory at Parel, near the Gas Works. In an open space in the compound a huge fire was kindled and therein was put a safe of the firm's manufacture containing paper. The safe remained in the fire for about three hours and was then removed red hot. On being opened the papers therein were found to be free from any effects of the strong heat. A prize worth double the value of a safe of any other make was offered to those who could compete successfully with this firm's safe in the fire test. The offer was not taken advantage of.'

A Government Test of Safes: 'The Director-General of Posts and Telegraphs held a fire test of Safes of different makers some years ago in Calcutta when a large number of fire-proof Safes had to be purchased for the protection of Savings Banks ledgers in the Post Offices in India and Burma. High Officials including the Government chemist were present at the test which proved conclusively the immense superiority of our Safes to those of other makers and the whole order for 372 Safes that were wanted was placed with us.

'Subsequently easy burglaries having occurred in several post offices it was decided to replace all the Safes in use in a large number of post offices in the country with our non-fireproof Safes (Safes made to resist burglars' tools only and not for protection against fire) and *over nine hundred such Safes* have been bought from us for that purpose.'

ARDESHIR B. GODREJ

Another Fire Test: 'This sheet of paper formed a portion of the contents of the safe manufactured by Messrs Godrej and Boyce Manufacturing Company, Parel, Bombay, which was subjected to a fire test in the Bombay Exhibition grounds on Sunday the 5th of February 1905. The safe was closed and the fire lighted in the presence of Mr Lallubhai Samaldas and after a ton of fire-wood had been consumed around it was opened in the presence of the Hon. Mr Vithaldas D. Thakersey and Khan Bahadur M.C. Murzban. The contents of the safe comprising 20,000 circulars, a number of pamphlets, a currency note signed by Mr Lallubhai

Samaldas, a watch, a quantity of raw cotton and some tissue paper were found intact and uninjured and showed no signs of the severe ordeal through which the safe had passed. The watch was going as usual and appeared unaffected.

We corroborate the above statement.

(Sd.) Vithaldas Damoder Thakersay
(Sd.) M.C. Murzban
(Sd.) Lallubhai Samaldas

Government House, Bombay, 21st November 1905

From the Military Secretary to His Excellency the Governor of Bombay

Messers GODREJ & BOYCE Mfg. Co.

Dear Sirs,

At the request of His Excellency Lord Lamington, Governor of Bomay, I have the pleasure of informing you that the safe provided by your firm for Her Royal Highness the Princess of Wales during the recent Royal visit to Bombay gave entire satisfaction.

It was subsequently placed at the disposal of Her Excellency Lady Curzon and Her Excellency the Countess of Minto with equally satisfactory results.

I am, Dear Sirs, your faithfully,

(Sd.) Richard Owen, Lieut-Colonel.

Success against Burglars in a Jungle

The Mela Ram Cotton Mills.
Lahore, 5th June 1906.

Messrs GODREJ & BOYCE

Dear Sirs,

Messrs Mela Ram's Sons having contracted to lay the Nagda Muttra Railway line, the safe that you supplied a few months back was sent to Baran station (in Rajputana) via. Bina. Between 4,000 and 5,000 men are employed on this contract in the jungles of Rajputana and thousands of rupees for the wages were put into this safe which remained day and night either in a tent or under a tree. Seizing the opportunity an armed band of the notorious Bhil robbers of Rajputana turned up one night last month and made most determined efforts to force open the safe with sledges and other tools; but it gives us great pleasure to say that they completely failed. Notwithstanding that they laboured during the whole night they could accomplish nothing beyond breaking the brass handle. Messrs Mela Ram's Sons are delighted that their trust was rightly reposed; they highly appreciate the thoroughness of the burglar resisting quality of your safes and desire me to convey to you their grateful thanks for being saved from what might have been a heavy loss.

Yours faithfully,

FAKIRJEE EDULJEE BHAROOCHA,
L.M.E., A.M.I.M.E.,
Mill Manager and Engineer,
Mela Ram Cotton Mills, Lahore.

Three days' attack on a Godrej Safe

Messrs GODREJ & BOYCE

Gentlemen,

I beg to send you the following facts thinking you will be pleased to know that one of your safes withstood successfully an attack by a number of burglars lasting two or three days and preserved the contents intact.

Plague having made its appearance at Veraval where I was in March last, I left that place with my family for Chorwad leaving behind me at Veraval a safe made by your firm containing ornaments of the value of Rs 4,000 and a number of important documents.

Taking advantage of our absence several burglars broke into my house and tried to break open the safe and from evidence they worked at it for three days but it proved to be too well made to yield to their efforts. The burglars made away with silk clothing of the value of Rs 1,150 that they found in cupboards. The police were at once informed of the burglary and now I hasten to communicate the information to you. Please accept my congratulations and assurance that I shall always be glad to recommend your safes.

Yours truly,

JETHALAL PREMJI BHAICHAND GANDHI,
C/O DHARAMSI RATANSI
No. 33, Laxmidas Khimji's Market

Appendices

Bombay Improvement Trust

Engineer's Office.
Bombay, 22nd August 1905

I have purchased one safe from Messrs Godrej and Boyce for my office and I am satisfied with the workmanship and design.

The price is moderate and the value excellent.

(Sd.) H. KEMBALL, C.E.,
Trust Engineer.

Government Central Press

Bombay 24th July 1906

Messrs GODREJ & BOYCE, Bombay

Gentlemen,

I have the honour to inform you that the large fire-proof safe recently purchased from you for this Press is quite up to my requirements in finish and other respects. I may also state that the experiments recently carried out in my presence at your workshop have satisfied me that the fire-proof composition used was sufficient to protect books and papers from fire.

Your most obedient servant,

(Sd.) E.E. COOMBOS,
Superintendent, Government Central Press

The Chamber of Commerce

Bombay, 20th January 1908

Messrs GODREJ & BOYCE
Safe Manufacturers, Bombay

Dear Sirs,

In reply to your inquiry I have much pleasure in stating that the safe supplied by you this office has proved satisfactory. The workmanship and locking arrangements are good and the general get-up of the safe is creditable to your factory.

I am, Dear Sirs,
Yours faithfully,

(Sd.) J.B. JESLIE ROGERS, Secretary

Improvement Trust

Bombay, 16th August 1906

Messrs Godrej & Boyce made a safe to order for the use of my office. The design and workmanship are both good and it compares very favourably with the more expensive safes of English manufacture.

(Sd.) S.M. EDWARDS,
Special Collector
Under the Land Acquisition Act

Bank of Upper India, Ltd.

Allahabad, 6th September 1906

Messrs GODREJ & BOYCE MFG. CO.

Dear Sirs,

We have much pleasure in giving you these few lines regarding the safes you supplied us. They are all that can be desired and compare well with the best English manufactured article.

Yours faithfully,

(Sd.) G.J.M. HAMILTON,
Agent.

Improvement Trust

Engineer's Office
Bombay, 12th July 1907

Messrs GODREJ & BOYCE SAFE MAUFACTURERS

In reply to their inquiry Messrs Godrej & Boyce are informed that owing to their not having sent men to open the safe supplied by them two years ago and of which the keys had been lost the undersigned was obliged to employ professional locksmiths to open it, which they did after 8 hours of hard work.

(Sd.) F. WATSON, A.M.I.C.E.,
Ag. Trust Engineer.

N.B.—The safe in question was our cheapest quality of burglar resisting safes

Appendices

Certificate of the Portuguese Consul embodying the opinion of an Expert

This is to certify that at the request of Goa Government I appointed an expert of long experience and got examined before being painted, thirty made to order safes by Messrs Godrej & Boyce Manufacturing Co., Parel, Bombay, for the communities of Ilhas de Goa.

In the opinion of the expert all thirty safes are so well constructed and finished that they would surpass many safes made in Europe.

(Sd.) M. GERARD,
Belgian Consul,
Acting Consul General for Portugal

Public Works Office

Bombay, 12th September 1905

Messrs GODREJ & BOYCE have supplied two strong room doors for the Coin Vaults in the Paper Currency Building, Bombay. They are of good design and excellent workmanship and compare very favourably with more expensive doors of English manufacture. The locks manufactured by this firm are all that can be desired. They are moderate in price, well finished and thoroughly reliable.

(Sd.) R.J. KENT, C.E.,
Executive Engineer, Presidency

Bombay, 29th November 1913

DEAR MR GODREJ,

The recent fire which took place yesterday in the Luxmidas Khimji Market we had our shop there possessing one Godrej Safe of C quality. After twenty-four hours when we got the possession of our safe we found it quite safe. When we opened the safe we found all our ornaments of pearls, diamonds and gold as well as our documents quite safe, without hurt effected by the fire. We certify your safe to be the best proof against fire.

Yours faithfully,
MATHURADAS MORARJEE

Expert Opinion

I have carefully examined an ordinary sample of the "Gordian" safe lock of Messrs Godrej & Boyce Mfg. Co. and find it in design, material and workmanship a most satisfactory piece of work. The strength and the wearing surfaces are ample and the springs of the levers being all in duplicate the risk of accident is practically eliminated. The keys which are drop forgings in steel are machine cut in the proper manner and not filed out by hand and the precautions taken to prevent fraud are both ingenious and effective.

As the keys of safes are frequently lent to subordinates there is always the risk of impressions being taken for fraudulent purposes. As a protection for the proprietor a second key is provided with which a turn from right to left so alters the lock that the proper key ceases to act. Another turn in the opposite direction restores the normal condition of the lock. Should the working key be stolen, the safe may at once be rendered secure from thieves.

All the locks are made to fit their keys, thus ensuring the greatest measure of security and wear.

I have also visited the factory of Messrs Godrej & Boyce and found an excellent organisation of tools and processes which should enable the firm to turn out work, both in quantity and quality, to satisfy the severest requirements of the various Indian Administrations.

(Sd.) JOHN WALLACE, C.E.,
Editor, *Indian Textile Journal.*

Appendices

Appendix D

On Ardeshir's Donation of Nasik Land to Parsi Punchayet

A merchant in Bombay, Mr Ardeshir Burjorji Godrej, died in 1936 and left behind a large estate.

According to the directive of the High Court to take care of his estate and to implement his charities as mentioned in his will, and how those estates should be sold, Mr Nadirshaw Cawasji and Mr Pestonji Limji Parekh had taken out originating summons against Shirinbai Keikhosrow Kooka, and this came up in the High Court before Justice Blackwell.

Mr Ardeshir Godrej was the founder and Managing Director of Godrej Soaps Ltd. His capital was Rs 5 lakhs consisting of 5,000 shares of Rs 100 each. Mr Godrej owned 3,500 shares. He was also an owner of two big farms, 370 acres farm at Pipalgoan in Nasik and 150 acres farm near Nasik at Mushrul.

According to his will, out of his estates, including his farms, for the poor families, an agricultural and horticultural institute is to be established.

At the time of the hearing of the originating summons with the consent of parties, honourable judge had given a "hukumnama" wherein among other things it was mentioned that farms at Nasik and his other estates should be used by the Trustees of Parsi Punchayet Funds and Properties so that the Parsi youths and the Parsi families can be inhabited and a colony can be established to train them there.

—from *Jame Jamshed*, 12.12.1939
p. 533 in *Parsee Prakash*
Vol. VI, Point V (1938-1940)

Parsi Punchayet Booklet

Since 1984, the Bombay Parsi Punchayet publishes accounts in the form of booklets. This volume made in 1951 contains extracts from this booklet of various happenings from 1908 to 1942.

This extract is from the year 1941. The estate of Mr Ardeshir Burorji Godrej at Nasik measuring 591 acres (15 guntha) were handed over to the Parsi Punchayet on 7.1.1940. On this farm a few apprentices are kept who get an allowance besides boarding and lodging and there they are trained.

A committee was formed to look after this farm by the trustees of the Parsi Punchayet consisting of the following persons: Mr Pirojsha Burjorji Godrej, Mr S.M. Bharucha, Seth Naoroji Pirojsha Godrej, Seth Bapuji B. Lam, Seth Feredoon R. Mehta, Dr Jal Phiroze Balsara. Over and above the committee, an advisory committee of the following was also appointed by the trustees: Mr Sohrab R. Gandhi, Dr Jamshed A. Daji, Dr Feredoon P. Antia, Seth Ardeshir B. Mehta and Seth S.D. Motafaram.

The members of the above committees have agreed to work on an honorary basis.

Parsee Prakash, Vol. VI, Point V (1938-1940)

Appendices

Appendix E

Extract from the Guinness Book on the 123-Hour Typing Marathon on the Godrej Typewriter

In 1986, Mr Shamboo Anubhawane, a job typist of Bombay, shattered the world record for continuous typing and entered the Guinness Book of World Records on a Godrej Prima Typewriter. He typed for 123 hours completing 8,06,000 strokes, a marathon achievement which started at 12.00 noon on Monday; August 18, 1986, and concluded at 3.00 p.m. on Saturday, August 23, 1986.

Appendix F

THE CAPTAIN
Remembering Naval Godrej

Who can escape the sting of fate?
At best we can but feint and dodge,
We know someday the barb will lodge.
For some it's soon, for others late
Though nature yields sometimes to reason
Not all transpires in timely season.

How dreadful—a slow, sapping death
Where every moment's full of strife
And breathing's all that's left of life
And life, itself, not worth a breath.
We must accept the soul is leaving,
But nothing can arrest our grieving.

For solace, there still is the past
And grief is foiled by reveries—
The treasure of sweet memories
Of which, our board is rich and vast.
Each day we can produce a jewel
And grief is bound to lose the duel.

But why not gaze the other way
And build for him a monument,
Complete the work for which he spent
His each and every living day,
And thus the wounds of grief we suture
By looking at the past and future.

No one quite knows where he can be
I have a vision—a quiet beach
He stands and gazes at the reach,
He boards a yacht, he's out at sea,
He navigates an endless ocean,
And I am lulled by this strange notion.

—*Nadir B. Godrej*

Appendix G

Selected Honours and Awards conferred on Mr S.P. Godrej

Jan., 1979	Officer de l'Ordre de la Couronne by Baudouin, Roi des Belges.
1983	Sheriff of Bombay.
May, 1988	Ordre National de la Legion d'Honeur by the President of the Republic of France.
April, 1989	Commandeur de l'Ordre de Leopold II by Royaume de Belgue.
July, 1989	Lok Shree Award for Social Commitment by the Institute of Economic Studies, New Delhi.
June, 1991	WWF 25th Anniversary Benefactor Award by HRH Prince Philip, the Duke of Edinburgh.
Nov., 1991	The Indira Gandhi Paryavaran Puraskar Award for 1991 by the Government of India.
April, 1992	Indian Merchants' Chamber Diamond Jubilee Endowment Trust Award for outstanding contribution by a businessman in enhancing the image of the business community by personal service.
Nov., 1992	The Jawaharlal Nehru Birth Centenary Award for 1992-93 by the Indian Science Congress Association.
June, 1996	'The Order of the Rising Sun, Gold Rays with Neck Ribbon' for his outstanding contribution to Indo-Japanese friendship.

Appendix H

Selected awards conferred on Burjorji P. Godrej

1. Awarded inclusion in *The International Who's Who of Intellectuals Volume VII* of the International Biographical Centre, Cambridge, England, in recognition of distinguished achievements.

2. Awarded the Excellence Award '89 on the occasion of the Jawaharlal Nehru Centenary for enhancing India's prestige and contribution towards national development. London, 17th June 1989.

3. Awarded inclusion for the second time in the second edition (1990) in the *First Five Hundred International* published by the International Biographical Centre of Cambridge, UK, in recognition of distinguished service and outstanding achievement.

4. Awarded membership of the World Institute of Achievement, Division of American Biographical Institute, Inc., Raleigh, North Carolina, USA.

5. Awarded inclusion in the second and third world edition of *International Book of Honour* published by the American Biographical Institute, Raleigh, North Carolina, USA.

6. Awarded the International Cultural Diploma of Honor by the American Biographical Institute selected on the basis of Introduction of the Art of Living for a Better and Peaceful World. Invented a Process for Detergent Manufacture, Epoch-Making for the World. I.O.M., (International Order of Merit), International Biographical Centre, Cambridge, England.

7. Selected the Man of the Year 1992 based on his outstanding accomplishments to date and the noble example he has set for his peers and entire community by the American Biographical Institute, USA.

BIBLIOGRAPHY

Auletta, Ken (1984): *The Art of Corporate Success: The Story of Schlumberger*, G.P. Putnam's Sons, New York.

Brendon, Piers (1991): *Thomas Cook: 150 Years of Popular Tourism*, Martin Secker and Warburg Limited, Great Britain.

Carnegie, Andrew (1901): *The Gospel of Wealth*, Frederick Warne, London.

Desai, Ashok V: *The Origin of Parsi Enterprise*.

Desai, Shahpur F. (1977): *History of the Bombay Parsi Punchayet (1860-1960)*, Bombay Parsi Punchayet Funds and Properties.

Desai, T.B.: *The Economic History of India*.

Douglas, James (1900): *Glimpses of Old Bombay and Western India With Other Papers*, Sampson Law, London, Marston.

Dutt, Romesh (1960): *The Economic History of India, Volume One: Under Early British Rule 1757-1837*, reprinted by the Publications Division, Delhi.

——(1970): *The Economic History of India, Volume Two: The Victorian Age 1837-1900*, reprinted by the Publications Division, Delhi.

Eras, V.J.M. (1957): *Locks and Keys Throughout the Ages*, (translated from the original in German).

Gandhi, M.K. et al: *Swadeshi—True and False* (articles reprinted from *Young India* and *Harijan*).

——(1973): *Thoughts on Trusteeship (In Humanised Society Through Trusteeship)* reprinted by G.B. Deshpande for Trusteeship Foundation, Bombay.

Gokhale, Gopal Krishna: *The Swadeshi Movement*.

Gupte, Pranay (1984): *The Crowded Earth*, W.W. Norton & Co., New York.

Hopkins, A.A. (1928): *The Lure of the Lock*.

Jeejeebhoy, J.R.B. (1952): *Bribery and Corruption in Early Bombay*, the author, Bombay.

Karanjia, B.K. (1970): *R.P. Masani—Portrait of a Citizen*, Bombay Popular Prakashan, Bombay.

Kumar, Dharma and Desai, Meghnad (1983): *The Cambridge Economic History of India*, Cambridge University Press.

Lala, R.M. (1981): *The Creation of Wealth*, IBH Publishers Pvt. Ltd., Bombay.

Martin, G: *Modern Soap and Detergent Industry*.

Masani, R.P. (1939): *Dadabhai Naoroji—The Grand Old Man of India*, George Allen and Unwin, London.

——(1960): *Britain in India—An Account of British Rule in the Indian Sub-Continent*, Oxford University Press, London

Martineau, Harriek (1857): *British Rule in India*.

Naoroji, Dadabhai (1901): *Poverty and UnBritish Rule in India*, Swan Sonnenschein and Co., London.

Pal Bipin Chandra (1954): *Swadeshi and Swaraj (The Rise of New Partiotism)*, Yugayatri Prakashak Ltd., Calcutta.

Peters, Thomas J. and Waterman Jr. Robert H. (1971) *In Search of Excellence: Lessons from America's Best Run Companies*, Harper & Row Publishers, New York.

Read, Leonard: *Meditations on Freedom*.

Sarkar, Sumit (1973): *The Swadeshi Movement in Bengal (1903-1908)*, People's Publishing House, New Delhi.

Swaminathan, Sed.: *The Collected Works of Mahatma Gandhi*. Volume 20, Navjivan Trust, Ahmedabad.

Tikekar, Aroon (1984): *The Cloister's Pale: A Biography of the University of Bombay (Post-Centennial Silver Jubilee Publication)*, Somaiya Publications, Bombay.

Whipple, Allen O. (M.D.), Dr Euween, Heen (1941): *History of Surgery*.

Articles

Davar, A.J.: 'Non-Zorastrians in Zorastrian Precepts and Practices,' *Spenta*, Vol VI, Nos. 3, 5, 6.

Mehta, Raj and Belk, Russell W. (1991): 'Artifacts, Identity and Transition: Favourite Possessions of Indians and Indian immigrants to the United States,' *Journal of Consumer Research*, Vol. 17, March 1991.

INDEX

Adi Godrej 144, 156, 157, 233
alpha olefins 144, 145
Ameeta Madhok 103
American Biographical Institute 148
—The International Cultural Diploma of Honour awarded to Burjor in 1991. 148
American Typewriter Company 120
Annie Besant 11, 50
—Theosophical Society 11
Ardeshir Godrej 1 ff., 12, 16, 22, 24-5, 28, 105, 111, 173
—locks 29-32;
—safes 33;
—soaps 47;
—death 56;
—well-versed in Persian 61
Asian flu 106
Aspi Golwala, Dr 110

Bachubai Godrej 57;
—Rajabai Tower Tragedy Fund 37
Bahadurjee, Dr 9
Bharuch 2
Bartle Frere, Sir 5
Bipin Chander Pal 63
Bombay 1, 2, 3, 6, 7, 10, 11, 14, 193, 194;
—over-reclamation 177;
—Sheriff of, 7, 186
Bombay Management Association 120
boycott 64

Breach Candy Hospital 219;
—Pirojsha Memorial Wing 222
British rule 65
Burorji Godrej 114, 135 ff.,
—bold approach to technology 7;
—Chairman of J.G. Kane Memorial Trust 146;
—conscious culture of research and development at the factory 136;
—Honorary Consul-General of Austria 146;
—interests in philology specially Indo-European languages 145;
—International Award of the International Biographical Centre, Cambridge 148;
—latest scientific management system 149;
—licence for exclusive use of G-11 in India 139;
—personal traits 147;
business,
—social responsibility of, 188

Central Bank of India 92;
Charles Darwin 105
Charles Morgan 108
China 164, 176, 178
Cinthol/Cinthol toilet soap 142
—computers 223
—consumer 125, 188, 189, 192
Cooverbai Vakil 94, 107

Cornelia Sohrabji 10
culture-building process 103
customers 162
—corporate philosophy regarding, 162

Dadabhai Naoroji 16-19, 22, 53, 59, 161
dealers 152
Desai, T.B. *Economic History of India* 13-14
Dinshaw Daji 86
Direct taxes/taxation 190, 191
Dosa Godrej 77
drain 16-18
Dutta Samant 219-21

environment, environmental
  environmentalist 78, 174-5, 177, 182, 183, 194, 208
  degradation 185

East India Company 4, 15
European Economic Community (EEC) 166, 167

Facit 124
Factory Acts 17
family planning 91-3, 175, 178, 179, 182;
  —Family Planning Association of India 179
Ford Foundation 92-3, 94
fatty acids 49, 137, 138, 139
foreign trade 17, 63, 164, 167
forests 177
Foundation for Research in Community Health (FRCH) 210
FTPA 191, 192

G-11 germicide/hexachlorophene 76, 114, 139-42
Gandhi/M.K. Gandhi/Mahatma 21, 23, 50, 61, 62, 177, 178
Gerald Fryer 3
Germany 50, 136
global presence 158, 166
Godrej 1 ff.
Godrej & Boyce Mfg. Co. Ltd., 68, 109, 113, 156, 159, 233
Godrej Kaizen System 158
Godrej Soaps 77, 142
  —change of control 113;
  —Burjor's control 135;

—bold approach to technology 139
Guderz 2
Gopal Krishna Gokhale 18, 23, 63
Glycerine 137-8
glycerol 138
GE Appliances 233

'halalkores' 3
Halda 114, 121, 124
Henry Mill 115-6
Herbert Spencer 105
Home Guards for Civil Defence 95
Homi Bhabha 224

Immunization programme 95, 179
Indian Institute of Science, Bangalore 97
Indian economy 163, 166
industrial policy 164
industry 102, 166;
  discrimination against 165
Indian Soap and Toiletry Makers Association (ISTMA) 48, 142, 143, 144
In Search of Excellence 224
Indian Machine Tools Association 198

Jaganath Shankarshet 11
Jai Burorji 95, 207, 145
James Fergusan, Sir 10
Jamshetjee Jeejeebhoy, Sir 8
Jamshyd Godrej 216, 230, 233, 208, 156
Japan 119, 163
Japanese 163, 164
  —Kaizen system 149
Jehan Dastoor 83
Jussawal, Dr 110
Jyotsnaben Mehta 94
J.R.D. Tata 96, 179, 192

Kaikhushroo Naoroji 89
Kalyaniwalla and Mistry 87
karkhanas 160, 174
Kekhushro Navroji Katrak 85-6
Kerse Naoroji 81, 86, 103
K.R. Gokulam 84-5
Khurshed Bardy 79-81

Labour, free of labour trouble till 1972. 104
Lalbaug 27, 31, 40, 75, 79, 88-91, 101, 105, 106, 145, 173, 203, 226
Land Revenue 16
Lavji Nusserwanji Wadia 4

Index

Levers, Lever Brothers 13, 74, 144, 147
Leprosy control 212, 178
Locks 29-32
 —business left for Pirojsha 34
Lokmanya Bal Gangadhar Tilak 23, 61;
 —Tilak Swaraj Fund 61, 62

machine tools 84, 153, 168-70, 196-200;
 —IMTEX 198-9, 202
 —stepping up of R&D 200-2
managers 102, 152, 154, 156, 157
Managing Agency System 154
management 156-8, 178
Mandwa 210, 211, 230
mangrove forests 183, 194
'marketing myopia' 228
marketing 153;
 —aggressive strategies 157;
 —depots taking over as clearing agents 158;
Mashrul 53, 55
Mechanical presence and press brakes 197,
 —shearing machines 197-8
Merwanji Cama 24
Mountstuart Elphinstone 10
multinationals 155

Nadir Godrej 156, 223
Nariman Sahukar 81-3, 101
Nani Palkhivala 229,
 —National Conservation Centre 183
Naval Godrej 92, 95, 104, 108, 113, 119, 120, 128, 130, 132, 153, 154
 —climax of industrial career 202;
 —given charge of indigenous manual typewriter 77
 —IMTEX hosted at Pirojshanagar 199
 —listing factors for why machine-tool industry had lagged behind 199-200;
 —manufacturing process equipment under leadership of, 197;
 —philanthropy 208;
 —productivity 204;
 —rapport with workers 202
 —Sixth IMTEX, 1986. 199
 —Spokesman for machine tools 199
Nehru Jawaharlal 28, 73, 114, 163
Noshir Antia, Dr 210-12

Parsi, parsis 8, 62, 213-14
Parsi Punchayat 56, 62, 213-16, 229

Patents (Godrej) 35, 42
Phadke, Dr G.M. 92
Pheroza Godrej 207
Pherozshah Mehta 9, 86, 88, 89, 99, 171
Pirojsha Godrej 8, 37, 86, 88, 89, 93, 94-98, 99, 100-12, 171, 174, 175;
 —Pirojsha Godrej Foundation 8
Pirojshanagar 95, 97
pollution 173
population 175, 176, 181, 185
Pragati Kendra 92, 94, 175
private sector 163, 189, 193
public sector 163
P.D. Muncherji 151
PUF 128, 133

Queen Victoria's Jubilee 6

railways 8, 17
Rajkot 5-6
Ranade 22
refrigeration 129
refrigerator 130-34, 153
 —price-war 134
Remington 114, 12, 124
Rotary 184-6
Russel W. Peterson 176
Rustom Sanjana 101, 83, 204, 226

sales,
 —approach 150-1;
 —branches 151;
 —dealers 152;
 —decentralisation 156;
 —force 151;
safes 2;
 —breaker 227;
 —burglar-resistant quality 38;
 —deposit vaults 42;
 —fire resistant 38-42
Savak Desai 84
secret circular 62
self-sufficiency 201;
 —Japan and Germany 201
Shamboo Anubhavane 126
sheet metals working machinery 197-8
 —agency agreement from foreign manufacturers like LVD of Belgium and L Schuler of Germany 198

Sholes 116-17; 'lady typewriters' 117
ship-building 4-5, 14
Shivlal Shah 59, 60
soaps, toilets washing 49, 51, 142-4, 147;
—eco-labelling 143
—ISTMA 142, 143
social concerns of Godrej 97, 186
—Ardeshir and Pirojsha conscious of total responsibility to business community 187
Sohrabji Godrej 88, 102, 107, 108, 110, 114, 142, 155, 159, 160, 162, 165, 169, 172, 174, 175, 177, 181, 182, 187, 192, 193, 194
—a marketing expert 195;
—a Rotarian 185
—an active member of Indian Heritage Society 194;
—closer to Europe, IFTA 168;
—President of Indo-French Technical Association de Bombay 168;
—'F.P. Godrej', 175;
—invited by World Wildlife Fund-International to be President of World Wildlife Fund-India 182;
—'Mr Environmentalist' 175;
—population-environment nexus 183
—plea that concept of professional management should be interpreted in terms of application, attitudes and approaches 156
—scientific management 114;
—Sheriff of Bombay 186
Soonuben Dastoor 92, 93, 95, 203, 205, 207
Soonabai 107, 109, 160, 161
—Soonabai Godrej Trust 183, 209;
—Soonabai Pirojsha Godrej Foundation 209
Soonawala, Dr R.P. 92
steel
—cupboard 71;
—furniture and equipment 73;
—Godrej's association with 162;
—import from Taiwan, Japan, Korea and Indonesia 171
—office furniture 170;
Storwel 91, 100
strike 104
Swadeshi 21, 43, 47, 48, 99;
—Ardeshir 22; 63-5;
—Pirojsha 67;

S. Khursetji 10
S.F. Desai 129

Tanya Godrej 156
Thana 109
Thomas J. Watson 98
trade balance 167
trade missions 76, 166,
—wide spectrum of industry 166
trade-unions 146, 181
trade relations 167
typewriter 77, 114, 115
—electronic typewriters 72;
—first Godrej typewriter 121;
—Godrej AB 122-3;
—Godrej PB 123;
—Godrej Prima 124;
—in collaboration with Buro Maschine Werke of East Germany 121;
—in Indian and foreign langauges 127;
—'lady typewriters' 117;
—Woodstock machine 120

Udayachal Schools 92-3, 97, 107, 182, 206, 207, 208
'Upchargraha' 94, 179

Vanamahotsav 95
Veerbaiji 107
Victoria Jubilee Technical Institute 28
Vijay Crishna 233
Vikhroli 84, 92, 93, 95, 100, 119, 144, 179, 204, 217, 222, 226
V.N. Gogate 85

welfare of people 187
wild life 182
WWF-India National Steering Committee on Population and Environment 182
Workers Welfare 91, 99, 100
—Provident Fund 205
—safety committee 91
workers 78, 95, 102-4, 188;
housing of employees 209;
—Soonuben looking after workers children 205
World Typing Championships 125, 126

Zanzibar 1, 19
Zorastrian/Zorastrianism 208, 213, 230

FORTHCOMING

GODREJ: A HUNDRED YEARS
Volume II
B.K. Karanjia

The first volume dealt with the first and second Godrej generations. The second volume will deal with the succeeding generations. But the division, however, between the two volumes is not only chronological; while this volume concerns itself with great manufacturing towards making the country self-reliant, the next one shifts the emphasis to marketing in a changed and highly competitive global environment, and to meet unforeseen challenges with unorthodox methods.

The trials and tribulations of this corporate pilgrimage undertaken by succeeding generations make for engrossing reading. How the industries grew and the man grew with them or; more correctly, how the men grew making the industries grow with them—justify the truth of poet Edwin Markham's evocative words, which are quoted to preface the next volume as they did this one:

> Why build these cities glorious
> If man, unbuilded, goes?
> In vain we build the world, unless
> The builder also grows.